NARRATIVE OF THE EMBASSY
OF
RUY GONZALEZ DE CLAVIJO
TO THE
COURT OF TIMOUR

AT SAMARCAND,
A.D. 1403-6.

TRANSLATED, FOR THE FIRST TIME,
WITH NOTES, A PREFACE, AND AN INTRODUCTORY LIFE
OF TIMOUR BEG,

BY

CLEMENTS R. MARKHAM, F.R.G.S.

GYAN

Published by

GYAN

Gyan Publishing House
5, Ansari Road
Daryaganj, New Delhi-110002
Phone: 011-47034999, 9811692060
E-mail: books@gyanbooks.com

Distribution Network
gyanbooks.com
India, USA, Canada, UK, Australia, France

ISBN : 978-81-212-3805-2 (PB)
First Published, 1859

2nd Impression 2020

Printed at: Gyan Press, Delhi.

The book at your disposal is the edition of an old book originally published long back. The Text quality of this book may not be at par as compared to our other books but many readers approached us to reprint this important book so that it could satiate their hunger. We request all the readers of this book to help us to improve its quality by providing the necessary text of those pages which are not properly visible. Your valuable support in this case will be highly appreciated and acknowledged and our future readers will be benefitted immensely.

NARRATIVE OF THE EMBASSY
OF
RUY GONZALEZ DE CLAVIJO
TO THE
COURT OF TIMOUR

Narrative of the Embassy

OF

RUY GONZALEZ DE CLAVIJO

TO THE

COURT OF TIMOUR,

AT SAMARCAND,

A.D. 1403-6.

TRANSLATED, FOR THE FIRST TIME,

WITH NOTES, A PREFACE, AND AN INTRODUCTORY LIFE OF TIMOUR BEG,

BY

CLEMENTS R. MARKHAM, F.R.G.S.

LONDON:
PRINTED FOR THE HAKLUYT SOCIETY.
M.DCCC.LIX.

THE HAKLUYT SOCIETY.

CONTENTS.

PREFACE.

THE account of the journey of Ruy Gonzalez de Clavijo, in his embassy to the court of Timour, at Samarcand, is the oldest Spanish narrative of travels of any value. Indeed the literature of Spain then consisted only of ballads, and a few chronicles. John II, the poet, and patron of literature, was in his cradle; and the exquisite *serranas* of the Marquis of Santillana were still unwritten.[1] None of the great historians and poets, who afterwards raised Spanish literature to such a height of excellence, had appeared, and no Spaniard had yet produced a narrative of travels which is at all worthy of remembrance.

It was in the earliest dawn of Spanish literature that the good and trusty old knight, Ruy Gonzalez de Clavijo carefully wrote the journal of his embassy; and this fact alone gives a peculiar interest to the

[1] John II was born in 1405; Santillana in 1398.

work. In a historical point of view it is also important, because the descriptions of the Spanish knight corroborate many of the statements of Ali of Yezd, Mirkhond, and other eastern writers; and, as a narrative of what he saw and heard, his journal describes travels which are equal in interest to those of Marco Polo and of Sir John Mandeville.

The peaceful reign of Henry III[1] of Castille is famous for the attempts of that prince to extend the diplomatic relations of Spain to the remotest parts of the earth. Mariana tells us that he sent embassies to the princes of Christendom, and to the Moors, to gather information respecting their affairs, and to collect all the knowledge that could be useful for the good government of his own country. Amongst other embassies, Henry sent two knights, named Pelayo de Sotomayor, and Fernando de Palazuelos to the east, to report upon the forces, customs, and intentions of

[1] In 1388 peace was concluded between John I of Castille and the king of England; and Henry of Castille, aged twelve, was married to Catharine of Lancaster, aged fourteen. As the heirs of England were called princes of Wales, Henry, in imitation, was created prince of the Asturias. In 1390 John died of a fall from his horse, at Burgos; and Henry III ascended the throne. Under his reign Spain enjoyed peace, and the queen gave birth to a son named John, in 1405. Henry III died at Toledo, on Christmas day 1407, leaving three children, John, Maria, and Catalina. He was affable and liberal, with a handsome face, well spoken, and eloquent.—*Mariana.*

the rulers, in those distant countries. These ambassadors were present at the battle of Angora, between Timour and the Turk Bayazid, in the year 1402. The conqueror treated them with distinction, and dismissed them, on their return to Spain, in company with an envoy of his own, named Mohammed al Cazi, who brought a complimentary letter,[1] and rich presents of jewels and women, to the king of Castille.

Amongst these presents there were two Christian ladies, who had been rescued by Timour, from the harem of the brutal Turk, named Angelina and Maria. Angelina was the daughter of Count John of Hungary,[2] and Maria was a Greek. The Hungarian, Angelina, was one of the most beautiful ladies of the age, and her loveliness was celebrated by many poets.[3] After landing at Seville, the lovely strangers set out for the Castillian court, in company with their protector, the envoy Sotomayor; and on the road they came to a town called Xodar, where they were hospitably received by Sotomayor's cousin, the young lord of

[1] Argote de Molina gives this letter in full.

[2] Probably taken prisoner at the fatal battle of Nicopolis, in 1386.

[3] Amongst others a Genoese knight, named Francesco Imperial, who lived at Seville, wrote some *coplas* in her honour. Argote de Molina gives them, but they are devoid of merit.

Xodar and Carpio. Angelina's tent was pitched near a fountain, and Maria's was close by. Here Sotomayor declared his love for the beautiful Grecian, and he had a son by her. This love passage by the village fountain, is celebrated in an ancient song,—

> "En la fontaña de Xodar
> Vi la niña de ojos bellos:
> E finqué herido dellos,
> Sin tener de vida, una hora."

Angelina married a Spanish knight of noble family, named Diego Gonzalez de Contreras, magistrate of Segovia; and the inscription on her tomb may still be seen in the chapel of St. John, in that city.[1] There were several children by this marriage, and the descendants of Angelina, with Hungarian christian names, and bearing the arms of their mother, long resided in the town of Arevalo. The fate of these lovely captives may perhaps be considered sufficiently interesting, to excuse this short digression.

On the return of Sotomayor and Palazuelos, king Henry determined to send another embassy to the court of the mighty Timour. The persons who were selected to represent the majesty of Castille at Samar-

[1] Translation:—"Here lies Dona Angelina, of Greece, daughter of count John, and niece of the king of Hungary. Wife of Don Diego Gonzalez de Contreras, magistrate of this city." The arms, a lion, *or*, on a field, *azure*.

cand, on this occasion, were Ruy Gonzalez de Clavijo, a knight of Madrid,[1] Gomez de Salazar, and a master of Theology named Fray Alonzo Paez de Santa Maria. Timour's envoy, Mohammed al Cazi, accompanied them, and they sailed from the port of Seville, on the 22nd of May, 1403.

Clavijo resolved to write a description of all the countries he passed through, that his travels might be had in memory; and a most curious chronicle of his journey to Samarcand was the result. He begins with an account of the occurrences of each day, during the voyage from Cadiz to Constantinople; gives a minute description of all the public edifices of the great capital of the empire of the east, before it fell into the hands of the Turks; graphically describes the dangers of his voyage in the Black Sea; recounts his adventures in the long journey from Trebizond to Samarcand, and enters fully into all the magnificence of Timour's court. He introduces some historical narratives; and repeats many stories concerning lands which he did not visit, received at second hand.

Mariana gives some account of this mission, and says that Clavijo "minutely related the particulars of

[1] Clavijo was a very ancient name in that city.—*Hijos de Madrid*, iv, p. 302.

the embassy, and many other wonderful things, if true."[1]

The historian of Spanish literature says of Clavijo, —"we may trust to his faithfulness, as much as to the vigilant and penetrating spirit he shows constantly, except when his religious faith, or his hardly less religious loyalty, interferes with its exercise."[2]

Oviedo, the Spanish chronicler,[3] relates that Clavijo had heard that Timour had a ring, with a stone which had the property of becoming dim when any lie was told in its presence. He, therefore, related many things concerning the grandeur of Spain, which, though not strictly true, were so in a metaphorical sense. As what he said was true to some extent, Timour saw that the stone preserved its bright colour, and was much surprised.

Clavijo said that the king had three vassals who brought six thousand knights into the field, with golden spurs, alluding to the masters of Santiago, Alcantara, and Calatrava: he said that there was a

[1] *Mariana*, lib. xix, cap. xi. The old Spanish historian devotes this chapter to an account of the "great Tamerlane." Gibbon derived his knowledge of Clavijo's embassy from Mariana.

[2] *Ticknor*, i, p. 187.

[3] Gonzalo Fernandez de Oviedo, chronicler to the catholic kings, in his general history of Spain, relates this anecdote. Argote de Molina repeats it, but confesses that it is unworthy of a place in a serious history.

bridge in Spain, forty miles broad, on which a thousand head of sheep found pasture, alluding to the land under which the river Guadiana flows, until it appears again: that there was a lion and a bull in Spain, which were maintained every day by the milk of many cows, meaning the famous cities of Leon and Toro; that there was a town surrounded by fire, and built upon water, alluding to Madrid, where there are many springs, and which is surrounded by a wall of flint: and that there were three wolf dogs (*canes*), which fought in the field, each with two hundred lances; meaning the three towns named Can de Roa, Can de Muño, and Can de Zurita.

Clavijo's Itinerary was first published by Gonzalo Argote de Molina, "the careful antiquary of the time of Philip II,"[1] in Seville, in the year 1582 (folio), with "a brief discourse, drawn up for the better understanding of this book."[2] There is only one other edition, a very good one, published by

[1] *Ticknor*, i, p. 183.

[2] Argote de Molina dedicates the Itinerary of Clavijo, to Antonio Perez, Secretary of State to Philip II. He says, "As the history of Tamerlane, promised by Juan de Barros, has not yet appeared, I have brought this itinerary, written by Ruy Gonzalez de Clavijo, to light; the original of which is in my possession." Argote also gives a life of Tamerlane by Pero Mexia, and another by Pablo Jovio, bishop of Nochera. The edition of 1582 contains sixty-eight folio pages, with double columns.

Antonio de Sancha at Madrid in 1782 (quarto). In this edition there is an additional notice of Timour, by Garcia de Silva y Figueroa, a Spanish envoy, who was sent by Philip III to the court of Shah Abbas the Great of Persia in 1618, to urge him to continue his wars with the Turks, so as to check their encroachments in the Mediterranean.

I have carefully compared my edition of 1782, from which this translation has been made, with the edition of 1582 in the King's Library, at the British Museum.

Having performed this most remarkable journey, Clavijo landed in his native country on the 24th of March, 1406, after an absence of nearly three years; and proceeded at once to the court of his sovereign, at Alcala de Henares. He remained at court for about a year, as chamberlain to the king, but on the death of Henry in 1407,[1] he retired to his native city of Madrid, where he rebuilt the chapel of the monastery of San Francisco,[2] in a most costly

[1] Clavijo was one of the witnesses to king Henry's will, which was signed at Toledo, in December 1406.

[2] This chapel was pulled down in 1760. "Clavijo's house stood on the spot where the chapel called 'of the bishop' was afterwards erected, in the parish of St. Andrew. It was so handsome that it subsequently served as a residence for Don Enrique of Aragon, cousin of king John II.—*Hijos de Madrid*, iv, p. 302.

way. After a few years his remains found a resting place in this chapel, with those of his fathers, in a rich marble tomb, bearing the following inscription:—

"Here lies the honourable knight, Ruy Gonzalez de Clavijo, whom God pardon. He was chamberlain to the king Don Henry, of happy memory, and to Don John his son. The king Don Henry sent him on an embassy to Tamerlane, and he died on the 2nd of April, in the year of our Lord 1412."

His arms were placed over the tomb—quarterly, on a field *gules*, a half moon *or*, and on a field *argent*, three girdles *gules*. His tomb was, a few years afterwards, removed from the chapel, to make room for that of Juana, queen of Henry IV. In 1573 it was placed in the centre of the church of San Francisco, and in 1580 it was finally put in the wall, near the pulpit, where at length it found a resting place.

A brief sketch of the life of Clavijo was written by Don José Antonio Alvarez y Baena, in the end of the last century;[1] but the old knight's claim to be remembered by posterity, must rest on his bold and adventurous journey, which he has so fully and so pleasantly described. This narrative, independently

[1] *Hijos de Madrid,* por Don José Antonio Alvarez y Baena, vecino y natural de la misma villa.—*Madrid,* 1791, tom. iv, p. 302.

of any intrinsic value which it may possess, is interesting as the first of a long series of chronicles of Spanish voyages and travels in every quarter of the globe, when Spain was in the height of her glory, and when her sons might proudly exclaim—

> "Quæ regio in terris, nostri non plena laboris?"

INTRODUCTORY LIFE

OF

TIMOUR BEG.

BEFORE accompanying the good old Spanish knight from his native land, through the regions of the far east, to the court of Timour, it will be well to refresh the memory with a brief sketch of the life of that mighty conqueror.

At his birth, the enormous empire of his predecessor in universal conquest was rapidly falling to pieces; and the numerous kingdoms formed by the energetic sons and grandsons of Zengis Khan,[1] were for the most part in a state of helpless anarchy, under the nominal sway of their degenerate descendants. The last great wave of those devastating floods of conquest which, for centuries, had periodically burst forth from

[1] *Zengis Khan.* His name is so written by Abulghazi, who says that *Zen* means "great," and *gis*, the "superlative." Fadlallah asserts that *Cheng* means "strong," and that *Chengez* is the plural. D'Herbelot, who is followed by Gibbon, spells the name *Genghiz Khan.*

the wilds of central Asia, to spread terror and desolation over the eastern world, was rapidly subsiding. The most contemptible puppet descendants of the mighty Zengis sat on the thrones of Persia, Samarcand, and China; while their former vassals were beginning to assert their independence in every direction.

The country between the rivers Oxus and Jaxartes, known to the Arabs as Mawur-ul-naher,[1] had fallen to the share of Zagatai, on the death of his father Zengis Khan in 1227, and the land had been ruled by his descendants for more than a century, when Timour was born in 1337; but each succeeding Sultan of Mawur-ul-naher had become more degenerate, and more contemptible than his predecessor, while the insolent independence of powerful vassals, at the head of large bodies of cavalry, kept the country in a state bordering on anarchy.

The most famous of Timour's ancestors was Karachar Nevian, the minister of Zagatai, and the first

[1] Grand Tartary extended from the Volga to the ocean, and from the Gihon to Siberia. Ptolemy divided this vast region into Scythia beyond, and this side the Imaus. North of the sources of the Ganges, a range of mountains extends to Kashgar, where it turns to the north-east, towards the river Ili; this chain was called by Ptolemy, the Imaus. That part of Scythia on this side the Imaus, which lies between the Oxus and Jaxartes, was known to Roman geographers as Transoxiana, and to the Arabs as Mawur-ul-naher.

In 706 the Arab conquerors first crossed the Oxus, under the command of Catiba, who introduced Islamism into the countries of Bokhara, Samarcand, and Fergana.

convert to Islamism amongst the wild conquerors. He ruled with justice and moderation for many years, and established his own tribe of Berlas round the town of Kesh, near Samarcand.[1] He became *Sepah Salar* or general of Zagatai's forces, and the title was made hereditary in his family; but his great grandson, Teragay, who was Timour's father, appears to have resigned the office, preferring the retirement of Kesh, and the society of learned men, to the turbulent strife of the court of Samarcand.

Teragay, the chief of the tribe of Berlas, is said to have been a man of distinguished piety and liberality, and he inherited an incalculable number of sheep and goats,[2] cattle and servants. His wife, Tekina Khatoum, was virtuous and beautiful; and on the 8th of April, 1336, she gave birth to a son, at their encampment, near the verdant walls[3] of the delicious town of Kesh. This child was the future aspirant for universal empire.

Timour was of the race of Toorkish wanderers, and he was of noble lineage, amongst a people who thought much of their descent. His countrymen lived in tents, loved the wandering lives of warlike shepherds, better than the luxury and ease of cities; and, even in the countries which they had conquered, preferred an encampment in the open plains, to a

[1] Karachar Nevian outlived Zagatai, and died in 1270.

[2] Sir Thomas Brown ridicules the idea that Timour was a common shepherd, because his father possessed flocks and herds."—*Vulgar and Common Errors*, book vii, chap, xvi.

[3] "In spring the walls and terraces of Kesh are all green and cheerful."—*Baber's Memoirs*.

residence in the most splendid palaces. Brought up amidst such feelings, a youth of undoubted genius would naturally turn the whole force of his vigorous intellect to the achievement of military glory; but if Timour had not been a great conqueror, he would inevitably have become famous in some other way; and under any circumstances, he would have left the impress of his genius on the history of the Asiatic races. Timour was no vulgar conqueror, no ordinary man: his history, as displayed both in his own writings, and in those of his biographers, proves that, if not in his acts, certainly in his thoughts and opinions, he was in advance of his age and country.

When the man child was born to the chief of the tribe of Berlas, he took it, with its mother, to pay their respects to the holy Sheik Shems-ud-Deen;[1] who was reading the 67th chapter of the Koran, and repeating this verse,—"Are you sure that he who dwelleth in Heaven, will not cause the earth to swallow you up? and behold *it shall shake*" (*Tamurū*). The Sheikh then stopped, and said, "we have named your son Timour."[2]

In his seventh year Timour's father took him by the hand, and led him to school, where he was placed

[1] Teragay was devoted to the society of this worthy, who was a famous *peer* or religious man.

[2] Timour's titles, in the height of his power, were Sultan Kamran Ameer Kutb-ud-Deen Timour Kurkhan Sahib Keraun. *Sultan* means "lord;" *Kamran*, "successful;" *Ameer*, "commander;" *Kutb-ud-Deen*, "pole star of the faith;" *Timour*, "it shall shake;" *Kurkhan*, "of the lineage of sovereign princes;" and *Sahib Keraun*, "master of the grand conjunctions."—*D'Herbelot.*

in charge of the Mollah Ali Beg. The Mollah, having written the Arabic alphabet on a plank, placed it before the child, who was much delighted, and considered the study as an amusement. In his ninth year he was taught the daily service of the mosque, and always read the ninety-first chapter of the Koran, called the *Sun*.

The child very early began to entertain an innate feeling of superiority, and a sort of presentiment of his future greatness. He himself afterwards described his recollection of this feeling, in quaint terms. "At twelve years of age," he says, "I fancied I perceived in myself all the signs of greatness and wisdom, and whoever came to visit me, I received with great hauteur and dignity. At eighteen I became vain of my abilities, and was very fond of riding and hunting. I passed much of my time in reading the Koran, and playing at chess, and was also very fond of horsemanship."[1]

At about this time a change came over his habits of thought; he repented of his past life, left off playing at chess, and made a vow never to injure any living creature. The future destroyer of thousands of his fellow men, was seized with a feeling of tender regard

[1] *Timour's Memoirs.* I believe there is no doubt as to their authenticity. The manuscript, brought from India by Major Davy, is an octavo volume of four hundred and fifty-seven pages, in the Persian hand. It begins with Timour's birth, and ends in his forty-first year, omitting the last thirty years of his life. The manuscript was found in the library of Jafir, Hakim of Yemen, by Abu Taleb ul Husseini, in the Toorki language, and was translated into Persian; and into English by Major C. Stewart in 1830.

for the most insignificant of God's creatures, and when the kind-hearted youth once unintentionally trod upon an ant, he was so deeply grieved, that he felt as if his foot had lost all its power.

Such was this young man's character when, in 1355, at the age of twenty, his father, Teragay, made over to him a number of tents, sheep, camels, and servants, and, in short, gave him a separate establishment. Then it was that his energetic mind found other work than meditations on Budhistic vows; he began to long for some wider field of action, and to form plans of rebellion against what he considered the tyranny of the Zagatai Sultan. He could not then find any one to join him; but another turbulent spirit, named Ameer Kurgan, one of the greatest chiefs of the tribe of Zagatai, defeated and killed the tyrant, and ruled the kingdom for ten years, in the name of another puppet named Danishmundche Khan.[1]

Timour was deputed by his father to wait upon Ameer Kurgan, on business connected with the tribe of Berlas; and the new ruler took a liking for the young chief, and gave him his grand-daughter in marriage. This lady proved a faithful and loving companion, following her lord in all his wild adventures, and sharing his dangers and misfortunes.[2] Timour

[1] He was not of the house of Zagatai, but was descended from Octai, another son of Zengis Khan. In this year (1356) Timour's mother died. He says, "I was for some time very melancholy, and gave up my ambitious intentions."

[2] Her name was Aljaz Turkhan Aga, daughter of Ameer Mashlah, grand-daughter of Ameer Kurgan, and sister of Ameer Hosein.

now began to experience all the realities of a Toorkish chieftain's life, in the chace and in the battle field, and his restless spirit ever thirsted for the excitement of action. He has himself recorded some of his adventures. On one occasion he lost his way, out hunting, in a heavy snow storm. After wandering about for many hours, he reached the hut of some wandering shepherds, half dead with cold, fatigue, and hunger; and was revived by the kindly Toorks with a large supply of hot soup, of which he ate plentifully. On another day he was sent against a band of invaders from Irak, charged them at a gallop, and, after a few cuts, put them to flight, and took possession of their plunder.

It was not, however, until 1358, when he was twenty-three years of age, that Timour's ambitious views began to take a wider range than the government of his native tribe of Berlas. In that year Ameer Kurgan determined to invade Khorassan, and gave the command of a thousand horse to young Timour, who was delighted with his new command. The men became exceedingly attached to him; he wrote a list of their names, and kept it folded in his pocket; and he was so elated by finding himself at the head of so many faithful followers, that he resolved, when the ruler of Khorassan was dispossessed, to grasp the sovereignty for himself.

The ruler of Khorassan was expelled; and Timour was left in possession of Herat, while Ameer Kurgan returned to the Oxus, where he was treacherously murdered by two Toorkish chiefs. Timour was justly indignant at this base act, and, with his accustomed energy, collected his native tribe, induced several other leading men to join him, and marched to Samarcand, where the victorious chiefs divided the whole empire amongst them.

Timour's ambition was now roused. Eager to assume the sovereign power, and to distance all competitors, his wisdom yet taught him the necessity of keeping on terms with the chiefs who were as powerful as himself, whilst he endeavoured to throw the ball of contention amongst them, and to rise to the head of affairs amidst the general confusion. At this time Ameer Hosein, the late Kurgan's grandson, and brother to Timour's wife, advanced from Cabul, and was encouraged by his relation to invade Badakshan, which he did in 1359. "This," says Timour, "was the greatest error I committed during my whole reign; for the man was of a vile disposition, proud and miserly, but I did not then know his character."

While the petty chiefs were thus contending for superiority, the commander of a vast army, named Tugluk Timour Khan, of the lineage of Zengis, encamped on the banks of the Jaxartes, and summoned them all to his presence. His power was felt to be irresistible, and the chiefs selected young Timour to wait on him, and to endeavour, by his ingenuity, to prevent the country from being overrun.[1] The envoy repaired to the encampment of the invader, who gave him the command of the whole country; and the

[1] At this time Timour's father died, and was buried at Kesh.

astute Timour, by his address, became sovereign of his native land, while the formidable Tugluk retired into the deserts of the east.

Thus far the ambitious projects of the young chieftain had been crowned with success. He was now not only the hereditary head of the tribe of Berlas, but he had, with extraordinary ease and rapidity, obtained a prize beyond which his youthful dreams could scarcely have dared to soar. But the difficulties which surrounded his position, and the precarious tenure by which he held his power, were not disguised from himself, and he prudently deferred having the Khotbeh read, and coin struck in his name,[1] until he had subdued all the nomade tribes. He appears to have been, at this time, very decisive in his operations, and quick to remove persons, whom he could not trust, out of his way. He says, "I went to assist Ameer Hosein, in Badakshan, and at this time Kai Kobad, son of Kai Khosro Khutelany, who had killed the king of Badakshan, waited on me, and began to flatter me, but as I had no confidence in him, I put him to death."

Timour was as yet too weak to establish order amongst his unruly countrymen. Hajee Berlas, his own uncle, was in rebellion, and was only defeated after two days hard fighting; other chiefs tried to inveigle Timour into their power, in order to assassinate him; and the heads of the villages came to

[1] These are the customary marks of sovereignty in the east. The *khotbeh* is a prayer, offered up in the mosques for the reigning sovereign. It means, literally, *written*, from *kataba* (*he wrote*).

him, declaring that the land of Mawur-ul-naher was desolate, and that in every district there was some tyrant, who unjustly plundered the people. Finding it quite impossible to restore order single handed, Timour wrote to Togluk Timour Khan, representing that the country was ruined, but offering, with his assistance, to make it productive.

The formidable chief advanced from the deserts of the east, with a great army, to the banks of the Jaxartes. The petty chiefs either fled or submitted. Hajee Berlas escaped into Khorassan, where he was murdered by some villagers;[1] and another chief had his head cut off, for delaying to give up the gates of Samarcand. Timour, at first, received the command of all the hordes of Mawur-ul-naher, and he then naturally began to think of a pretext for inducing his formidable ally to leave the country; but some of his proceedings created suspicion, and he was ordered to be killed. He, therefore, fled with a few followers towards Kharism, and met his brother-in-law Ameer Hosein on the road, who was also a fugitive.

Timour was now to learn the bitter lessons of adversity. His misfortunes seem to have brought out some of the finest points in his character; and this time of disaster is the most interesting period in the life of the great conqueror.

Although Timour and Ameer Hosein had only sixty followers between them, they resolved to attack

[1] When Timour conquered Khorassan, he punished these people, and gave their village, in perpetual jagheer, to the grandson of his uncle, Hajee Berlas.

the fort of Orgunge,[1] and they fought with such desperation that only twelve of them were left, at the end of the day. Ameer Hosein's horse was wounded, but his wife immediately gave up hers, and was remounted on the same horse with Timour's wife. They then retreated to the top of a hill in the desert, and continued to fight with the enemy, until only seven men were left. With this devoted little band, Timour at length retired, and fled across the boundless deserts. This took place in the year 1362.

The region of Kharism or Khiva, in which Timour had taken refuge, is seven hundred and fifty miles long, by six hundred broad; and, with the exception of the narrow tract bordering the Oxus, and the well watered sands of Merve, it consists of a wide desert plain, without rivers or springs, woods or mountains. Between Merve and Khiva it is a broken surface of deep sand, with a small growth of underwood;[2] and it was over this cheerless waste that Timour's little party wandered, until they came, hungry and thirsty, to a well in the desert. The weary fugitives at length found rest and refreshment, the water was delicious; a shepherd gave them part of a goat, which they roasted between stones, and, as Timour says, "we enjoyed ourselves exceedingly."

But their future prospects were most disheartening. Aljay Turkhan Aga, the faithful and devoted wife of Timour, cheered him up in this darkest hour of his life, and said,—"Surely our fortunes are now arrived at the lowest point."

[1] Near the modern Khiva.

[2] Abbott's *Khiva*.

They wandered on for days and nights, without water or bread, and remained, for a month, in a ruined deserted village. At length they fell in with a troop of wild Toorkmans, under one Ali Beg Ghurbany, who took the fugitives prisoners, and confined Timour and his wife in a wretched cow house, full of fleas and vermin, for more than two months.

This was the lowest ebb to which his fortunes sank, and from this time the tide began to flow, which bore him on to the empire of Asia. He escaped from his durance, collected twelve horsemen, whose numbers soon increased to a hundred, and raised the standard of royalty.

For the next seven years, from 1362 to 1369, when he was finally seated on the throne of Samarcand, Timour was engaged, first in expelling the invaders from his native land, and afterwards in a death struggle with his brother-in-law Ameer Hosein.

Togluck Timour Khan, who had driven Timour into the desert, was ruler of Kashgar, and of the boundless pastures further east, and he was at the head of a great army, composed of a race called Jetes, or Calmucks, who were unconverted to the faith of Islam. Togluck, who was of the race of Zagatai, left the country of Mawur-ul-naher, under the rule of his son Alyus Khwajeh, returning to the pastures east of Kashgar.

The first result of Timour's assumption of royalty, was a quarrel with Ameer Hosein, who took offence, and left him. Many old followers, however, continued to flock to his standard, and, after passing some months in hunting along the banks of the Oxus, he entered Seistan at the head of a thousand horsemen, in 1362.[1] He took several forts from the Beloochees of Seistan, but was eventually defeated, and wounded in the hand and foot; which obliged him to retire into the Gurmseer, or hot regions of the coast of the Arabian sea, where he remained to recover from the effects of his wounds.[2]

Having recruited his strength, and collected forty horsemen, he marched towards Balkh, and was joined

[1] Seistan is a territory, between Persia and Affghanistan, surrounded, except on the north, by wide deserts. It is a flat country, with low hills here and there. One third of its surface is moving sand, and the other two thirds are composed of compact sand and clay, covered with thickets of tamarisk, and abundant pasture. The Helmund, which is by far the finest river between the Tigris and the Indus, flows through Seistan, and falls into the lake of Zurrah. The river banks are clothed with luxurious vegetation, and the lake, which is about ninety miles long by sixty broad, is bordered by forests of reeds, beyond which there are pastures and tamarisk thickets. The original inhabitants of Seistan were Taujiks; but the country has long been occupied by savage tribes of Beloochees. Seistan is well known to the admirers of Ferdosi, as the country of Zal and Rustam.—*Ferrier; M. Elphinstone.*

[2] This gave rise to the story that Timour was wounded in the leg by a shepherd, when stealing sheep, and to his name of *Timour-lenc* (lame), corrupted into *Tamerlane.* This name was first given him by the Syrian Ahmed ben Arabshah, who wrote a life of the conqueror in 1440, called *Ajaib-al-Mukhlukat* (wonders of the creation), which was translated from Arabic into Latin by Golius in 1636, and by Mangin in 1767 and 1772. Arabshah hated the memory of Timour for the devastation caused by his armies in his native land of Syria, he takes every opportunity of blackening his character, and his history is a coarse satire, little worthy of credit. See Clavijo's account, p. 77 of this volume.

by a hundred men, under his kinsman Sadyh Berlas. They encamped under the shelter of a hill, on the banks of a rivulet, and lived by the chace; while their numbers gradually increased to fifteen hundred cavalry, and Timour found himself in a position to face the Jete armies under Alyas Khwajeh, the son of Timour Togluk, which were now in possession of his native land. The spirits of the young chief rose in proportion, the companions of his early days flocked around him, his ambitious hopes seemed once more to be near their accomplishment, and his heart was filled with gladness. Before encountering the enemy, he passed ten days in feasting and rejoicing, with his old companions in arms.

In 1363 he determined to fight a decisive battle with Alyas Khwajeh, but the odds were fearfully against him, as his force only numbered six thousand men, while that of the Jetes consisted of thirty thousand victorious horsemen. Timour took up an intrenched position near the Oxus, between Khulm and Koondooz, where he was attacked by the Jetes. His troops showered arrows upon them, which forced them to retire, and on the following morning he took them by surprise in their own camp, and put them to flight. Alyas Khwajeh, overwhelmed with shame at having been defeated by such an inferior force, retreated to within twelve miles of Timour's native city of Kesh.

At this time news came that Timour Togluk was dead, and Alyas Khwajeh, therefore, marched away with all his forces; closely followed by Timour, whose army rapidly increased in numbers. Once the retreating Jetes turned to face their foe, but Timour charged at the head of his troops, and finally drove them across the frontier. His native country was thus delivered from the invaders; once more the young chieftain was sovereign of the land. The citizens of Samarcand came out to meet him, and, amidst the general rejoicings, his faithful wife, who, since the disaster in Seistan, had taken refuge in the Gurmseer, came to share the prosperity of her lord.

The pretensions of Timour were disputed by his brother-in-law, Ameer Hosein, and the feud continued for five years, although the rivals were obliged to unite their forces, more than once, to resist an invasion of their common enemies the Jetes. In 1364 Timour crossed the Jaxartes, and fought with the Jete army, during the whole day. Night closed in with a heavy fall of rain, and the chief passed the hours of darkness in the open plain, with a saddle for his pillow. The rain had converted the land into a swamp, but the Zagatais charged through it, and engaged the Jetes, who had received large reinforcements, during the whole of the following day. Timour lost two thousand men, and was obliged to retreat to Kesh where he refreshed his troops, and eventually succeeded in clearing the land of the enemy.

Ameer Hosein, stirred up by jealousy, had now become Timour's implacable enemy; and Timour himself declared that, "as there was only one God in the universe, so there should only be one monarch in a kingdom." He defeated his rival in 1366,[1] and forced him to retire across the Oxus.

In 1667 Ameer Hosein again attacked his brother-in-law, and Timour retreated to Tashkend, where he passed a month in pleasant idleness, hunting and hawking over the plains, and receiving forty eggs, and a tureen of soup every morning, from the Khet Khoda, or ruler of the district. His peace was, however, again disturbed by Ameer Hosein, but his followers deserted him, and he gave himself up to Timour, requesting permission to be allowed to retire to Mecca. His successful rival at first consented; but many of the rude chiefs had cause to hate the wretched captive, who had been cruel and insolent, as well as avaricious, in the days of his prosperity. Timour appears to have been desirous to save his life, but he gradually yielded to the clamours of his officers, and Ameer Hosein was killed by three chiefs, who dragged him out of a minaret, where he had taken refuge.

Timour had now cleared his native land of seditious aspirants to the throne, as well as of foreign invaders. From the year 1369 until the day of his death, he held the sovereignty of Samarcand, while he extended his dominion over half the continent of Asia. He was formally enthroned in the city of Balkh, by four of the most revered Syuds, or descendants of the prophet, and all the people held up

[1] In this year Timour's faithful wife, the illustrious Aljay Turkan Agha, departed this life. "Verily we belong to God, and to him shall we return," was Timour's pious reflection.—*Memoirs.*

their hands in prayer for his prosperity. When this ceremony was over, he crossed the Oxus, and marched to Samarcand, which he made the capital of his empire.[1] "From my twelfth year," he says in his Institutes, "I travelled over countries, combatted difficulties, and hazarded my person in the hour of danger, until I vanquished empires, and established the glory of my name."

Timour's first important act, was to assemble a *Couroultai*, or general meeting of all the principal chiefs, and of the Ameers or commanders of Tomauns (ten thousand men), and Hazarehs (one thousand men); and he then proceeded to regulate the affairs of his empire.[2]

Although Timour was the real sovereign, he only took the title of Ameer, and, until the day of his death, all the affairs of state were conducted in the name of a puppet descendant of Zengis Khan, who was sometimes permitted to reside at Samarcand, but who was more frequently to be found serving in Timour's army. Yet Timour established all the outward forms of etiquette in his court, and each rank had its established place when they appeared before him. A council of state was formed, a code of regulations was drawn up for his government, favours were conferred on his friends, permanent grants of

[1] For a description of Samarcand, see Clavijo, p. 164 *et seq.*

[2] Timour frequently convoked a *Couroultai*, or diet of his nobles; as was also the custom of his predecessors. "He always addressed them in a speech calculated to attain their cordial assent; and, through them, to animate the zeal and courage of their followers." —Malcolm's *Persia*, i, p. 476.

land were made for charitable purposes, and the army was carefully organized.

Timour's army, as the chief instrument of his power and his conquests, received the greatest share of his attention, and a large portion of his Institutes is devoted to the details of its organization.[1] It was divided into detachments of ten, a hundred, and a thousand men, each under separate officers, called respectively *Oun-bashees*, *Euz-bashees*, and *Ming-bashees*, over whom there were many Ameers, four Begler Begs, and an Ameer-ul-Omrah, who had authority over the whole army, and acted as the deputy of his sovereign.[2] The Ameer-ul-Omrah was distinguished by a standard; the subordinate Ameers by spears with figures on their points, denoting the rank of those to whom they belonged; the Ming-bashees by a trumpet; and the inferior officers by drums.

Great attention was also given to the supply of arms and provisions for the soldiers. Each man had two horses, a bow, quiver of arrows, sword, saw, axe, awl, thread, ten needles, and a leathern knapsack;

[1] Timour thus announces his intention, in drawing up his "Institutes." "Be it known to my sons and descendants, that I have collected together these laws and regulations, for the well governing of my dominions, as a model for others. Let them make these regulations the rule of their conduct in the affairs of their empire."

[2] The army of Zengis Khan was divided on the same principle into ten thousand men, called a *Tomaun,* under a Tomaun Aghassee; one thousand, called a Hazareh, under a *Ming Aghassee;* one hundred, under an Euz Aghassee; and ten, under an *Oun Aghassee;* and these divisions are said to have existed even before the time of Zengis.—*De Guignes,* ii, p. 73.

and every eighteen men were provided with a tent between them. Each Oun-bashee was supplied with a tent, a coat of mail, sword, bow, quiver, and five horses; the Euz-bashees had ten horses apiece; the Ming-bashees, twenty; and the Ameer-ul-Omrah, three hundred. Rules were laid down for guiding the tactics of the commanders when in the field; and, in choosing a position, they were particularly enjoined to take care to be near water, on a situation more elevated than that of the enemy, that their flanks and rear were covered, and that the ground in their front was extensive and open. But the noblest, and, considering his age and country, the most remarkable part of Timour's army regulations, was the treatment of the conquered. It is but too true that in the heat of battle the orders, recorded in his Institutes, were frequently disregarded, but the fact of their existence proves that Timour's ideal standard of right was far in advance of other conquerors of his race and creed. He ordered that every soldier who had performed his duty, and fought with valour on the side of the enemy, if he sought shelter under his authority, should be treated with honour and regard, since he had performed his duty, and acted with fidelity to his former master.

The civil departments of Timour's government also received their share of attention at his hands, and he gave minute instructions respecting all the details of his administration. He superintended everything himself with a watchful eye, and, in the frequent audiences which he gave to his officers, every rank had a regular place assigned to it. The sons and other relations of the sovereign sat round the throne, the Syuds and learned men stood on the right hand, the Ameer-ul-Omrah, Begler Begs, and Ameers on the left hand, the Dewan Beggee, Viziers, and other civil officers opposite the throne, the magistrates behind the viziers, and the soldiers, with the title of Bahadur,[1] in the left rear of the throne.

The council of ministers, for the administration of civil affairs, was presided over by the Dewan Beggee, under whom there was an Erz-Beggee, or presenter of petitions, who communicated the complaints of the people, and four Viziers. The first superintended the state of the husbandmen, the produce, the levy of duties, the merchandize, and the police; the second had charge of the pay of the troops, the supply of provisions, and the state and strength of the army; the third took possession of the effects of absentees and of the dead, received taxes, and restored the effects of the dead to their lawful heirs; and the fourth superintended the receipts and general expenditure of the household of the sovereign.

Although an enormous revenue was derived from the spoils of conquest, and from the dues levied on the transit of merchandize; yet the largest item was probably the land tax, as is the case in all eastern countries. In Timour's Institutes the tax was fixed at a third of the produce on all irrigated land, besides a certain due for using water from the public reservoirs; but any cultivator who built a tank,

[1] A reward for valour in the field.

planted a grove, or brought new land under cultivation, paid no revenue for the first and second years.[1]

[1] The land tax has, from the most remote ages, been the chief source of revenue in all Asiatic countries.

The Sassanian kings of Persia established the tax at a third of the value of the produce, but when calamity overtook the crops, the cultivators received advances from the treasury.

By Mohammedan law the produce of the land is liable to two imposts, namely, the *Ooshr* or tithe, a poor rate due only on the actual produce of the soil; and the *Khiraj* or tribute, generally imposed on land within reach of irrigation or running water. No land can be subject to both *Ooshr* and *Khiraj* at the same time. The *Khiraj* was imposed on Syria by Omar, on Egypt by Amru; but Arabia is *Ooshree,* a very small part of it being under the influence of running water.

The *Khiraj* is of two kinds, *Mookassimah* and *Wuzeefa.* The former is due on the actual produce only, and resembles the *Ooshr;* the latter is due, whether there is any produce or not.

The Caliph Omar levied the *Khiraj* in Syria and Persia, the rate varying according to the value of the produce.

The Hindoo kings exacted one sixth of the produce, besides a poll tax, which was *Mookassimah;* but the Mohammedans converted it into *Wuzeefa,* in the time of Shere Shah; and the emperor Akbar, while adopting the same system, carried it into effect with greater precision and exactness.

In Persia, in the days of Timour, the land tax amounted to one tenth the produce of the soil; but the husbandman was loaded with a number of other taxes, which altogether exceeded half the produce.

In India Timour's descendant, the emperor Akbar, abolished all arbitrary taxes, and fixed the revenue according to the value of the different lands; which were divided into four classes.

1. *Poolej,* which never lies fallow.

2. *Perowty,* kept out of cultivation a short time, for the soil to recover its strength.

The *Poolej* and *Perowty* were each of three kinds; best, middling,

Ruined bridges were repaired, and serais for travellers were erected on the roads, at the expense of the sovereign. The collection of taxes, when necessary, was enforced by menaces and threats; but Timour ordered that the whip and scourge should never be used, saying that the "governor whose power is inferior to the power of the scourge, is unworthy to govern."

Having firmly established his government, and thoroughly organized his immense army, the sovereign of Mawur-ul-naher began to aspire to universal conquest, and the empire of the world. His mind was filled with an inordinate lust of power; he felt his superiority to all other men, and that his genius was equal to his ambition; but, at the same time, he differed, in this respect, from a mere vulgar conqueror, that he was anxious that his name should go down to posterity as a benefactor, rather than as a scourge to the human race; and part of his Institutes are taken up with a defence of his system of conquests.

Timour voluntarily defended himself at the bar of

and bad. The produce of a beegah of each sort was added together, and a third of the sum was considered as the average produce of *Poolej* or *Perowty* land; one third of that being the revenue. Shere Shah exacted rather more.

3. *Checher* was land which had suffered from inundations, or excessive rains; and received grants of remissions for five years.

4. *Bunjer* land, which had suffered from great inundations, and enjoyed still larger remissions.

Rewards were granted, by Akbar, for high cultivation, and the land settlement was made for periods of ten years. *Ayeen Akbery; Neil Baillie on the Land Tax.*

public opinion, and displayed some anxiety that the judgment of posterity might be in his favour. He said,—"if in any kingdom, tyranny, and oppression, and iniquity shall be predominant, it is the duty of a prince, from a regard to justice and the law, to expel and extirpate the authors of that iniquity, and to assault that kingdom. It is the duty of a victorious king to bring under his authority, every kingdom where the people are oppressed by their rulers; and thus I delivered Khorassan, and purified the kingdoms of Fars and Irak, and Shaum."[1] The fact that this great conqueror should have felt the necessity of framing some excuse, to soothe his own conscience, and to justify his conduct before posterity, is a proof that his was not the mind of a mere barbarian; and his wars were at least as excusable as many which have been undertaken in more modern times, and amongst more civilized people.[2]

[1] *Institutes*, p. 331.

[2] The history of Timour's conquests is chiefly derived from the writings of two eastern authors, namely, Ali of Yezd, and Mirkhond.

Mollah Shereef-ud-Deen Ali of Yezd wrote the life of Timour at Shiraz, by order of his grandson, Ibrahim Meerza, in 1424, nineteen years after the conqueror's death. His work was entitled *Zaffah Nameh*. It was translated into French by M. Petis de la Croix, a famous oriental traveller and scholar, in 1722.

Mirkhond, who was born in 1432, flourished at the court of Hosein Meerza at Herat, and wrote a general history of Persia from the Creation to the year 1471, entitled *Rauzat-us-Safa*. After many years of disappointment from want of patronage, he was at length befriended by the munificent minister Ali Shir Beg, who obtained him a suitable dwelling near Herat, and assisted

For several years the operations of Timour's army were confined to incursions into Kharism, and frequent invasions of the country of his ancient enemies the Jetes; but in 1376 he undertook a more important enterprise. Jojy,[1] the eldest son of Zengis Khan, received the sovereignty of a vast territory from his terrible father, called Desht Kapchak,[2] which extended from the Caspian sea, over the greater part of southern Russia, to the shores of the Dnieper. He died in 1226, six months before Zengis; and his son Batou carried the Mongol arms into Russia and Hungary, and spread terror through all the Christian countries of Europe. Batou died in 1256, and his descendants of the golden horde continued to tyrannize over Muscovy, until they were finally sub-

him in collecting materials. Mirkhond died in 1498, and his son, Khondemir, wrote an abridgment of his father's work, called *Khulasat-al-Akhbar*.

Texeira, a Portuguese traveller, published a translated abstract of Mirkhond, and there is an English translation of Texeira, by Stephens; but the best translation of that portion of Mirkhond's work, which relates to the history of Timour's conquests, was published in Major David Price's Mohammedan history, in 1821. There is also a translation of Mirkhond's history of the early kings of Iran, published by David Shea in 1832.

[1] *Jojy* means *stranger* in Mongol, and he was so called because his mother was in captivity when he was born. Few names have had a greater number of spellings. D'Herbelot calls him *Giougi*, his name is spelt *Dgoudgy* by Petis de la Croix; *Zuzi* by the translator of Abulghazi Khan; *Jugi*, *Tushi*, and *Chuchi* by the authors of the *Universal History*.

[2] *Desht Kapchah*. *Kapchah* is a Turkish word, and *Desht* means a wide uncultivated plain.

dued, and confined to the Crimea, by the Czar Ivan in 1552. In 1318 Uzbeg Khan[1] was lord of Desht Kapchak, and he introduced the religion of Mohammed into his dominions. On the death of Uzbeg Khan in 1342, his son, and afterwards his grandson, followed him, but in 1360 Urus Khan, descended from a younger son of Jojy, became sovereign of Kapchak. He reigned peaceably for several years, but at length Tokatmish, a member of his family, rose in rebellion, was defeated, and took refuge at the court of Timour, the new sovereign of Mawur-ul-naher.

Timour saw, in this feud, a means of extending his power, and he received the fugitive with great honour. Urus Khan led an army against Timour, and the hostile forces met on the plains beyond the Jaxartes, but a terrible storm of snow and hail, accompanied by a hard frost, obliged Urus to retreat, and he died a few months afterwards. Timour then established Tokatmish as sovereign of Kapchak, and thus extended his influence, and the fame of his arms, through all the nomade tribes which wander over the interminable steppes of central Asia. Yusuf Soofy, the ruler of Kharism, alone defied the authority of Timour, and in 1378, the now powerful sovereign crossed the Oxus, and laid siege to his enemy's

[1] The seventh in succession from Jojy. He was much revered by his subjects, and from that time, according to Abulghazi Khan, who is partly supported by Khondemir, they called themselves Uzbegs. Eventually the Uzbegs expelled the descendants of Timour from Mawur-ul-naher, and they still retain possession of Khiva, Bokhara, and Kokan.

capital. Yusuf challenged him to single combat, and Timour, in spite of the warnings and entreaties of his Ameers, rode up to the edge of the ditch, but no one came out to fight him, and he returned, amidst the applause of his own army. During the siege Yusuf died, and, the place having been taken by assault, was utterly destroyed, the inhabitants being removed to Kesh, Timour's native town, which he had enlarged and beautified, and made his summer residence, when not engaged in war.

No chief in the boundless regions of Touran could now dispute the supremacy of the sovereign of Mawur-ul-naher; and Timour's ambition, increasing with his power, led him to contemplate the conquest of Iran.

If Timour's theory of conquest could be admitted, that, "it is the duty of every prince to invade any country where tyranny, oppression, and iniquity are predominant," Persia certainly offered all these pretexts for aggression, to the lord of Touran.

More than a century before, Holagou Khan, a grandson of Zengis, had founded a dynasty in Persia, and put an end to the rule of the caliphs at Bagdad. After a life of conquest and devastation, Holagou had fixed his capital at Maraga in Azerbijan, philosophers and poets assembled at his court, and his friend and adviser, Nasser-ud-Deen, was the most famous astronomer of the age. Holagou retained the pure theism of his grandsire, and, though tolerating both Christians and Mohammedans, he never embraced either of their religions. In 1264 he was succeeded by his son Abaka, a wise and prudent prince, who strove to remedy the evils caused by the conquests of his father; and Arghoun, Ghazan, and other princes of this dynasty, were equally illustrious; but Abu Said, the last prince of the family who retained a vestige of power in Persia, died the year before the birth of Timour. From that time the fair provinces of Iran had been in a state of anarchy, and in 1380 Sultan Ahmed, a descendant of Holagou, ruled at Bagdad; the family of Mozuffurs enjoyed the sovereignty of Fars, with their capital at Shiraz; and the other provinces of Persia groaned under the rapacious tyranny of numerous petty chieftains.

Such was the state of things, when Timour, the lord of Touran, determined to conquer the land of Iran. In 1380 he sent his eldest son Miran, then aged fourteen, with some experienced Ameers, to assume the government of Khorassan. An excellent bridge of boats was thrown across the Oxus, the army advanced to Herat, and in 1381 the Persian provinces of Khorassan and Mazanderan submitted to the conqueror. In the following years he added Seistan, Candahar, Azerbijan, and Georgia to his rapid conquests, and in 1387 he encamped before the Persian city of Ispahan.

The inhabitants submitted, and Timour's forces entered the city, exacting a contribution from the people, but securing their lives and property. During the night of November 16th, a youth named Ali Cutchapa raised an unruly rabble, and massacred many of the Zagatay soldiers. Timour was furious at this breach of faith, and ordered a general massacre of the people. After having taken this terrible revenge, he marched to Shiraz,[1] confirmed the Mozuffurs in their government, and returned to Samarcand in triumph.

Iran had now become a province of the empire of Timour, and in 1389 he summoned a *Couroultai* at Akiar, near Kesh, to announce and celebrate his victories. The Ameers, and chiefs of Tomans and Hazarehs, were assembled at a solemn banquet, and two of the sons of the sovereign, Miran and Omar Sheik, received the government of the provinces of Khorassan and Andecan.

Timour now prepared for the greatest and most extraordinary military exploit of his life, the invasion of the illimitable wilds of Kapchak. During his absence in Persia, Tokatmish, regardless of the debt of gratitude he owed to his benefactor, made several incursions across the Jaxartes, and was held in check, with difficulty, by Timour's young son Omar Sheikh.

In 1390 preparations were made, on a great scale, for the invasion of Kapchak, and the punishment of its ungrateful Khan. The officers were ordered to collect a year's provisions, for the troops under their command; and each soldier was supplied with a horse, a bow and quiver of arrows, and a leathern water bottle. Every ten soldiers had a tent, two mattocks, a spade, a hand saw, a hatchet, a hundred

[1] During Timour's stay in the beautiful city of Shiraz, he had a complimentary interview with Persia's greatest poet, the divine Hafiz, who died two years afterwards.

needles, an awl, about fourteen pounds of rope, a leathern knapsack, a copper pot, and a baggage horse.

Having completed all the necessary preparations for his hazardous and daring campaign, Timour left Samarcand in 1390, crossed the Jaxartes by a temporary bridge at Khojend, and wintered at Tashkend, where he was attacked with a severe illness.

In January 1391, the army marched out of Tashkend, and for three weeks the intrepid Timour led his troops over the arid and uninhabited wastes, to the north of the Caspian Sea. At length he reached an isolated hill called Ulugh Tauk, whence he viewed the vast plains of Kapchak, stretching away as far as the eye could reach in every direction. He caused a lofty cairn to be erected at this spot, as a memorial to other times of his memorable expedition.

Hunting as he marched, Timour then crossed the river Yelanjouk, in 54° north latitude, and his provisions at length began to fail him. His soldiers' rations were reduced to one bowl of broth a day; and great hunting parties were organized, encircling a vast space, and driving the game into the centre. Sheikh Daoud, a chief who had been brought up from a child amidst these cheerless solitudes, was sent on in advance, with a small troop of horse, to reconnoitre the enemy, who had hitherto remained invisible. He succeeded in discovering their camp, and in May 1391 Timour's army crossed the river Jaick, in 53° north latitude, and found itself face to face with the vast hordes of the Khan of Kapchak, who were greatly superior in numbers to the invaders. A brilliant series of cavalry engagements followed, which ended in the defeat and flight of Tokatmish, and the host of Kapchak was scattered far and wide over the plain. A small remnant escaped across the Volga.

The conqueror was enchanted with the verdure of the plains between the rivers Volga and Jaik; and was not a little astonished at finding that immediately the sun set, the dawn of day was clearly perceptible in the west. He passed the month of June in hunting along the banks of the Volga, and commenced his return march in July.

The plains were covered with his army. Great troops of cattle, sheep, and camels, were intermingled with the Zagatay cavalry and their prisoners, while the unwieldy portable pavilions of Timour and his Ameers were dragged along by twenty-two oxen, eleven abreast. The ruts of these enormous waggons were twenty feet apart, and the axletrees were as large as a vessel's mast. The conqueror returned to Samarcand in the end of 1391;[1] and, in the following May, he again departed with a large army, to subdue the western parts of Persia, where the Mozuffers had revolted. This was known as the expedition of five years.

The first year was passed in reducing the forest covered province of Mazanderan, along the southern shores of the Caspian, where an obscure town on the sea coast, near Amul, held out against his whole

[1] In the meanwhile Timour's generals had crossed the river Irtish, and penetrated into the wilds of Siberia.

army. For the first and only time in his life, Timour, the great commander of cavalry, was forced to have recourse to naval warfare. A brigade of boatmen with their boats, and a band of slingers of wild fire, were sent from the Oxus to the Caspian, where they embarked, and invested the little town by land. The garrison then surrendered, and, being followers of the accursed sect of Hassan Sabah,[1] a general massacre followed. The conquest of Mazaderan having been completed, Timour wintered in the valley of the Goorgaun.

The second year was occupied in the subjugation of western Persia. Passing through Fars and Hamadan, the invading army overran the province of Louristan, crossed the river Karoon at Ahwaz, and entered Dizful.[2] Meanwhile Mansur Mozuffur, the ruler of Shiraz, prepared to resist the invader, and a decisive campaign ensued.

In his march from Dizful, Timour followed in the footsteps of Alexander, making forced marches by Ram Hormuz and Zohra, to the foot of the almost

[1] Assassins.

[2] While Timour was in the province of Khuzistan, of which Dizful was then the capital, he repaired the famous dyke across the Karoon at Shuster, which had been constructed, many centuries before, by the Sassanian king Nourshirvan. It is made of hewn stone, cemented by lime, and fastened together by clamps of iron, and is twenty feet broad and one thousand two hundred long. In the centre there are two small arches, which allow part of the water to flow in the natural bed of the river, while the remainder is led off to irrigate the plains. The dyke was again repaired by Colonel Monteith, under the orders of Mohammed Ali Meerza, eldest son of the Shah of Persia, in 1810.

impregnable heights of Kalah-suffeed, which he assaulted and captured, after a desperate resistance. Mansur, the ruler of Fars, then engaged the mighty conqueror, but his Persians were defeated, and he himself was killed in single combat, by Shah Rokh, the son of Timour.

The conqueror then entered the beautiful city of Shiraz, exterminated the race of Mozuffurs, and completely subjugated the southern provinces of Persia. Timour did not remain long at Shiraz; the divine poet Hafiz, whose society he had enjoyed during a former visit, was dead; and the wrath of the sovereign was only appeased by the slaughter of the rebellious people. There was nothing, therefore, to induce him to prolong his stay; and in September 1393, his triumphant army was led against Ahmed, the sultan of Bagdad; who fled at his approach.[1] The Zagatay cavalry overtook the sultan on the plain of Kerbela near the Euphrates, and a skirmish with bows and arrows followed. The Sultan's followers again fled, rallied, and were again beaten off by the cavalry of Timour. A third time they rallied, and a desperate hand to hand conflict ensued, but Ahmed being by this time out of danger, his troops drew off. Timour's cavalry suffered the agonies of a raging thirst, in their return across the Mesapotamian deserts, to Bagdad.

Having rebuilt the mausoleum of the Imaum Hanbal, which had been ruined by the inundations of

[1] The cruelty and misgovernment of Ahmed led the people of Bagdad to beseech Timour to succour them.—*De Guignes*, ii, p. 288.

the Tigris, Timour marched into Georgia, in 1394, and drove all who opposed him into the fastnesses of the mountains. He sent the different corps of his army in various directions, to reduce the people to submission, while he relaxed the toils of conquest, by hunting and festivity. At this time the births of his two grandsons, Ulugh Beg and Ibrahim Sultan, were celebrated, with great splendour, on the plains of Kars. The throne of Timour was raised in the midst of magnificent tents, with lovely damsels ranged around it. Musicians and singers were grouped behind, and the Meerzas, Ameers, Nevians, and foreign lords from Iran and Touran, joined their voices in prayers for the prosperity of the mighty sovereign. The festivities lasted for eight days.

This short relaxation was interrupted by an irruption of the army of Tokatmish through the gates of Derbent, in the Caucasus. The Khan of Kapchak had recovered from the chastisement inflicted on him, during Timour's memorable campaign, and had once more renewed hostilities.

The conqueror, therefore, again prepared for war, and reviewed his vast army, on a plain about twenty-seven miles south of Derbent, in a line extending from the Caucasus to the shores of the Caspian. He then led his forces over the pass near Mount Elbourz, and again encountered the army of Tokatmish. The cavalry, on both sides, fought fiercely, and charged each other with desperate speed; but victory again declared on the side of her favourite, Tokatmish fled into the wilds of Siberia, and Timour, halting on the plains of Astrakhan, installed a son of Urus Khan, as the new Khan of Kapchak.

Before returning to his own dominions, the mighty lord of Touran entered Muscovy, penetrated to the shores of the Dnieper, and repassing the Caucasus, caused a great festival to be held on a plain in Georgia, to celebrate his victorious campaign. The sovereign was seated on a throne, in a splendid pavilion, the air was perfumed with rose water, and bottles of Georgian wine were uncorked, amidst songs and music.

The man, who had not many years before been a destitute wanderer in the deserts of Kharism, had now arrived at the highest pitch of earthly glory. The chiefs on the western and northern shores of the Caspian submitted to his sway, his eldest surviving son Miran was governor of Azerbijan, the wealthy city of Ormuz, in the Persian gulf, paid him tribute,[1]

[1] *Ormuz*, which was for ages the great emporium of trade in the Persian Gulf, was originally founded by a colony of Arabs, and the city appears to have enjoyed centuries of peace and commercial prosperity. In 1290 the Mongols invaded Ormuz, and the inhabitants fled to a barren volcanic island, at the mouth of the Persian Gulf, which was named Ormuz, in memory of the ancient city. The king of this new Ormuz considered it prudent to send tribute to Timour.

The city is described by Abdul Rizak, the ambassador sent by Shah Rokh to India in 1442, as a place which has not its equal on the surface of the globe. "The merchants of Syria, Egypt, Roum, Fars, Khorassan, Irak, and Mawur-ul-naher, as well as the inhabitants of Java, Bengal, Socotra, Tennaserim, Malabar, Guzerat, and Arabia all make their way to this port. They bring hither those rare and precious articles which the sun, and the moon, and

and all the people of central Asia acknowledged him as their sovereign. He returned to Samarcand in 1396, and occupied himself for some time in the arrangement of the internal affairs of his vast empire, and in erecting splendid edifices in the land of his birth. Superb mosques and palaces were built at Samarcand and Kesh, gardens were laid out full of fragrant flowers, marble was transported from Azerbijan, and porcelain to adorn the chambers, from the distant empire of China.

For a time the enjoyment of great power, and the opportunities to work much good, in establishing peace throughout his now enormous empire, had charms for Timour; but, after an interval of rest, the conqueror still found the lust of conquest strong upon him, and, from the heights of Mawur-ul-naher, he looked down, with longing eyes, on the fertile plains of India.

Having conceived the idea of conquering the rich empire of Hindostan, he asked counsel of his sons and nobles, but they all opposed it, except Shah Rokh.[1] His resolution, however, had been already taken, and his grandson Peer Mohammed crossed the Indus, and laid siege to Moultan. Meanwhile Timour led his army across the Oxus, and commenced a new

the rains have combined to bring to perfection."—See *India in the Fifteenth Century*, published by the Hakluyt Society. Also *Clavijo*, p. 94. At present a few ruins, scattered amidst wild deserts of salt, on a dreary islet, alone testify to the former greatness of Ormuz.

[1] "My design for reducing Hindostan. First I asked counsel of my sons and my Ameers, and Shah Rokh advised it, but the Ameers opposed, and I forgave them."—*Institutes.*

campaign, in 1398, by attacking the infidel mountaineers who inhabit the ravines of the Hindoo Koosh, that tremendous range of mountains, which was called by the Arabs, " the stony girdle of the earth."

It was in the month of March that Timour, with sixty-two thousand men, entered the defiles of that mighty range which rises in a bold and precipitous line, with sides bare, black, and polished, from the plains of Balkh and Koondooz. At that time of year, and until the end of June, the passes are clear of snow, but they are destitute of vegetation, and mural precipices rise up perpendicularly on each side of the road, to a height of two thousand or three thousand feet. The summits of the peaks are covered with eternal snow.

On the approach of the invaders, the mountaineers retired into the deep ravines, where they were protected by snow drifts. No difficulties, however, could daunt the intrepid conqueror, or turn him from his purpose. True, the precipices, which he must pass to reach the retreat of the infidels, were perpendicular, but the resources of Timour's mind were inexhaustible, and he resolved upon a plan as audacious as it was novel. He ordered his army to be lowered down the rocky walls, by ropes, from ledge to ledge. The sovereign himself was lowered down on a stage of planks, secured together by iron rings, and the operation was five times repeated. The whole party was now on foot, except Timour himself, whose horse had also been lowered down; and this put them on equal terms with the mountaineers, who were, however, so amazed at the unexpected appearance of the invaders, that they abandoned their stronghold, sued for mercy, and humbly submitted to the authority of the mighty "lord of the conjunctions."[1] Timour then continued his march to Cabul, and prepared for the invasion of India.

Hindostan had been ruled by Moslem conquerors since the days of Mahmud of Ghizni, and at this time Mahmud, of the house of Togluk, reigned at Delhi over a disorganized empire, consisting of a Moslem army, a Hindoo population, and various Rajpoot states, which were virtually independent.

Timour crossed the Indus in 1398, and united his army with that of Peer Mohammed, on the banks of the Sutlej. He then marched to Delhi, slaughtered a vast number of prisoners who hindered his progress, and encamped on the banks of the Jumna, in January, 1399; where he found the Indian army, under king Mahmud, drawn up in order of battle, with ten thousand horse, forty thousand foot, and a brigade of elephants.

Timour, to use his own words, "resolved to appear weak in the sight of the Sultan of Delhi," and he surrounded his army with a ditch. This stratagem filled the Indians with presumptuous confidence, they

[1] *Sahib Keraun*, which was one of Timour's titles, means "lord of the grand conjunctions." The Easterns believe that in all the great conjunctions of the planets, there is a great revolution in the world. Thus Abraham, Moses, Zoroaster, Christ, and Mohammed, came into the world in a grand conjunction. Kayomurs, Solomon, Alexander, Zengis, and Timour, were each in their turn, *Sahib Keraun*, or "masters of the conjunctions," and of all the great events during their respective reigns.—*D'Herbelot.*

marched into the plain, were charged furiously by the Zagatay cavalry, and utterly defeated. Delhi fell into the hands of the conquerors, and an accidental collision with the citizens led to a general massacre. The holy city of Muttra met with the same fate, and Timour, satisfied with having become a *Ghazee*, or slayer of infidels, determined to return to Samarcand. He marched by the sources of the Ganges, Cashmere, and the Punjab, and crossing the Indus by a bridge of boats, he made a triumphal progress, through the defiles of the Hindoo Koosh, to his capital, which he reached in April 1399.

"Spoils above measure" were brought from India by the conqueror, who commenced the erection of a grand mosque at Samarcand. Ninety captured elephants[1] conveyed the stones from the quarries. This splendid edifice, the monument of Timour's conquests, consisted of a vaulted roof, supported on four hundred and eighty pillars of hewn stone, with doors of brass, walls decorated with inscriptions in relief, and lofty minarets at the four corners. It is now a mere heap of ruins.

After a brief season of repose, the conqueror was again obliged to take the field, owing to the deplorable misgovernment of his eldest son Miran Meerza, in Azerbijan,[2] and having tranquillized that province, he prepared to invade the territory of the Ottoman Sultan Bayazid. The towns of Bagdad, Aleppo,[3] and

[1] See *Clavijo*, p. 156. [2] See *Clavijo*, p. 95 of this volume.

[3] D'Herbelot has recorded an interview between Timour and some doctors of law, after the capture of Aleppo, during which the

Damascus were taken, and the Turk was utterly routed at Angora, on the 20th of July, 1402.[1] These transactions are faithfully recorded by the Spanish ambassador;[2] who followed the conqueror on his return march to Samarcand. The events which followed, the magnificent festivities, and grand rejoicings, at which Clavijo was present, and which are also fully described by the eastern historian Ali of Yezd, concluded the career of this extraordinary man.

Clavijo gives an account of the insolent message of the Chinese envoys, which excited the wrath of the aged warrior, who resolved upon invading the celestial empire in the depth of winter. He marched out of Samarcand, on the 8th of January, 1405,[3] in a heavy fall of snow, and, crossing the Jaxartes upon the ice, he encamped at a place called Otrar. In February he was attacked by fever and ague, and

conqueror declared that he had never undertaken any war without deliberation. *Bib. Or.*, ii, p. 517. Gibbon repeats a portion of this curious conversation, chap. lxv.

[1] The story of the iron cage, in which Bayazid is said to have been confined, is not mentioned by any early historian of the life of Timour, except Ahmed ben Arabshah. The fable afterwards appeared in a modern Ottoman chronicle, translated by Leunclavius.

D'Herbelot stated that it was not even mentioned by Arabshah, but Sir W. Jones has detected the error of the French orientalist, and quotes the passage in his works.—*Sir W. Jones's Works*, v, p. 547.

[2] See *Clavijo*, p. 73 *et seq.*

[3] He took with him several thousand loads of corn, intending to sow it along the line of march, as a supply for his troops on their return.—*Ali of Yezd.*

he died on the 17th of that month, in the year 1405, aged sixty-nine, leaving thirty-six male descendants. Timour's body was embalmed with musk and rose water, wrapped in linen, laid in an ebony coffin, and sent to Samarcand, where it was buried.

According to Ali of Yezd, Timour was tall and stout, but well shaped. His complexion was ruddy and fair; he had a large flowing beard, broad shoulders, and was very strong. He could not bear a lie, but loved the naked truth. He was bold, courageous, feared, and respected.

This picture was drawn by a friendly hand; he is described in very different colours by his enemy Ahmed ben Arabshah, who makes the spirit of winter address the dying conqueror thus:—

"Stop thy rapid career, thou unjust tyrant! How long dost thou mean to carry flames over an unhappy world? If thou art a spirit of hell, so am I. We are both old, and our occupation is the same, that of subjugating slaves. But proceed to extirpate mankind, and make the earth cold! yet thou wilt find at last that my blasts are colder. If thou canst boast of countless bands, who, faithful to thy orders, harass and destroy, know that my wintry days are, with God's aid, destroyers also;—and by the Almighty that liveth, I will abate thee nothing! Thou shalt be overwhelmed with my vengeance, and all thy fire shall not save thee from the cold death of the icy tempest."[1]

[1] Malcolm's *History of Persia*. Goethe gives a poetical version of this speech (*Gedichte*, p. 394); and Sir W. Jones has translated it into Latin.

Undoubtedly Timour's conquests were the cause of much suffering to the human race; but, on the other hand, he certainly was not the remorseless tyrant he is represented by Arabshah, and his other enemies. His boundless ambition led him to contemplate the subjugation of the whole world, and he lost no opportunity of extending his power; yet there is evidence that he had loftier aims than the mere gratification of his lust for conquest. He at least persuaded himself that in conquering Mohammedan countries, he delivered them from oppressive misrule, while religion prompted him to destroy the cities of infidel Hindoos. He was idolized by his soldiers, and by his own family, and he was free from the more despicable vices of eastern sovereigns; but the most marked feature in his character was his untiring energy and activity. "When I clothed myself in the robes of empire," he says in his Institutes, "I shut my eyes to safety, and to the repose which is found on the bed of ease."[1]

The name of Timour is frequently coupled with that of Zengis Khan; yet the latter was a rude uncultivated barbarian, while there is evidence that the former was versed in all the knowledge of his age and country. We know, from his Memoirs, that Timour was taught to read the Koran; he appears to have cultivated his own language, and he under-

[1] Malcolm, in his *History of Persia*, thus sums up the character of Timour. "Though one of the greatest of warriors, he was one of the worst of monarchs. He was able, brave, and generous; but ambitious, cruel, and oppressive."

stood and admired the Persian odes of Hafiz. His native language was the "Zagatai Toorki," which, at that time, prevailed from the Ulugh Tagh mountains to the Hindoo Koosh, and from the Caspian to the Cobi desert. The period between the reign of Timour and that of Baber, was the golden age of Toorki literature, and the princes of the great conqueror's family wrote poetry in their own tongue, and gave liberal encouragement to its cultivation amongst their courtiers. Ali Shir Beg, the Grand Vizier to Hosein Meerza, composed a poem in the Toorki language, and also wrote a complete prosody; and the other Ameers, at the courts of the Timouride princes, while they studied the literature of Persia, did not neglect the poetry of their native Toorki. Timour seems to have given the first impulse to these intellectual pursuits amongst his countrymen, and, though he owes his fame chiefly to his conquests, it would be unfair to forget his liberal encouragement of learned men, his love of the game of chess, and his claims to literary merit, in the composition of his Memoirs and Institutes. He has no right to the title of a reformer or of a benefactor to the human race, but neither was he a coarse and ruthless destroyer of his fellow creatures, like Zengis, and so many other Asiatic conquerors. He lived in an age and amongst a people to whom mercy and toleration were unknown. The realization of his own ideal of a perfect sovereign would have been impossible; yet he has some claim to the admiration of posterity, and, with Gibbon, we may excuse a generous enthusiasm in the reader of the Institutes, for their great author.

On the death of Timour his vast empire soon fell to pieces; yet the greatest and best princes that ever reigned in Mohammedan countries, are to be found amongst his descendants. His son, the good and virtuous Shah Rokh, during a reign of more than forty years in Khorassan, preserved peace and order in that unhappy country.[1] Ibrahim Meerza encouraged literature at Shiraz, and caused Ali of Yezd to write the life of the mighty conqueror.[2] Ulugh Beg, who reigned at Samarcand, was the greatest astronomer of his age.[3] Hosein Meerza, who reigned at Herat from 1487 to 1506, was a patron of learned men; and his court was frequented by such poets and historians as Jami and Hatifi, Mirkhond and Khondemir.

[1] "Shah Rokh is not more celebrated for his piety and liberality, than for his courage and military virtues. He died in 1446, having reigned over Khorassan since 1397."—*D'Herbelot.*

[2] Ibrahim Meerza, the son of Shah Rokh, reigned at Shiraz for twenty years, and died in 1435. He built a famous medrassa or college there, and encouraged literature.

[3] The astronomical tables of this prince, called *Zig Ulugh Beg,* are divided into four parts. The first treats of the æras and epochs; the second of the knowledge of the times; the third of the course of the planets; and the fourth of the fixed stars, in two hundred sections, A.D. 1437.

They are considered the most correct of all those which have been given us by the Mohammedans, and they agree very well with those of Tycho Brahe. John Greaves, the great English mathematician, translated the tables of fixed stars, given by Ulugh Beg, in 1650. Ulugh Beg had an observatory at Samarcand, and, amongst other instruments, he used a quadrant, the radius of which equalled in length the height of the dome of St. Sophia.—*D'Herbelot; Life of Greaves,* two vols., 1737; *Insignorum aliquot stellarum loca ab Ulugh Beg observata,* A.H. 841.

Baber, the founder of the empire of the great Moguls in India, was, after Timour, the greatest genius of his race; and his memoirs, which he wrote during the latter part of his life, compose one of the most curious and interesting works in eastern literature.[1] Lastly, the illustrious Akbar, the enlightened, the generous, the liberal emperor, was the brightest ornament of the family of Timour.

Akbar died in 1605, and from that time it would be well if a veil could be drawn over the history of the house of Timour. His three successors Jehanghir, Shah Jehan, and Aurungzebe, retained great power; but it was bought at the price of endless crimes, and, from the death of Aurungzebe in 1707, the great moguls became contemptible, as well as wicked. Escaping, through their submissive cowardice, the whirlwinds of Nadir, of Ahmed Shah, and of the Mahrattas, they subsequently continued to batten on an enormous pension granted by the British government, until, having, in 1857, added treason and murder to their other crimes, they will at last disappear from history unheeded and unpitied.

Such is the melancholy end of the descendants of the mighty Timour, the heroic Baber, and the illustrious Akbar.

After nearly five centuries of sovereign power the Timourides have ceased to reign; and of all the countries over which the members of this family

[1] *Vakeat Baberi* (Baber's Occurrences) was translated by Dr. Leyden and W. Erskine, Esq. R. M. Caldecott, Esq. wrote an abridgment of it, which was published in 1844.

once ruled, India alone has made any advance in material prosperity, since the days of their power. Samarcand, the capital of Timour, is a desolate heap of ruins. Andecan, the beloved home of Baber, is in the possession of Uzbeg savages. The once rich and opulent Herat, the abode of learning, the brilliant capital of Shah Rokh and Hosein Meerza, the native land of poets and historians, is now the ruinous fortress of a truculent Afghan. Shiraz, the beautiful city, made immortal by the songs of Sadi and of Hafiz, where Ali of Yezd wrote the life of the mighty Timour, is reduced to the condition of an impoverished provincial town, in the kingdom of the bungling Kajar Shahs of Persia. India, however, has passed into the hands of masters who do not require the fulsome flattery of Abul Fazl to show that their rule is more enlightened and beneficent than that of Akbar. The irrigating canals of Feroze and Shah Jehan have been restored and improved, after centuries of decay and disuse; a canal for irrigation and navigation, the largest work of the kind in either the old or the new world, now passes through eight hundred miles of the former empire of the great Moguls; the tax on land is lighter and less burdensome than the assessment imposed by Shere Shah or Akbar; good roads have been made; schools and hospitals founded; the more revolting forms of crime rooted out; valuable plants introduced from the remotest parts of the earth, more useful than the melons which Baber brought from Fergana; and the literature both of the Hindoos and of their Moslem conquerors has been carefully preserved by the wise strangers from the west. Whatever may be the shortcomings of the English in India, they need not fear to compare the present state of their acquired empire, with the same country in the best days of the rule of the descendants of Timour.

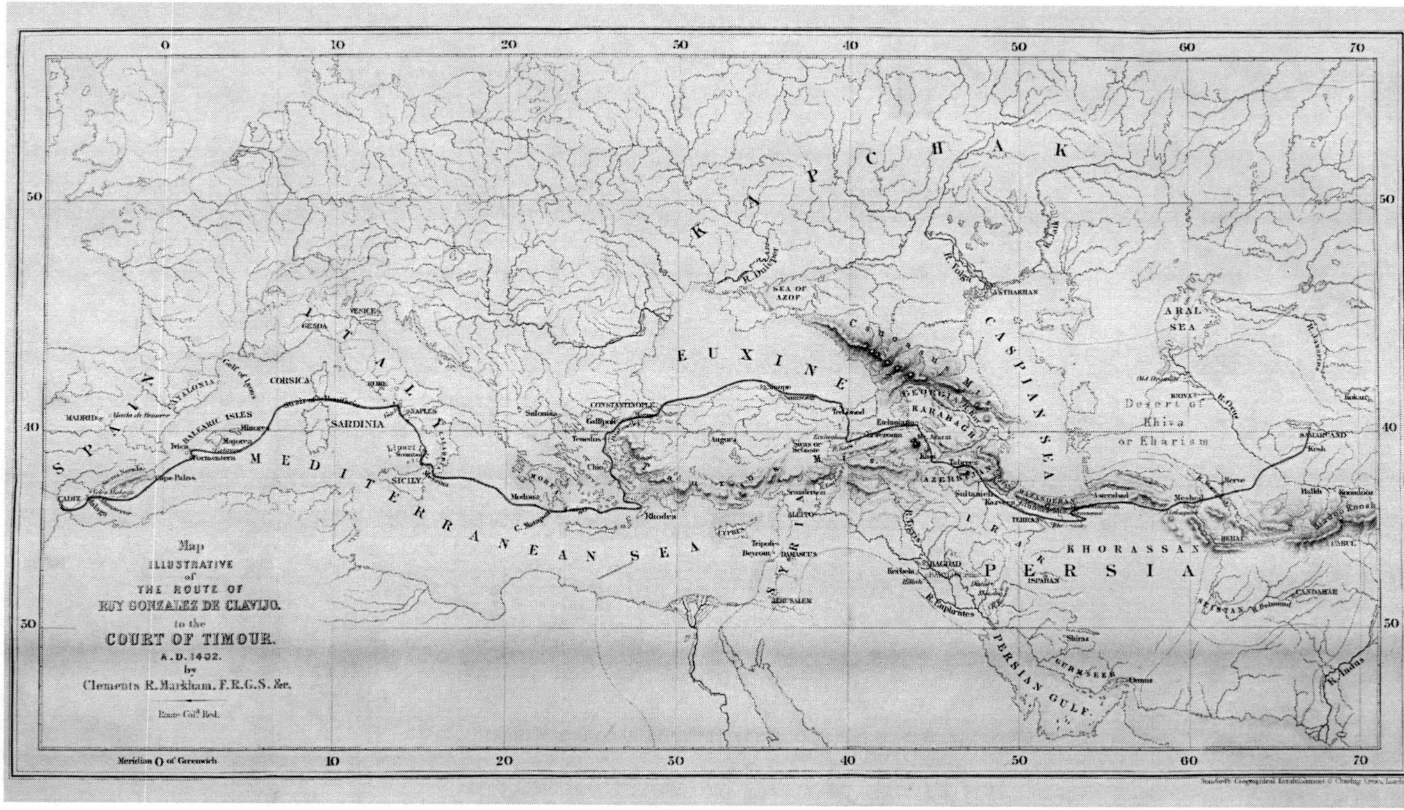

Map
ILLUSTRATIVE
of
THE ROUTE OF
RUY GONZALEZ DE CLAVIJO
to the
COURT OF TIMOUR.
A.D. 1402.
by
Clements R. Markham, F.R.G.S. &c.
Meridian 0 of Greenwich
KAPCHAK
EUXINE
CASPIAN SEA
ARAL SEA
SEA OF AZOF
MEDITERRANEAN SEA
PERSIAN GULF
SPAIN
ITALY
PERSIA
KHORASSAN
SARDINIA
CORSICA
SICILY
BALEARIC ISLES
CONSTANTINOPLE
SAMARCAND
ASTRAKHAN
Desert of Khiva or Kharism

LIFE AND ACTS

OF THE

GREAT TAMERLANE,

With a description of the Lands
of his Empire and Lordship.

Written by RUY GONZALEZ DE CLAVIJO,
Chamberlain of the most high and puissant
Lord Don Henry, third of that name,
King of Castille and Leon.

With a journal of what happened to the Embassy
which the said King sent to the said Prince,
otherwise called Timour Beg,
in the year of our Lord

1403.

I.

THE VOYAGE

FROM

CADIZ TO CONSTANTINOPLE.

THE great Lord Timour Beg, having killed the Emperor of Samarcand and seized upon his empire, where his own dominion commenced, as you will presently hear; and having conquered all the land of Mongolia, which is contained in the said empire, and the land of India the less; also having conquered all the empire of Khorassan, which is a great lordship, and having conquered and reduced to obedience the land of Tagiguinia,[1] with the territory and lordship of a land called Rei; and also having conquered and reduced all Persia and Media, with the empire of Tabreez and of Sultanieh; and also having conquered the lordship of Gheelan, with the land of Derbent; and also having conquered the land of Armenia the less, and the land of Arsinga,[2] and of Aseron,[3] and of Aunique, and reduced to obedience the empire of Merdi, and the land of Kurdistan, which is in the said Armenia; also having conquered in battle the lord of India the less, and taken a great part of his territory; also having destroyed the city of Damascus, and reduced to submission the cities of Aleppo,

[1] Kharism ? [2] Arzingan. [3] Erzeroum.

of Babylonia, and of Baldas; and having overrun many other lands and lordships, and won many other battles, and achieved many conquests, he came against the Turk Ilderim Bayazid (who was one of the greatest and most powerful lords in the world) in his land of Turkey, and gave him battle near his castle, which was called Angora, conquering him and taking him prisoner, together with one of his sons.

In this battle there happened to be present Payo de Sotomayor and Hernan Sanchez de Palazuelos, ambassadors whom the high and puissant Lord Don Henry, by the grace of God, king of Castille and Leon, whom God preserve, had sent to ascertain the power which the said Timour Beg and Turk Ilderim possessed in the world, that they might behold their magnificence, and the number of the hosts which they had brought against each other. It happened that in the battle, the great Lord Timour Beg had notice of the presence of the said Payo and Hernan Sanchez, and, for love of the said high lord the king of Castille, he treated them honorably, took them with him, entertained them, and gave them certain gifts; and received news of the high and famous king of Castille, and of the great consideration and power he had amongst the Christian kings; and, to obtain his friendship, after having conquered in the battle, he ordered an ambassador, with letters and a present, to be sent to secure an alliance with him.

With the ambassadors there went a certain Zagatayan knight named Mohamed Alcagi, with whom Timour sent his gifts and letters. The said ambassador went to the said king of Castille, and presented the letters which the Lord Timour Beg had sent, and his presents, and the women which he also sent according to his custom.

His highness the king, having received the said letters and presents, and having heard the good words which the said Timour Beg sent by his letters and ambassador, ordered that another present and ambassadors should be sent to the said Timour Beg, to increase the friendship which he had shown. He ordered that Fray Alonzo Paez de Santa Maria, master of theology, Ruy Gonzalez de Clavijo, and Gomez de Salazar, should convey the present and letters; and because the said mission is very arduous, and the journey very long, it is necessary to put in writing an account of all the places and countries through which the said ambassadors passed, and of the things which happened to them, that they may not be forgotten, and that there may be a complete knowledge concerning them.

To this end, in the name of God, in whose power are all things, and for the honour of the holy Virgin Mary his mother, I began to write from the day that the ambassadors reached the port of St. Mary, near Cadiz, to embark in a carrack, in which they had to cross the sea; and with them the ambassador, whom the said Timour Beg had sent to the said lord the king.

On Monday, which was the 21st day of the month of May, in the year of our Lord 1403, the said ambassadors arrived at the port of St. Mary, and on that day they caused part of their provisions to be sent on board the carrack, besides some which had been brought from Seville and Xeres, by some of their men.

On the following Tuesday, which was the 22nd of the same month, they got under weigh, together with Master Julian Centurio, the captain of the vessel in which they were embarked; and on Wednesday, at about sunset, they were off the cape called Spartel, with a fair wind.

On Thursday they were off Tangiers, and the hills of Barbary, and Tarifa, and Ceuta, and Algeziras, and Gibraltar; and they were so near the land that they could see those places very clearly, being within the straits; and the same day they were off the Sierra de la Fi.

On Friday, the 25th of May, when the day dawned, they were off Malaga, and anchored in the port, where they remained until the following Tuesday, as the captain had to land certain jars of oil and other merchandize. The said Malaga is a city on level ground, with one side facing the sea, and in one part, on a headland, there is a high castle with two walls; and outside the town there is another loftier castle called Alcazaba, and from one castle to the other there is a wall, which unites them together. At the other end of the town, facing the sea, there are some terraces, near which commences a wall with towers; and inside this wall there are many beautiful fruit gardens; and above the gardens and the town there are high mountains covered with houses, and vineyards, and gardens; and between the sea and the town wall there are a few warehouses belonging to merchants, and the city is very populous.

On the following Wednesday, the 29th of May, the carrack got under weigh, and was off the hill of Malaga, which is all covered with vineyards, and fruit gardens, and corn fields; she passed Velez Malaga, a high castle in these mountains; and Almuñecar, which is near the sea; and at sunset she was off the Sierra Nevada.

On Thursday she was off Cape Palos, which is near Carthagena, and on Friday she passed Cape Martin, which is a lofty headland in Catalonia.

On Saturday, at daylight, she was off an island called Formentera, which is uninhabited, and in sight of the island of Ivica; and she was in this place until Tuesday, sailing off and on, and unable to double a cape, so as to reach the port of Ivica, as the wind was foul: but on the said Tuesday, in the afternoon, they brought the carrack into port, being the 5th of June; and the captain discharged the merchandize which he brought, and got some salt on board. They remained in this port until Friday, as the wind was contrary; but on Wednesday, the 13th, they were under weigh, though the vessel was becalmed until the following Friday.

This island of Ivica is small, being five leagues long and three broad. On the day they arrived the ambassadors landed, and the governor, who was there for the king of Aragon, appointed them lodgings, and sent them men and beasts to convey them to the town. The island is a mass of hills covered with brushwood, and the town is built on a high hill near the sea, having three walls, and a castle on the most elevated part. The church is opposite to this castle, and has a high tower, and the town and castle are enclosed by one wall. In this island there are salt pans, where they make very fine salt from the water of the sea, which flows into them. These salt pans yield a great revenue, as many ships come from the Levant every year to get a cargo of salt. On the wall of the town there is a tower, which they call the tower of Avicena; and they say that Avicena was a native of this island; and on the walls and towers there are engines for casting stones, which the king Don Pedro caused to be used when he held the walls.[1]

[1] The Balearic islands were occupied by the Moors for four centuries. In 1229 James, king of Aragon, took Majorca, and pulled the Moorish king's beard, but his invasion, and subsequent flights of the Moorish inhabitants to Granada, reduced the population one half. James added much to the capital town of Palma, and built the cathedral. In 1232 he conquered Minorca, and in 1256 he established his younger son James in these islands, who became king of them by virtue of his father's will in 1276. In 1285 Alonzo, his nephew, a son of the king of Aragon, drove him out of the islands, and also conquered Ivica; but James was restored at the peace in 1291, paying tribute to his nephew, James II of Aragon. His title was *James, king of the Mallorcas and Count of Roussillon and Montpelier*. He was succeeded by his son Sancho, who governed the islands peaceably, and died in 1324 without children. The king of Aragon then gave the islands to James, son of Sancho's brother Ferdinand, and the young king married Constantia, daughter of Alonzo III of Aragon.

The young king James was finally deprived of his islands by Pedro IV of Aragon in 1345, and he died the following year. His son James married Joan of Naples in 1362, and, joining the Black Prince at Bordeaux, went with him to Castille, where he died in 1375.

After 1345, and at the time Clavijo visited Ivica, the islands were governed by officers appointed by the kings of Aragon.

On Saturday, the 28th of June, the vessel was off the island of Majorca, and so near that it could be seen very clearly; and on Sunday she was off an island called Cabrera, on which there is a small castle; and on Monday and Tuesday she made little way, owing to light winds; but on Wednesday she was off the island of Minorca, and entered the gulf of Lyons. From Thursday to Saturday she passed across the gulf of Lyons with a fair wind; and on Sunday, which was St. John's day, she was off an island called Linera, which is subject to the authority of the viceroy of Aragon.

At daylight on Monday the vessel was between two islands, the one called Corsica, where there is a castle named Bonifacio, in possession of a Genoese, and the other Sardinia, where there is a castle belonging to the Catalonians named Luecigosardo.[1] These castles on the two islands are near the sea, the one opposite the other; and the strait between them, which is narrow and dangerous, is called in those parts the strait of Bonifacio.

On Tuesday she was off an island called Ponza, which is uninhabited, but in former times it was peopled, and there were two monasteries on it, and grand edifices erected by Virgil; and on the left of this island some high mountains were in sight which are on the main land, and are called Montecarzel, where there is a castle called St. Felice, in the dominions of king Lanzalago.[2] A little further on she passed other mountains, also on the main land, and came in sight of a town which is called Taracena,[3] in the Roman territory, and twelve leagues distant from Rome. Between the sea and the town there were fruit gardens and tall trees, and between these gardens and the town there was a monastery, which was once occupied by nuns, but they had all been carried off by the Moors of Barbary.

On Wednesday, the vessel continued her course, and on

[1] Longosardo. [2] Ladislaus. [3] Terracina.

Thursday, the 27th of June, at sunset, she was off the port of Gaeta, and anchored so near the town that they were able to place a gang board on the city wall. The ambassadors went on shore, and lodged in an inn outside the town, where they remained sixteen days, because the captain and some merchants in the carrack had to land some of the cargo, and to get on board a cargo of oil.

This city of Gaeta, and its port, is very beautiful. The entrance of the harbour is narrow, but becomes wider inside, and is enclosed on every side by high hills, where there are castles and fine houses, with many fruit gardens. On the left hand there is an eminence, surmounted by a great tower, said to have been built by Roldan, for which reason it is called the tower of Roldan. Opposite this hill there is another, where the city is built, and the gate and houses facing the harbour are so close to the water, that the walls are washed by it; and two towers stand out from the walls, rising from the sea about a sling's throw from each other. When it is necessary, a chain is stretched from one tower to the other, inside which the galleys and boats take refuge, in time of war. Between the town and the tower of Roldan there is a castle with high towers, battlements, and turrets, and a wall surrounds the whole, to guard the city. Towards the sea there are high rocks, so that no vessel could enter the port in time of war; and another wall runs along the sea face, within which there is a hill covered with vineyards and olive gardens, and between this hill and the wall there is a street, with many houses and shops. In this street there is a church, where the people perform their devotions. It is called Santa Maria la Anunciada, and opposite to it there is another church called San Antonio, and above the church of Santa Maria there is a handsome monastery of Franciscans. At the end of this street the city wall goes over the hill to the sea on the other side, and this wall is built to prevent vessels, in time of war, from coming to damage the city. At the end of the wall, where the walls unite which encircle these hills, there is a church called Trinidad, and near it there are some houses and towers, like an *alcazar*.[1] Not far from this church there is a fissure made in the rock, about ten *brazas* in depth, and fifty paces long, and so narrow that only one man could get into it at a time; and a hermit lives there named Santa Cruz. It is said that there is a record in the city, showing that this opening was made on the day on which Jesus Christ suffered his passion. Within the walls there are many beautiful houses and gardens, containing oranges, lemons, citrons, and vines, which are very pleasant to look upon. Outside the walls, and facing the sea, there is a very handsome street containing palaces, houses, and gardens; and this street extends to a place called Mola, two leagues from the city. It is thickly inhabited, and paved throughout, and beyond it there are hills covered with villages; and all these things are visible from the city, presenting a most pleasant and wonderful view.

The ambassadors went to see everything while they were there; and beyond Mola there was a town and a high castle, and other places on the hills. At the entrance of the port, on the right hand, there was a very high look-out tower, called the tower of Carellano;[2] and these places once belonged to the Count of Fondi, but they are now subject to king Lanzalago, who seized upon them during the war with king Louis.[3] The houses of Gaeta are very handsome to look at outside; they are very high, with windows towards the

[1] *Al casr*, Arabic for a palace.

[2] Carigliano.

[3] Margaret, daughter of Mary, the sister of Joan queen of Naples, married Charles Duke of Durazzo, and on his murder in Hungary in 1386, she caused her son Ladislaus or Lancelot, who is called Lanzalago by Clavijo, to be crowned; and fled with him to Gaeta. In 1390 Louis of Anjou was crowned king of Naples; but in 1401 Ladislaus recovered the whole kingdom, and died in 1414, leaving no children.

sea. The finest street is that which runs parallel to the sea, the others being steep, narrow, and bad for walking. In the chief street there is much merchandise, and the city has a considerable trade during the whole year. When king Lanzalago was at war with king Louis, he lost all his kingdom except this city; and he marched out from it, and recovered all his dominions again.

When king Lanzalago was in this city, and married to Madame Gostanza, daughter of Monfrey de Charamente, he parted from her, and married her by force to his vassal, the son of Louis de Capua; and they say that the king himself, being in the church of Trinidad, took their hands and married them in sight of a great concourse of people; and afterwards, on the day of the marriage, that he took her by the hand, and danced with her. The said woman, his wife, said many ugly things in the streets; and they say that the king did this by the advice of his mother, the lady Margarita. Afterwards the king married the sister of the king of Cyprus, named Doña Maria; and he had no children by his wife, the lady Gostanza, during one year and a half, but by his second wife king Lanzalago had a daughter named Doña Juanela, married to the Duke of Sterlic and Babera, and she is reported to be a very beautiful woman.[1]

[1] Margaret married her son Ladislaus or Lanzalago to Constantia, the daughter of Manfred de Claramonte, a Catalonian, who governed Sicily. Manfred, who was Count of Modica, resided at Catania, and had made several successful expeditions against the Moors. He died at Palermo in 1391. In 1392 Constantia was sent to a private house at Gaeta, by advice of Margaret, on the pretext that since Manfred's death her mother had become the mistress of Martin, Duke of Monblanco, brother of John king of Aragon; and that it was dishonourable for king Ladislaus to have the daughter of a concubine for his wife. Two years afterwards Constantia, who had been so basely treated, married Andrew, Count of Altavilla. When he led her home, she declared, before all the courtiers, that he ought to consider himself a fortunate knight, as he had got his sovereign's wife for his mistress. This is the story alluded to by Clavijo.

In 1402 Ladislaus married Mary, sister of the king of Cyprus, but she died in 1404.

On Friday, the 13th of July, the carrack got under weigh at noon, and leaving Gaeta, continued on her course.

On Saturday she passed by an island which is called Ischia, and another called Procida. They are both uninhabited. The same day she was off an inhabited island called Trape,[1] in the dominions of the king of Naples, where there is a fine town. On the same day, she passed Cape Minerva[2] on the main land, and two high hills, between which there is a city called Amalfi, where they say the head of St. Andrew is preserved. At the hour of vespers, they beheld two masses of smoke fall from the heavens and reach the sea, and the water rose with violence, and with a great noise, and obscured the heavens, covering them with clouds: so they luffed the vessel as much as they were able, because they said that if those masses reached the carrack, they would surely sink her.

On Sunday, at daylight, they passed between two uninhabited islands, bare and without trees, named Arcu and Firucu; and a little further on, on the left hand side, another came in sight, with a high hill, which is called Stromboli; and it has a mouth out of which comes smoke and fire; and in the night great flames issued out, with a mighty noise. They also saw another island on the right hand, called Lipari, which is inhabited, and subject to king Lanzalago. In this island the veil of the blessed Saint Agueda is kept: and the island used to burn, but, owing to the prayers of the blessed Saint Agueda, it ceased to burn, together with other neighbouring islands; and when the other islands burn they take out this veil, and presently the fire ceases.

On Monday they passed amongst certain uninhabited islands called Salinas, Strangolin, and Bolcani,[3] and a great

[1] Capri?

[2] Cape Minerva, now called Cape Campanella, opposite Capri. "Once ennobled by the celebrated temple of Minerva."—*G. Knight*, p. 111.

[3] Salina, Stromboli, and Vulcano.

smoke issued from them, with much noise; and the same day they passed two desert islands called Paranea and Panarin.

On Tuesday, the 17th of July, the vessel was becalmed between these two islands; and in the night a heavy gale of wind sprung up, which lasted until the morning.

At noon on Wednesday the sails of the carrack were split, and she ran under bare poles, being in great danger. The storm lasted until Wednesday night, and the islands of Strangol and Bolcante[1] sent forth great volumes of fire and smoke; and during the tempest the captain caused the litanies to be sung, and every one sought mercy from God. The prayers being concluded, and the tempest still raging, a bright light appeared on the mast head of the carrack, and another light was seen on the bowsprit, which is that part of the ship ahead of the forecastle; and another on the yard arm, which is over the poop; and all who were on board the carrack saw these lights, for they were called up to see them, and remained some time to see if they would disappear; but they did not cease to shine during the storm; and presently all those on board went to sleep, except the captain and certain mariners, whose duty it was to keep watch. The captain, and two mariners, who were awake, heard the voices of men in the air, and the captain asked the mariners if they heard that noise; they replied that they did; and all this time the tempest did not abate. Soon afterwards they again saw those lights, returned to the places where they had been before; so they awoke the rest of the crew, who also saw the lights, and the captain told them of the voices he had heard. These lights remained as long as it would take to say a mass, and presently the storm ceased. The next day they were near the said islands, and in sight of Sicily, with fine weather and a fair wind. But they continued amongst these islands

[1] Stromboli and Vulcano.

until the following Thursday, owing to the calms which prevailed.

On Friday afternoon, the vessel was off the island of Sicily, and in sight of a tower which is called the tower of Faro, which is at the entrance of the port of Messina; but owing to the strong current which flows out of the strait, and the light winds, they were unable to reach the port of Messina that day. At night the wind rose, and a pilot, who had come out from the city of Messina to take the carrack into port, caused sail to be made; and, the vessel being off the tower of Faro, she struck the ground and the rudder jumped out of its case. They all expected to be lost, but the wind being light and the sea smooth, they got her off, and let go two anchors, waiting for daylight. At dawn the wind increased, so they made sail, and reached the port of Messina.

Opposite the tower of Faro is the land of Calabria, which is the main land, and between Calabria and Sicily the sea is only a league across; and in the tower there is a light all night, that vessels may know the entrance. The land of Calabria appeared to be sown with corn, and to be covered with many vineyards and fruit gardens. The city of Messina is near the sea, and its wall, with many well built towers, is washed by the waves. The houses are very high and handsome, built of stone and mortar; and they look beautiful from the sea. The windows of the houses face the sea, and the principal streets run parallel to the shore, and there are five or six gates opening towards the sea. At the end of the city there are terraces; and outside the walls there is a monastery of black Monks, called San Salvador, who say their prayers after the manner of the Greeks. In the city there is a strong castle.

The following Monday, being the 22nd of July, they made sail and departed from this port, with a fair wind. On the right hand was the island, and on the left was Calabria, and a city called Reggio. They entered the gulf of Venice, and continued in it until Thursday. On Friday afternoon they were off Mondon,[1] a land belonging to Venice; and the same day they came in sight of an island called Sapiencia,[2] and of two others called Benetico[3] and Cerne, and the Cape of Galo;[4] and they also saw the main land, called Coron.[5]

On Saturday, they were off Cape Matapan, and Cape St. Angelo, which are on a territory belonging to Venice; and at noon they passed close to an inhabited island called Cetul,[6] between it and a high rock called Lobo.[7] On this island of Cetul they saw a small castle, with high towers, on a lofty rock facing the sea. A little further on, in a plain near the sea, there appeared a great mass of ruins; and they say that this is the temple which Paris destroyed, when he seized upon Helen, and broke the idol, at the time that king Priam sent him to make war upon Greece. After passing this island, the vessel sailed between three rocks called Tres, Dos, and As.[8]

On Sunday, the 29th of July, they were off an uninhabited island called Cequilo, which is composed of high hills, where falcons breed. They tried to pass between this island and a high rock near the shore, where there was a strong current, which drove the vessel towards the land; and when they wished to go about, she passed so close to the shore, that some young falcons, which were sitting on a rock, began to scream. The vessel was in such danger that the captain, and some merchants and sailors, stripped off their clothes; and, when they stood off the shore, they understood that God had shown great mercy.

On Monday, the vessel was between two inhabited islands called Nillo,[9] and Ante-Nillo, which formerly belonged to

[1] Modon, near Navarino. [2] Sapienza. [3] Venetico.
[4] Cape Gallo. [5] Koroni, at the entrance of the gulf of Koroni.
[6] Cerigo? [7] Ovo? [8] *Three*, *Two*, and *Ace*.
[9] Milo and Anti-Milo.

the dukedom of the Archipelago, but they are now held by the Venetians, and are well covered with flocks of sheep. The vessel was becalmed between these islands for two days; and on Thursday she was off three inhabited islands, belonging to the dukedom of the Archipelago, called Mo,[1] Centuriona,[2] and Christiana;[3] and at noon she was off an island called Naxia, which is very large, and the capital of the dukedom.

On Friday, the 3rd of August, at daylight, the vessel was off an inhabited island called Calamo,[4] which is covered with corn fields; and on the same day she was off the island of Lango, which is held by the knights of the order who possess Rhodes; and on the left hand they sighted a part of the main land of Turkey, which is called Nisari and Lucrio. The islands are so close to the main land that they did not attempt to pass through the passage between them during the night: but they passed close to some other islands belonging to the lordship of Rhodes, called Piscopia,[5] and St. Nicholas de Carquini, and Pimia; and on the same afternoon the carrack was anchored in the port of the island of Rhodes.

When the ambassadors arrived in port, they sent to the city, to know if the grand master was there; and an answer came that the master, with certain galleys, and a great part of his troops, together with certain carracks and galleys of Genoa, led by captain Buchicate,[6] were gone to make war on the kingdom of Alexandria.

[1] Nio? [2] Santorini. [3] Christiana.

[4] Kalimno? [5] Piscopi.

[6] In 1396 the French seized upon Genoa. In 1401 John le Meingle, surnamed Boucicault, a marshal of France, entered Genoa as governor, and became so acceptable to the people, that they induced the French king to make him governor for life. In April, 1403, Boucicault sailed from Genoa with a fleet against the king of Cyprus, and forced him to a peace. He then went to Candelorum, in Cilicia, forced the lord of it to ally himself with France and Genoa, plundered Beyrout, and returned

On Saturday the ambassadors went on shore, and proceeded to the great palace of Rhodes, to see the lieutenant who had been left there by the grand master,[1] and to speak with him. The said lieutenant, and the friars who were with him, when they knew that the ambassadors were approaching, came out to meet them, and told them that the grand master was absent, but that, for the sake of the king of Castille, all their desires should willingly be complied with. The said ambassadors replied that they wished to go on shore, to obtain news respecting Timour Beg, and to collect information. The lieutenant, therefore, ordered them to be lodged in an inn belonging to a knight of the order, in which there was a church dedicated to the blessed St. Catherine. The ambassadors went to this lodging on Sunday, the 5th of August, and remained there until Thursday the 30th; and all that time they could obtain no news, except such as was brought by some who had come from the fleet, from parts of Syria, and from the Jerusalem pilgrimage. These said that Timour Beg intended to invade Syria, to reduce the Sultan of Babylon, that he had already sent his ambassadors, with a message demanding that the Sultan should coin his money, use his arms, and pay a certain annual tribute, and that, if the Sultan refused, he, the great Timour Beg, would not

towards Genoa with a galley from Chios, and another from the Knights of Rhodes. In 1410 the Genoese rebelled against him, and expelled the French.

[1] In 1396 the grand chapter at Rhodes elected Philibert de Naillac, grand prior of Aquitaine, to be Grand Master. He was immediately invited by the Pope to join a league against Bajazet, which he did with great readiness, and ordered his galleys to be equipped. Naillac fought with bravery at the fatal battle of Nicopolis; and escaped, with Sigismund king of Hungary, in a fisherman's boat to the mouth of the Danube, where the Christian fleet received him. The Grand Master then combined with Boucicault, to ravage the coasts of Syria. They were repulsed from Tripoli, but plundered Beyrout. In 1409 the Rhodian Knights made an advantageous peace with the Sultan. Naillac died in 1421, at a good old age.

wait until the summer, but would presently invade Syria. Such were the rumours amongst the Moors of Jerusalem, but they were only from hearsay, and the ambassadors did not consider them to be certain.

While they were in Rhodes, four great carracks and two Genoese ships arrived, with news from the fleet. They said that the fleet had sailed to Candelor, a castle of Turkey, and besieged it for twelve days; when the lord of Candelor came out and fought those of the fleet, and certain Frenchmen and Genoese were killed. Thence the fleet sailed to Ripuli,[1] a town in Syria, and attacked it. The people of Ripuli crossed a river which flows near the town, attacked the invaders, and did them much harm. The commanders of the fleet, therefore, took council together, and decided that as the carracks and ships sailed better than the galleys, they should go on ahead, towards Alexandria,[2] and wait off that port for nine days; while the galleys should proceed to the attack of Beyrout, a town of Syria, which is the port of Damascus. The said carracks made sail for Alexandria, and the galleys attacked and destroyed the town of Beyrout. The carracks waited for nine days off Alexandria, and, as they received no news of the galleys, as the horses died for want of water, and as their provisions were running short, they returned to Rhodes. Before the ambassadors departed, these carracks arrived at Rhodes; and as the ambassadors were unable to obtain any certain news respecting the great Timour Beg, they determined to go to Carabaqui,[3] a place which is in Persia, where he is accustomed to winter, and where they would learn certain intelligence respecting him.

This city of Rhodes is not very large; it is built on a plain near the sea, and it has a large castle, which is partly

[1] Tripoli, in Syria.

[2] Alexandretta, or Scanderoon, in Cilicia? previously attacked by Boucicault.

[3] Karabagh.

without, and partly within the city. Here is the palace of the grand master, and of his friars, and also a convent, and a beautiful church, and a great hospital for the sick. The friars are not allowed to go abroad, without permission from their superior. The harbour of this city is large, and well guarded from the walls, and it has two very fine moles, which enter the sea. On one of these moles there are fourteen windmills; and outside the town there are many houses, and very beautiful fruit gardens, and many citron, and lime, and lemon, and other fruit trees. The people of this city and island are Greeks, and most of them belong to the Greek church. The city is a great mart for merchandize, which comes from many countries; for no ships go to Alexandria, or Jerusalem, or Syria, without touching at this island; and the land of Turkey is so near that it can be clearly seen; and on the island there are other towns and castles, besides the city.

On Friday, the 31st of August, the ambassadors hired a ship to carry them to the island of Chios, which was in possession of a Genoese named Leonardo Gentil. They sailed from Rhodes; but the voyage from Rhodes to Chios is dangerous, as the land of Turkey is very close on the right hand; and there are many islands, both inhabited and desert, on the other side; so that it is dangerous to sail over this route, at night, or in bad weather.

From Friday to Tuesday the wind was contrary, and they tacked up and down the whole time, unable to double a cape of the land of Turkey.

On Wednesday the 5th of September, they were off the island of Lango, belonging to Rhodes; on which there is a town, in a plain near the sea, with a small castle; and between the castle and the town there is a large salt lake; and there are many houses, and gardens, and vineyards round the town. As they were unable to make head against the foul wind, they put into the port of Lango, and got on board fresh water and meat. There are always one hundred friars from Rhodes on this island, and a lieutenant, who holds the town and castle.

They sailed from Lango on Thursday, the 6th of September, but made little way during that day, owing to a contrary wind; and on Friday they also gained very little ground, as they were obliged to go about constantly, owing to the numerous islands, and to the land of Turkey being so close; and at noon, being near an island called "the Isle of Beasts," the contrary wind increased, and forced the vessel on the coast of this island, so that they expected to be lost, and were obliged to anchor. They remained off this island, which is without wood or water, during a whole day.

At noon on Sunday they got under weigh, and sailed all day amongst desert islands, and in sight of an inhabited island belonging to Rhodes, which is called Calamo.[1]

On Monday morning, they were off a city on the land of Turkey, called "Palacia nueva,"[2] and they were told that Timour Beg was in that city, when he conquered the Turk, and seized upon Turkey.

On Tuesday they were off an inhabited island, belonging to Rhodes, called Berro,[3] and, that they might not lose the ground they had gained, the wind being contrary, they anchored in the port of that island, and took in water. This island of Berro has a town, and a very strong and lofty castle, held by a friar of Rhodes: the inhabitants are Greeks, and they say that the Turks of Palacia have ravaged, and done much mischief on this island; and that this very year a galliot from Palacia had arrived, and the Moors had carried off many sheep, and the men who were working in the fields.

They departed from this island on Thursday, and on Friday morning they found themselves off a desert island called Madrea, where there is pasture for sheep, and fresh water;

[1] Kalimno. [2] Palatia. [3] Lero.

the same day they sighted another island called Tatanis,[1] which is inhabited by Greeks. Next day they were off a great island called Samos, inhabited by Turks; and in sight of another island called Micarea,[2] possessed by a lady, on which there appeared to be many farms; on the same day they were in sight of many other islands, large and small.

On Saturday, the 15th of September, and on the following Sunday, they were unable to proceed on account of the calms, and remained amongst these islands; and on Saturday afternoon a fair wind sprung up, but only lasted for a short time; and on Monday morning they were off a cape of the land of Turkey, which is called Cape Xanto,[3] and the island of Chios was in sight.

On Tuesday morning, at the hour of mass, they reached the port of Chios, and the ambassadors landed, and caused everything they had on board the vessel to be taken on shore.

There is a small town on the island of Chios, and the island itself is small, and belongs to the Genoese. The town is on a plain facing the sea, and it is divided into two wards, and is surrounded by many vineyards and fruit gardens. The land of Turkey is so close to Chios, that it is clearly visible.

In this island there are villages and castles, and the mastick grows here on certain trees. The town is well fortified with a wall and towers, but it is in a plain. In this island the ambassadors received news that the eldest son of the Turk, who was conquered by Tamerlane, was dead, and that his brothers were fighting for the succession to the land.

The ambassadors wished to depart from Chios at once, but they did not find a vessel ready, and remained on the

[1] Patino or Patmos.
[2] Nikaria, the ancient Icaria.
[3] Cape Blanco ?

island until the 30th of September, when they engaged a small Castilian vessel, commanded by a Genoese named Boquira de Marta. On Sunday the vessel got under weigh in the middle of the night, and made sail with a fair wind. At daylight they were off an inhabited island called Metella,[1] and two other islands were in sight on the left hand, called Pixara and Antipixara. In the afternoon they were near a cape of the land of Turkey called Cape St. Mary; and at dusk the wind increased so that the sails were split, and blown into the sea. As the strait of Romania[2] was near, and the wind increased as the night advanced, the captain feared he might not be able to find the mouth of the strait, and therefore determined to work off and on until daylight. A little before midnight the wind increased to a gale, and they found themselves off the island of Merdi, and resolved to make for the island of Metellin, to mend their sails and procure a pilot. Before reaching the port, a castle called Mollenos came in sight on the said island, and presently they saw another castle called Cuaraca. At noon they anchored in the port of Metellin, and remained there until Friday, repairing damages.

The town of Metellin is built on a high hill near the sea, and is surrounded by a wall with many towers; and outside there is a large suburb. This island is three hundred miles round, and contains several villages and castles, and there are many gardens and vineyards in the neighbourhood of the city. Near the town there have been very large houses and churches, and it would seem that, in former days, the island was thickly populated; and at one end of the city, in a plain near the fountains and gardens, there are the ruins of great palaces, and in the middle of the ruins there are about forty blocks of white marble;—they say that on the top of those blocks of marble, there was once a platform, where those of the city met in council. The people

[1] Mytilene. [2] The Dardanelles.

of this island are Greeks, and were formerly subject to the empire of Constantinople; but they are now under a Genoese named Juan de Catalus, whose father married a daughter of the emperor. They tell a strange story concerning this Genoese: that about twenty years ago, when this lord, and his father and mother and two brothers were asleep in the castle, the earth shook and threw down the castle, killing them all except this Genoese lord, who escaped in the cradle in which he slept; and was found next day in a vineyard at the foot of the castle: and it was a great wonder that he thus escaped.

When the ambassadors arrived, they found the young Emperor of Constantinople, who had married a daughter of the Lord of Metellin, and who resided a good deal in this island. A short time before, his father-in-law and brother-in-law had sailed with two galleys and five galliots, to take the city of Salonica, which belongs to the old Emperor of Constantinople;[1] and the reason they went

[1] 1355-91, John Palæologus, Emperor of the East, was a wretched vassal of the Turk, "the careless spectator of the public ruin." Andronicus, his eldest son, formed a guilty friendship with Sauzes, son of the Turk Murad, and the two youths conspired against the lives of their fathers. Sauzes was blinded, and John obeyed the Turk, by doing the same to Andronicus. Manuel, the second son, became heir. Their territory was about fifty miles long, and thirty broad, between the Euxine and Sea of Marmora. Manuel succeeded in 1391, and reigned till 1425.

In 1393 Bajazet besieged Constantinople. Christian princes marched from Hungary to assist Manuel; but were utterly routed at Nicopolis. John, son of Andronicus, agreed to give up Constantinople and retire to the Morea, if Bajazet would help him to drive out Manuel. To save Constantinople, Manuel gave up the city to John, and embarked for Venice.

In 1395 Bajazet threatened to besiege Constantinople, and Boucicault was sent to its relief. His presence caused the blockade to be raised; but the Turks soon returned; and Manuel and Boucicault retired to France to seek aid. The invasion of Timour saved Constantinople. In 1400 Manuel passed through Italy, France, and even visited England, Henry IV and his court receiving him on Blackheath. In 1402 he returned to the Morea and Constantinople, dethroned John, and banished

to attack that city, was as follows:—This young emperor lived with the Turk Murad, and, being in a city of Turkey called Solombria,[1] Mosen Buchicate, governor of Genoa, arrived there with ten galleys, and took away the said emperor to Constantinople, by force. He made friends with the emperor his uncle, on condition that the town of Salonica should be given to him as a residence. Mosen Buchicate conveyed the old emperor to France, to seek aid from the king; and the young emperor was left in charge of the government until his return. The old emperor being in France, the young emperor agreed, when Murad and Timour Beg were about to fight, that if the Turk should be victorious, he would deliver up the city of Constantinople to him, and would pay him tribute. When the old emperor heard this, on his return to Constantinople, he was very angry, and ordered his nephew never to appear before him again, but to depart from his territory to the island of Estalimen; and he deprived him of the city of Salonica. As he had previously promised him the city of Salonica, and would not now give it, he and his father-in-law determined to take it, if possible. The said Juan, lord of the said island, had sent a galliot to Mosen Buchicate, in which there was an ambassador, who was ordered to say that Buchicate knew well how the old emperor had promised the city of Salonica to his son-in-law, in his presence; but that he would now only give the island of Escalines; Juan, therefore, asked him to come and assist in taking the city, and added that he would wait for him in the island of Escalines. While the ambassadors were in the island of Metellin, the galliot, which had gone on this embassy, arrived, with the news that Buchicate had arrived in

him to Mytilene. Manuel reigned for many years in peace, and died in 1425.

His son Andronicus was invested with the principality of Thessalonica, and died of leprosy soon after the sale of that city to the Venetians.

[1] Selymbria.

Rhodes, and had sailed again, but it was not known whither he had gone.

On Saturday, the 6th of October, at dawn, they made sail, and directed their course between the land of Turkey, and the said island of Metellin, until they reached Cape St. Mary. On Sunday they doubled the cape, and came in sight of a desert island called Tenio,[1] on the left hand; and an inhabited island, belonging to Constantinople, called Nembro.[2] The wind was foul, and continued to increase during the afternoon; and, having made little way, they wished to take shelter under the island of Tenio, which was near, but they were unable owing to the wind and current, so they anchored between the land of Turkey and the said island of Tenio, in a Strait, near which stood the great city of Troy. From this place they saw the edifices of Troy, with parts of the wall, having doors at intervals, and towers, and other buildings like castles. It is built in a plain near the sea, and extends towards some high mountains; and at the other side of the city, a high and sharp peak rose up, where it is said that there used to be a castle, called Elion.

The island of Tenia, which is opposite the said city, used to be the port of the city, to which ships resorted. It was occupied by king Priam, who built a great castle on it, called Tenedos, for the defence of the shipping. This island used to be full of inhabitants, but it is now deserted. The boat was sent from the ship to procure water and wood, and some of the attendants of the embassy went to see the island, and found many vineyards and fruit trees, and game such as partridges and rabbits, and the ruins of a great castle.

The reason why this island of Tenia is uninhabited, is as follows:—About twenty-two years ago, the emperor of Constantinople promised to give the said island to the Genoese, for assisting him with some galleys in his war against the Turk; but he afterwards sold it to the Venetians,

[1] Tenedos ? [2] Imbro.

who settled on it, and fortified the town and castle. When the Genoese heard this, they declared that the island belonged to them, and that the emperor had promised it to them, and that he had no right to sell it to any one. Thus there was discord between the Genoese and Venetians, and they both began to arm their fleets, and committed great slaughter amongst each other, upon this island. Peace was made on condition that neither should have it; that the town and castle should be laid in ruins, and that the island should be left uninhabited. This is one of the causes why, at this day, there is enmity between the Genoese and Venetians.

On Wednesday they were unable to make sail, as the wind was still foul, and they were thus detained until Sunday. On Sunday afternoon a vessel arrived in the port of Tenio, and they sent to ask where she came from. She was from Gallipoli, a place belonging to the Turk, but on Grecian land, and was bound for Chios, with a cargo of wheat; and she brought news that a great pestilence raged at Gallipoli. The ambassadors were detained for thirteen days more, owing to the foul wind; and from the said island of Tenio they could see a very high mountain called Monteston,[1] which is in the land of Greece, and where there is a monastery of Greek monks, who lead very holy lives, and will not allow a woman, nor a dog, nor a cat, nor any tame thing which has young, to come near them: and they do not eat meat. This monastery is very rich, and they say that it is two days journey from the foot of the mountain to the summit, where the monastery stands; and, besides this one, there are fifty or sixty monasteries, where the monks all dress in black, and do not drink wine, nor eat meat, nor oil, nor fish, with blood; and these things were related by some Greeks who were in the said ship, who had lived some time on that holy mountain.

[1] Mount Athos, or Monte Santo?

On Wednesday, the 22nd of October, there was a light fair wind, so they made sail, after having been fifteen days between this island of Tenio, and the land of Turkey. On the same day, at noon, they were off a desert island called Mambre. The next day there was a calm, so that they could not enter the strait; but on Friday a fair wind sprung up, at the hour of vespers. They entered the strait of Romania,[1] and the entrance is so narrow that it is not more than eight miles across. On the right hand side is the land of Turkey, and there appeared a castle, on a high hill facing the sea, with a large town built round it, and a fortified wall. A year and a half ago they say that eight Genoese galleys arrived, and plundered the town. The castle is called "the end of the roads;" and when the Greeks came from their country to destroy the city of Troy, they had their camp in this castle, and in front of it the Greeks made some great caves, leading towards Troy; three in number. On the opposite side of the strait, there was another castle, on a hill near the sea, called Xetea; and these two castles guard the strait of Romania. A little further on, on the Turkish side, there are two great towers, with a few houses near them, and this place is called Dubeque. They say that the city of Troy extended from Cape St. Mary to this place, which is a distance of sixty miles. At sunset the vessel was off a tower near the sea, on the Greek side, called the tower of Vituperio.

On Saturday they were off Gallipoli, a castle and town on the Grecian side, but it is occupied by the Mussulman Ahalali, eldest surviving son of the Turk. In the said port of Gallipoli, the Turk has all his fleet of ships and galleys, forty in number; and the castle is strongly fortified, with a large garrison. Gallipoli was the first place occupied by the Turks, in the land of Greece; and it is not more than ten miles from this castle to the land of Turkey. By taking this

[1] The Dardanelles.

castle, the Turks have gained all the places which they occupy in Greece, and if they should lose it, they would lose all their other conquests; as they have their fleet here, and can thus quickly bring over succour from the land of Turkey, which is so near. From the entrance of the strait to Gallipoli it is very narrow, but from this place forward, the sea is a little broader. Above Gallipoli there are two castles, called Satorado and Examilli. The Turkish side appeared to consist of high hills, while the Grecian side was more level, and covered with corn fields.

At night they were off a cape on the Turkish side, called Quinisco; and they say that when Timour Beg defeated the Turk, certain troops, who were in the battle, fled to this cape, and converted it into an island. On Sunday they were off an inhabited island called Marmora, and this island yields the jaspers and marbles of Constantinople.

On the same afternoon they were off a place, belonging to the emperor, called Redea; and in sight of an island called Calonimo,[1] off the land of Turkey. On Monday morning they were near the same place, as there was little wind, so they anchored about two miles from the shore, and fifteen miles from Constantinople. The ambassadors then sent forward, to secure lodgings in the city of Pera, and to acquaint the emperor of their approach.

On Wednesday, the 24th of October, they put all their luggage on board a large boat, and went on to Pera, where lodgings were prepared for them; and they did this because the wind was foul, and the vessel was unable to reach the port. It was necessary to lose no time in obtaining information, and completing their preparations for the rest of their journey.

[1] Kalolimno.

II.

CONSTANTINOPLE.

On Sunday, the 28th of October, the Emperor of Constantinople sent for the ambassadors, and they went from Pera to Constantinople in a boat, and found a crowd of people waiting for them, and horses to convey them to the palace. The emperor had just returned from hearing mass, and he received them very well, in a chamber apart, which was lofty and covered with carpets, on one of which there was the skin of a leopard, and in the back part pillows were placed, embroidered with gold. Having conversed with the ambassadors for some time, the emperor ordered them to return to their lodgings, and he sent them a large stag, which had been brought in by some of his huntsmen. The emperor had with him, the empress his wife and three small children, the eldest being about eight years old. On the following Monday he sent some courtiers to the ambassadors, to answer what they had said to him.

On Tuesday, the 30th of October, the ambassadors sent to the emperor to say that, as they were desirous of seeing the city, and the churches and relics which it contained, they hoped that he would graciously order them to be shown; and the emperor directed his son-in-law, a Genoese named Ilario, who was married to one of his illegitimate daughters, to accompany them, and show them what they wanted.

The first thing they went to see, was the church of St. John the Baptist, which they call St. John of the stone, and which is near the emperor's palace. On the top of the first doorway of this church there was a very rich figure of St. John, well designed in mosaic; and near this doorway there was a lofty capital, raised on four arches; and the roof and walls are covered with beautiful images and figures in mosaic. This mosaic work is made of very small stones, which are covered with fine gilt, and blue, white, green, or red enamel, according to the colour which is required to depict the figures, so that this work is very marvellous to behold.

Beyond this place there is a great court, surrounded by houses, and containing many cypress trees: and opposite the door into the body of the church there is a beautiful fountain, under a canopy raised upon eight white marble pillars, and the pipe of the fountain is of white stone. The body of the church is very lofty, and near the entrance there are three small chapels, each containing an altar, and the door of the centre chapel is plated with silver; and by the side of the door there are four marble columns inlaid with small jaspers, and silver crosses, and precious stones: and there are curtains of silk across these doors, placed there that the priest may not be seen when he goes in to say mass. The roof is very rich, and inlaid with mosaics. On the roof of the body of the church there is a figure of God the Father; and the walls are inlaid in the same manner nearly to the ground; and the floor is enriched with jaspers. The chapel was surrounded by seats of carved wood, and between each chair there was a brazier with ashes, into which the people spit, that they may not spit on the ground; and there are many lamps of silver and of glass.

There are many relics in this church, of which the emperor keeps the key. On this day the ambassadors were shown the left arm of St. John the Baptist, from the shoulder to the hand. This arm was withered, so that the skin and bone alone remained, and the joints of the elbow and the hand were adorned with jewels set in gold. This church also contains many relics of Jesus Christ; but the ambassadors were not shown them on that day, because the emperor had gone out hunting, and had left the keys of the church with the empress, but he forgot to give her the keys of the place where these relics were kept. But on another day they were shown, as will presently be related. This church belongs to a monastery, and the monks have a very large hall, in the middle of which there is a table of white marble, thirty paces long, and there are many wooden seats round it; and there are three other small tables. Within the precincts of this monastery there are gardens, and vineyards, and other things which there is not space to describe.

The same day they went to see another church called Peribelico, dedicated to St. Mary. At the entrance to this church there is a great court, containing many cypresses, walnut trees, elms, and other trees. The outer walls of the church are covered with images and other figures, in gold, blue, and other colours. On the left hand side of the entrance to the church there are many figures, and amongst them an image of St. Mary, with one of the emperor and another of the empress on each side. At the feet of the image of St. Mary there are representations of thirty castles and cities, with the names of Grecian cities written under them. They say that these cities and castles formerly belonged to this church, having been given by an emperor called Romanus, who lies interred here. At the feet of the image there were certain documents written in steel, and sealed with seals of wax and lead, which described the privileges enjoyed by this church over those cities and castles.

There are five altars in the body of the church; which is

very large and lofty, supported on pillars of various coloured marble, and the walls and floor are inlaid with jasper; and the ceiling is inlaid with very rich mosaics. On the left hand side, at the end of the church, there is a handsome stone monument, where the body of the emperor Romanus is interred: they said that this monument was formerly covered with gold and precious stones, but that when the Latins captured this city, ninety years ago, they plundered this tomb. In this church there is another great stone tomb, in which another emperor is interred, and this church also contains the other arm of the blessed St. John the Baptist, which was shown to the ambassadors. This was the right arm, and it was fresh and healthy; and, though they say that the whole body of the blessed St. John was destroyed, except one finger of the right arm, with which he pointed when he said "Ecce Agnus Dei," yet certainly the whole of this arm was fresh and in good preservation, but it wanted the thumb. The reason given by the monks for the thumb being gone was this,—they say that at the time when idolatry prevailed in the city of Antioch, there was a terrible dragon, to which one person was given every year, to be eaten. They drew lots who should be the victim, and the person on whom the lot fell, could not be excused from being eaten by the dragon. Once the lot fell upon the daughter of a good man, and when he saw that his daughter must be given up to the dragon, he was very sad, and gave her to a church of christian nuns, who were then in that city, saying to the nuns, that he had heard that God had performed many miracles through St. John, and that he wished to believe, and to adore the arm of that saint, which they possessed. He prayed that, in addition to the other miracles which God had performed through him, he would save the girl from being eaten by this ferocious dragon, and deliver her from danger. The nuns, taking compassion on him, showed him the arm, on which he threw himself down to worship it, and bit off its thumb, without letting the nuns see him. When the people were going to give the maiden to the dragon, and the monster opened its mouth to eat her, the good man threw the thumb of the blessed saint into its mouth; upon which the dragon turned round, and fled, which was a great miracle: and that man was converted to the faith of our Lord Jesus Christ.

In this same church they were shown a small cross, a *palmo* in length, ornamented with gold, with a small crucifix; and it was placed in a recess which was covered with gold, so that it could be taken out and replaced at pleasure. They say that it is made of the wood of the true cross, on which our Lord Jesus Christ was placed, and its colour is black. It was made when the blessed St. Helen, mother of Constantine, who built this city, brought the whole of the true cross from Jerusalem to Constantinople. They were also shown the body of the blessed St. Gregory, which was whole and undecayed. Outside the church there is a cloister, where there are many beautiful representations of history, among which is the root of Jesse, showing the lineage whence came the blessed Virgin Mary. It was figured in mosaic; and was so wonderful, so rich, and so well drawn, that it surpassed all the other works. There are many monks belonging to the church, who showed the above things to the ambassadors; and also took them into a very large and lofty refectory, in the midst of which there was a table of white marble, very well made, being thirty-five *palmos* long, and the floor was of marble flags. At the end of this refectory there were two small tables of white marble, and the ceiling was covered with mosaic work; and on the walls pictures were represented in mosaic work, from the salutation of the blessed Virgin Mary by St. Gabriel, to the birth of Jesus Christ our God, together with his journeys with his disciples, and all his blessed life, until he was crucified. In this refectory there were many flag stones, made to place meat and other food upon;

and in the monastery there were many cells, where the monks live; and gardens, and water, and vineyards, so that this monastery is like a large town.

On the same day the ambassadors visited another church called St. John, to which a monastery is attached. The first part of the church is very lofty and richly adorned, and beyond it there is a courtyard, leading to the body of the church, which is round, and surrounded by three great naves, all under one roof. It contains seven altars, and the ceiling is covered with rich mosaic, representing many historical events; and the body of the church is surrounded by twenty-four marble pillars of green jasper, and the naves have the same number of pillars. The walls are adorned with mosaics; and beyond the body of the church there is a beautiful chapel, embellished with mosaics of marvellous workmanship, and containing a figure of the holy Mary, for whose service this chapel was built. The monastery contains a large refectory, with a white marble table; and on the walls there are mosaics representing the last supper, in which our Lord Jesus Christ is seated at a table with his disciples, and this monastery contains houses, gardens, fountains, and many other things.

On another day the ambassadors went to see a plain called the Hippodrome, where they joust. It is surrounded by white marble pillars, so large that three men can only just span round them, and their height is two lances. They are thirty-seven in number, fixed in very large white marble bases; and above, they were connected by arches going from one to the other, so that a man can walk all round, on the top of them; and there are battlements, breast high, of white marble, and these are made for ladies, and maidens, and noble women, when they view the jousts and tournaments which are celebrated here. In front of these seats, there is a row of pillars, on which is a high seat, raised on four marble pillars, surrounded by other seats, and at each corner there are four images of white marble, the size of a man; and the emperor is accustomed to sit here, when he views the tournaments. Near these pillars, there are two blocks of white marble, one on the top of the other, of great size, each one being the height of a lance, or more; and on the top of these blocks there are four square blocks of copper. On the top of these blocks there is an immense stone, sharp at the end, at least six lances in height. It is not fixed in any way; so that it was marvellous to think how so great a mass of stone, yet so sharp and fine, could have been placed there. It is so high that it may be seen above the city, from the sea. This column has been placed there in memory of some great event; and on the base there is an inscription, announcing who it was who caused this stone to be placed there, and for what reason; but as the writing was in Greek, and it was getting late, the ambassadors could not wait to have it read to them. But they say that it was raised to commemorate some great deed. Beyond it the range of columns continues, though they are not so high as the first, and the deeds of the knights are painted on them; and between these columns there are three copper figures of serpents. They are twisted like a rope, and they have three heads, with open mouths. It is said that these figures of serpents were put here, on account of an enchantment which was effected. The city used to be infested by many serpents, and other evil animals, which killed and poisoned men; but an emperor performed an enchantment over these figures, and serpents have never done any harm to the people of the city, since that time.

The plain is very large, and is surrounded by steps, one rising above the other to a considerable height; and these steps are made for the people of the city; and below them there are great houses, with doors opening on the plain, where the knights who are going to joust are accustomed to arm and disarm.

On the same day the ambassadors went to see the church which is called St. Sophia, which is the largest, most honoured, and most privileged of all the churches in the city; and it has canons who do duty as if it was a cathedral, and a patriarch, whom the Greeks call *Marpollit.*

In a court, in front of the church, there are nine very large white marble pillars, the largest I ever beheld, and it is said that a great palace used to stand on the top of them, where the patriarch and his clergy held their meetings. In this same court, in front of the church, a wonderfully high stone column stands, on the top of which there is a horse made of copper, of the size of four large horses put together; and on its back there is the figure of an armed knight, also of copper, with a great plume on his head, resembling the tail of a peacock. The horse has chains of iron round its body, secured to the column, to prevent it from falling, or being moved by the wind. This horse is very well made, and one fore and one hind leg is raised, as if it was in the act of prancing. The knight, on its back, has his right arm raised, with the hand open, while the reins are held with the left arm. This column, horse, and knight, are so large and high, that it is wonderful to see them. This marvellous horse is said to have been placed here by the Emperor Justinian, who erected the column, and performed great and notable deeds against the Turks, in his time.

At the entrance to this church, under an arch, there is a small but very rich and beautiful chapel, raised upon four marble columns; and opposite this chapel is the door of the church. It is very large and high, and covered with brass, and in front of it there is a small court, containing some high terraces; beyond which there is another door covered with brass, like the first. Within this door there is a broad and lofty nave, with a ceiling of wood, and on the left hand there are very large and well built cloisters, adorned with slabs of marble and jasper of various colours. The body of the church contains five lofty doors, all covered with brass, and the centre one is the largest. The body of the church is the loftiest, most rich, and most beautiful that can be seen in the whole world. It is surrounded by three large and broad naves, which are joined to it, so that mass may be heard in all parts of the church. The arches of the naves are of green jasper, and unite the roofs of the nave with that of the body of the church; but the summit of the latter rises much higher than that of the naves. It is dome shaped, and very high, so that a man must have good eyes who looks up from beneath; and the church is one hundred and five paces long, by ninety-three broad; and the dome is supported by four pillars, very large and thick, covered with flags of many coloured jaspers; and from pillar to pillar there are arches of green jasper, which are very high and sustain the dome. In the arches there are four very large slabs, two on the right hand and two on the left, which are coloured with a substance made from a powder, artificially, and called porphyry. The dome is covered with very rich mosaic work, and, over the high altar, the image of God the Father, very large, is wrought in mosaics of many colours; but it is so high up, that it only looks about the size of a man, or a little larger, though really it is so large that it measures three *palmos* between the eyes; but to him who looks at it, it does not appear to be more nor less than a man, and that is owing to the very great height it is placed above the ground.

On the floor, in the centre of the part under the dome, there is a pulpit placed on four columns of jasper; and the sides of it are covered with flags of jasper; and this pulpit is surmounted by a capital, raised on eight very large jasper columns; and here they preach, and also say the gospel on feast days. The walls and floor of the church are lined with flags of jasper, worked all over with ornaments, very beautiful to behold. The part between the arches, which supports the dome, was of very handsome white stone, on which many appropriate figures were inlaid, and above that there was very rich mosaic. The arched roofs of the naves surrounded the dome, except where the high altar stood, all which was worth seeing. The said arched roofs were ninety paces broad, and four hundred and ten paces round, and they were beautifully inlaid with mosaics. In the wall, on the left hand side, there is a very large white slab, on which, among many other figures, was drawn, very naturally, without any human artifice of sculpture or painting, the most sacred and blessed Virgin Mary, with our Lord Jesus Christ in her most holy arms, with his most glorious forerunner, St. John the Baptist, on one side. These images, as I said before, are not drawn, or painted with any colour, or inlaid; but the stone itself gave birth to this picture, with its veins, which may be clearly seen; and they say that when this stone was cut, to be placed in this most holy place, the workmen saw these most wonderful and fortunate images on it, and, as this church was the most important one in the city, that stone was deposited in it. The said images appear as if they were in the clouds of heaven, and as if there was a thin veil before them.

This appeared most wonderful, as a thing which God himself had shown; and at the foot of these images there is an altar, and a small chapel, in which they say mass; and in this church was shown the holy body of a patriarch, which was entire, both in bone and flesh.

The ambassadors were also shown the gridiron on which the blessed St. Lawrence was roasted; and in the church of St. Sophia there are vaults and cisterns, and subterranean chambers, which are strange things, wonderful to see. Near the church there are many fallen edifices, and doors leading to the church, closed and ruined. In the church there is a very large cistern under ground, capable of floating ten galleys. All these works, and many others in this church, were shown, so that they can neither be related nor written briefly; and so great is the edifice, and the wonderful works in the church are so numerous, that they take a long time to see. The roofs are all covered with lead. This church is privileged, and any person, either Greek or of any other nation, who commits a crime, either of robbery or murder, and takes refuge here, may not be taken hence.

On the same day the ambassadors went to see another church, called St. George; in which, after passing the first gate, there is a large court, in which there are many houses and fruit gardens, and the body of the church is in the midst of these gardens. Opposite the church door, outside, there is a large and beautiful font, over which there is a canopy supported by eight marble pillars, inlaid with many figures. The body of the church is very high, and is all covered with mosaic work, and the ascension of our Lord Jesus Christ is here represented. The floor of this church is wonderfully made, for it is covered with flags of porphyry and jasper; and the walls are of the same material. In the centre of the roof is a figure of God the Father, in mosaic work; and over the door there is figured the true cross, which an angel showed to the apostles from the clouds of heaven, when the Holy Spirit descended upon them in a flame of fire. It is wonderfully made, in mosaic work. In this church there is a large tomb made of jasper, and covered with a silken cloth, where an empress lies buried.

As it was now late, the ambassadors waited until Wednesday to visit the gate called Quinigo; where they found the said Master Ilario, and the other courtiers of the emperor; and they then went to see the other things in the city, returning to Pera, where they lodged.

On another day the ambassadors were unable to pass to Constantinople, as they intended, because news came to the city of Pera, how that certain Venetian galleys had come upon the Genoese fleet, which was making war on the kingdom of Alexandria (of which Mosen Buchicate was captain), and that many persons had been killed near Mondon, and several galleys taken, together with Chastel Morate, the nephew of Buchicate.[1]

On account of this news, there was a great stir in the city, and the people seized upon certain Venetians who were there, and took their ships; and the governing power of the city seized a galliot in which the ambassadors were about to go to Trebizonde, because they wanted to send her with a message. This caused great annoyance to the ambassadors, for the time was short, and they were unable to find such a vessel as they required, so they were obliged to

[1] Jean le Meingle, surnamed Boucicault or Buchicate, has already been mentioned several times, by Clavijo, in the previous chapter. He was one of the greatest captains of the age, and was the son of a marshal of France, of the same name, who signed the peace of Bretigni.

After serving in many parts of Europe, Boucicault accompanied the Duc de Nevers to Hungary, and was taken prisoner at the fatal battle of Nicopolis. He was brought up before the brutal Turk, with the other Christian knights, to be murdered; but the Sultan was tempted by the hope of a great ransom promised by Nevers, and Boucicault escaped. On his return to France he was made a marshal of France, and was sent to Constantinople in 1399, to assist against the Turk. The Greeks received him with demonstrations of joy, and he was created Constable of the Empire. After passing a year in the East, he returned to Europe with the Emperor Emanuel, and was received at the French court with great distinction. At this time he instituted an order of knighthood for the protection of ladies, to be called "*De la Dame Blanche à l'Ecu vert,*" consisting of thirteen knights, who were bound by the statutes of the order for five years. Their device was "un écusson d'or, émaillé de verd, sur lequel étoit representé en émail blanc le portrait d'une dame modeste."

In 1401 Boucicault was appointed governor of Genoa, by Charles VI, at the request of the Genoese; and he distinguished himself in successful expeditions to Cyprus, and other parts of the Levant.

After leaving Genoa, he was at the battle of Agincourt in 1415, where he was dangerously wounded and taken prisoner. He died in England in 1421, aged fifty-five, and his body was embalmed and sent to France. It was buried with those of his father and mother at Tours.—*Froissart; Histoire du Marechal de Boucicault* (Paris, 1697).

seek for another ship, to enable them to proceed with the king's service. They, therefore, sent to master Ilario, to say that they could not go to Constantinople on that day, as they had promised, but that they would do so some other day; and he sent half a pig to the embassy, being one which had been killed lately.

Afterwards, on Thursday the 1st of November, the ambassadors went to Constantinople, and soon found Master Ilario, and others of the household of the emperor, at the gate of Quinigo, where they were waiting. They then mounted on horseback, and went to see a church called "Santa Maria de la Cherne," which is within the city, and opposite to a ruined castle, which used to be a lodging, used by the emperors. The said castle was destroyed by an emperor, because he found his son in it, in a manner that will be related to you presently.

This church of "Santa Maria de la Cherne" used to be a chapel of the emperor's, and the interior consists of three naves, the centre one being the largest and most lofty, and the other two being lower. They are vaulted, and the arches connect them together. These naves are adorned in the following manner. They are raised on great pillars of green jasper, and their bases are of white marble, inlaid with many figures. The ceilings and the walls, half way up, are covered with flags of jasper of many colours, with many figures and beautiful works artificially wrought upon them. The ceiling of the centre nave is very rich, made of timber in squares and beams, all gilded with very fine gold; and though parts of the church were much out of repair, this gilded ceiling looked as fresh and as beautiful as if it was just finished. In the centre nave there was a rich altar and a pulpit, also very rich; and all the furniture of the church is very rich and costly, and the roof was all covered with lead.

On the same day the ambassadors went to see the relics in the church of St. John the Baptist, which were not shown to them before, for want of the keys. When they arrived at the church, the monks robed themselves, and lighted many candles, and took the keys, singing and chaunting all the time. They then ascended to a sort of tower, where the relics were; and with them there was a knight of the emperor's household. They then came forth chaunting very mournful hymns, with lighted tapers, and many incense bearers before them, and they placed the relics on a high table covered with a silken cloth, in the body of the church. The relics were contained in a coloured chest, which was sealed with two seals of white wax, on two plates of silver. They opened it, and took out two large silver gilt plates, which were placed on the top of the relics. They then produced a bag of white dimity, sealed with wax, which they opened, and took out a small round golden casket, in which was the bread which our Lord Jesus Christ gave to Judas at the last supper, as a sign who it was who should betray him, but he was unable to eat it. It was wrapped in a red crape cover, and sealed with two waxen seals, and the bread was about three fingers in breadth.

They then took out a gold casket smaller than the first, in which there was a crystal case, which was fixed in the casket, and which contained some of the blood of our Lord Jesus Christ, which flowed from his side, when it was pierced by Longinus. They also took out another small golden casket, the top of which was pierced like a grater, and it contained the blood which flowed from a crucifix in the city of Beyrout, when a Jew once attempted to injure it. They also showed a little case of glass, which had a cover, and a little golden chain attached to it; in which was a small red crape cover containing some hairs of the beard of our Lord Jesus Christ, being those which the Jews pulled out, when they crucified him. There was also a piece of the stone on which our Lord was placed, when he was taken down from the cross. They then showed a square silver casket, two and a half *palmos* long, which was sealed with six seals made of six plates of silver, and it was opened with a silver key. They took out of it a board, which was covered with gold, and on it was the iron of the lance with which Longinus pierced our Lord Jesus Christ. It was as fine as a thorn, and of well tempered iron, and the handle was bored through, being about a *palmo* and two fingers long; and the blood on it was as fresh as if the deed which was done with it had just been committed. It was fixed on the board, which was covered with gold, and the iron was not bright, but quite dim. There was also fixed on this board, a piece of the cane which they gave our Lord Jesus Christ, when he was before Pilate. It was a *palmo* and a half long; and near it there was also a piece of the sponge with which Jesus Christ, our God, was given gall and vinegar, when he was on the cross. In the same case with this board, there was the garment of Jesus Christ, for which the knights of Pilate cast lots. It was folded, and sealed, that people who came to see it might not cut bits off, as had been done before, but one sleeve was left outside the seals. The garment was of a red dimity, like muslin, and the sleeve was narrow, and it was doubled to the elbow. It had three little buttons, made like twisted cords, like the knots on a doublet, and the buttons, and the sleeve, and all that could be seen of the skirt, seemed to be of a dark rose colour; and it did not look as if it had been woven, but as if it had been worked with a needle, for the strings looked twisted in network, and very tight. When the ambassadors went to see these relics, the people of the city, who knew it, came also, and they all cried very loudly, and said their prayers.

On the same day the ambassadors went to see a convent of old ladies, called *Omnipotens*, and they were shown a stone of many colours in the church, on which it was said that our Lord was placed, when he was taken down from the cross. On it were the tears of the three Marys, and of

St. John, which they wept when Jesus Christ, our God, was taken down; and these tears looked fresh, as if they had just fallen.

In this city of Constantinople there is also a church called "Santa Maria de la Dessetria"; it is small, and some religious canons live in it, who neither eat meat, nor drink wine, nor eat grease, nor fish containing blood. The body of the church is inlaid with very beautiful mosaic work, and contains an image of the holy Mary, which is said to have been designed and made by the hands of the glorious and blessed St. Luke. They say this image has performed many miracles, and the Greeks shew great devotion for it. It is painted on a square board, about six *palmos* in breadth, and as many long, which is covered with silver, and inlaid with emeralds, sapphires, topazes, pearls, and many other stones. Every Tuesday there is a grand festival and a great crowd of religious persons, and the clergy of other churches assemble, and take this image out of the church, to a court which is in front of it. It is so heavy that it takes three or four men to carry it, with leathern cords. They then place it in the middle of the court, and all the people say their prayers to it, with many tears and groans. Presently an old man comes and prays before the image; he then lifts it up as if it weighed nothing, and carries it to church. It is marvellous that a single man should be able to lift so great a weight; and they say that no other man, but this one, could raise it, because he comes of a lineage by whom it pleases God that it should be lifted. On certain festivals in the year they carry this image to the church of St. Sophia, with great solemnity.

In this church an emperor was buried, father of the emperor who wanders outside Constantinople. They say that the latter has a right to the empire. The present emperor is called Chirmanoli, which means Manuel, and his brother was emperor before him, and had one son, who was so disobedient to his father, that he intrigued against him. The

Turk Murad, father of him whom Timour Beg vanquished, also had a son at that time, who was disobedient; and the sons of the Turk and the emperor leagued together to depose their fathers. Murad and the emperor of Constantinople also joined together against their sons, and attacked them in the castle of Gallipoli, which now belongs to the Turk. The fathers agreed that when they captured their sons, they would put their eyes out. When this happened, the Turk put his son's eyes out; and the emperor had compassion on his son, and did not wish to hurt him, but ordered him to be put in a dark prison, and finally caused him to lose his sight, with hot basins. After some time he consented that his son's wife should go to him in prison, and she used certain remedies, which enabled him to see a little. One day, when this woman was with the emperor's son, she saw a great serpent come out of a large hole, and she told her husband; and he said to the woman that she must point out to him the place where the serpent had entered; and he waited there until it approached, and killed it with his hands. It was very large and wonderful, and they showed it to the emperor. When he saw it, he felt great compassion for his son, and ordered him to be liberated.

After a short time, the son returned to his evil practices, seized upon his father the emperor, and kept him prisoner for some time, until he was liberated by his knights, when the son fled. The father destroyed the castle in which his son had seized him, disinherited him, and left the empire to his brother Chirmanoli, who now enjoys it.

His son left a son whom they call Demetrius; and it is said that he now has a right to the empire, and the question is arranged in the following manner: that they shall both be called emperors; that after the death of him who now enjoys the sovereignty of the empire, the other shall be emperor; that after his death, the empire shall go to the son of him who is now emperor; then to the son of the other; and thus it is arranged, but I do not believe that any of these arrangements will ever take effect.

In this city there is a cistern, very beautiful to behold, which they call the cistern of Mohammed. This cistern is vaulted with cement, and paved with marble, and the ceiling is raised upon four hundred and ninety very large pillars; and here they are accustomed to collect a great volume of water, which suffices for many people.

The city of Constantinople is surrounded by a high and strong wall, with towers. The wall has three angles, and from angle to angle there is a distance of six miles, so that the whole city is eighteen miles in circumference, which is six leagues; two sides facing the sea, and one facing the land. At the angle which does not face the sea, on a hill, are the palaces of the emperor.

Though the city is so large, it is not all well peopled, for in the middle of it there are many enclosures, where there are corn fields, and fruit gardens. The most populous part is near the sea; and the greatest traffic is from the city, by the gates which open on the sea, especially the gates leading to the city of Pera, on account of the ships which go there to unload; and because those of both cities pass from the one to the other, with their merchandise.

This city of Constantinople contains many great churches and monasteries, but most of them are in ruins; though it seems clear that, in former times, when the city was in its youth, it was the most renowned city in the world. They say that even now there are three thousand churches, large and small; and within the city there are fountains and wells of sweet water; and in a part below the church which is dedicated to the Holy Apostle, there is a bridge reaching from one valley to another, over houses and gardens, by which water used to come, for the irrigation of those gardens.

In a street which leads to one of the gates of the city, opposite Pera, there is a pair of stocks fixed in the ground, for men who are to be imprisoned, or who break any of the city regulations, or who sell meat or bread with false weights. Such persons are taken to this place, and left there day and night, exposed to the weather. Between the city walls and the sea, opposite Pera, there are many houses, in which many things are sold, and warehouses.

The city of Constantinople is near the sea, as you have been told, and two sides face the sea; and in front is the city of Pera. Between the two cities is the port, and Constantinople is thus like Seville, and Pera is like Triana, with the port and the ships between them; and the Greeks do not call it Constantinople as we do, but Escomboli.

Pera is a small city, but well peopled and surrounded with a wall, and it contains good and handsome houses. It is inhabited by Genoese, and is a lordship of Genoa. It is peopled by Genoese and Greeks, and is so close to the sea, that between the wall and the water there is not sufficient breadth for a carrack to pass. The wall runs along the shore, and then ascends a hill, on the top of which there is a great tower, whence the city is watched. This hill, however, is not so high as another outside the town, which rises above it; and on that eminence the Turk encamped when he besieged Pera and Constantinople, and here they fought, and hurled missiles from engines. The Turk twice assaulted the city, and blockaded it by sea and land for six months, with four hundred thousand men on land, and sixty galleons and ships by sea; but they were unable to enter, nor even to occupy a suburb, so that it seems that the Turks are not good combatants, as they could not enter. The sea between Pera and Constantinople is narrow, not being more than a mile across, which is the third of a league; and this sea serves as the port for both cities; and I hold it to be the best and most beautiful in the world, and the most secure from all winds. Vessels lying in it are also secure from enemies, who cannot enter if both cities are of one mind.

It is very deep and clear, so that the largest ship can come close to the walls, and place a gangboard to the shore.

The land of Turkey is also very close to these two cities; and opposite Constantinople, on the land of Turkey, there is a plain near the sea, called Scutari. Many vessels pass from these cities to the land of Turkey every day.

The Genoese obtained the city of Pera in the following way. They bought the site, as much as a bullock's hide cut into strips would go round, from an emperor, and on it they have built the city; and they made two walls, in which they enclosed two suburbs which were near the city. But the primary jurisdiction over the city belongs to the emperor, and he has certain rights over it. The Genoese call this city Pera, but the Greeks call it Galata; and they give it this name because, before the city was built, there were certain places here, where flocks of sheep were collected every day, and they took the milk from those which they were going to sell in the city, and for this reason they call it Galata, which means the milk yard, for milk in their language is *gala*. It is now ninety-six years, a little more or less, since this city was built.

There are two very handsome monasteries in Pera, one dedicated to St. Paul, the other to St. Francis. The ambassadors went to see them both.

The monastery of St. Francis is richly ornamented, and contains several relics. First they were shown a glass case, very richly adorned, and set on a silver gilt stand, in which were the bones of the blessed St. Andrew and the glorious St. Nicholas, and the dress of the blessed and glorious St. Francis. In another case there were the bones of St. Catherine, of the blessed St. Louis of France, and of St. Li of Genoa; and in another there were the bones of the innocents. They were also shewn the arm of St. Pantaleon, the arm of St. Mary Magdalene, of St. Luke, three heads of the eleven hundred virgins, a bone of St. Ignatius, the right arm of St. Stephen, the first martyr, with the hand missing, the head and arm of St. Anne. The latter wanted one finger, and they say that the emperor of Constantinople took it away to put amongst his relics, and that there was a law suit about it. They were also shewn a silver cross inlaid with stones, in the centre of which a small cross was fixed, made of the wood of the most holy true cross; and a richly ornamented glass case, containing a bone of the glorious St. Basil. They then examined a richly gilded silver cross, inlaid with many stones, on which many relics of saints were fixed. Next they saw a glass case containing a silver hand, holding a bone of the blessed St. Llorente, relics of St. John, St. Dionysius, and many other things belonging to the saints.

They say that these relics were taken, when Constantinople was occupied by the Latins; that afterwards they were claimed by the Greek Patriarch, and that there was a law-suit about them. The ambassadors were also shown some very rich dresses, chalices, and crosses.

In this monastery is interred, before the high altar, the body of the grand marshal of France who fought the Turk, when he routed the French who came with the king of Hungary;[1] and in the monastery of St. Paul lies interred the body of the lord of Truxi, and many other knights slain by the Turk, after they had yielded, and he had received a ransom for them.

The said ambassadors were in the city of Pera, from the Wednesday on which they arrived to Tuesday the 13th of November, for during all that time they could not find a vessel to take them to Trebizond; and, as the winter was approaching, and the sea is very dangerous for navigating during the winter, they took a galliot to prevent further delay, the master of which was a Genoese named Nicolo Socato, and they caused him to obtain sailors and provisions; and they intended to have sailed on the said Thursday, had not several accidents prevented them.

[1] At the battle of Nicopolis.

III.

THE VOYAGE

FROM

CONSTANTINOPLE TO TREBIZOND.

ON Wednesday, the 14th of November, at the hour of mass, they made sail, and set out with a fair wind down the strait, which forms the mouth of the great sea. At the third hour they were off a tower, which stands close to the sea on the Grecian side, called Trapea. They went into port at this place, filled up with water, and had dinner. After dinner they continued their voyage, and soon afterwards they passed two castles on hills near the sea, the one being called "El Guirol de la Grecia," and the other "El Guirol de la Turquia," the former being in Greece, and the other in Turkey. The Grecian tower is ruined and deserted, but the Turkish one is inhabited. In the sea, between these two castles, there is a tower surrounded by the water; and at the foot of the Turkish castle there is a tower built on a rock, with a wall connecting them. Formerly a chain was stretched from one tower to the other, and when the land on both sides belonged to the Greeks, these castles were used to guard this strait; and any vessel passing from the greater sea to Pera and Constantinople, or from Pera to the sea, was stopped by a chain stretched across from one castle to the other, and was thus detained until the dues were paid.

At the hour of vespers they reached the entrance of the greater sea, but, as it was late, they anchored and remained until the next day. This strait is very narrow, and the land of Turkey is on the right hand, and the land of Greece on the left; and on both sides many churches were in sight, close to the sea.

In the middle of the night they entered the great sea, and their course was close to the land of Turkey. At the third hour, being under sail with a fair wind, the mast was sprung; and they went on under oars, close in shore, until they had fished the mast. A little after noon, next day, they were off a small castle, on the top of a rock, in the land of Turkey, and almost surrounded by the sea. It is called the castle of Sequello. As it was near the hour of Ave Marias they put into a port, in a small island belonging to the Genoese, called Finogia. The governor of the city of Pera had sent two armed vessels to this sea, to watch for the Venetian ships, which would have to come from the sea of Tana,[1] laden with merchandize; and which would be unsuspicious, as their captains did not know of the war. One of these Genoese vessels was at anchor off this island of Finogia.

On Friday they intended to sail, but the wind was foul, and they had to remain. This island of Finogia is a small island, and uninhabited, and two miles from the coast of Turkey. As this port was not safe, they intended to make for the port of Carpi,[2] about six miles distant, where the other Genoese carrack was waiting for the Venetian ships; but the boatswain said that it was better to remain where they were, than to go to Carpi, so they went a little closer in. In the middle of the night the wind rose, and the sea got up; and the boatswain, thinking they would be safer under the lee of the carrack, got the vessel under weigh, and tried to reach the carrack by means of oars; but they could not, for the wind increased to a gale; so that when

[1] Azoff. [2] Kirpe or Calpe?

they tried to return to the position which they had left, they could not. When they saw that they could neither reach the carrack nor the port, they let go two anchors. The gale still increased, and the anchors came home, so that the galliot was drifted close to the rocks; but it pleased our Lord God that the anchors at length found holding ground, so that the vessel did not touch the rocks; for if she had touched, she would have gone to pieces.

Meanwhile the gale increased in a frightful way, and every person commended himself to God our Lord, for they thought they would never escape; and the waves rose so high that they broke over the vessel, and she worked much, and made much water, so that the people could do nothing but wait, and hope for the mercy of our most blessed Lord God. If it had been clear they would have made sail, and stood in for the land; but it was dark, and they knew not where they were.

The carrack, which was off Carpi, being also in this storm, her people weighed her, and she was like to run foul of the galliot; but it pleased our Lord God to succour her, and she passed without touching; and they let go the anchors of the said carrack, but they would not hold, and she drifted on shore. Before day, she had gone to pieces, so that there was nothing left of her; but her people escaped in a boat, losing all they had on board. The mast and bowsprit of the carrack floated close to the galliot, and if they had touched her, she would have been destroyed; but it pleased our Lord God, and his blessed Mother, to protect the galliot from the wreck of the carrack, so that it did her no damage. But the galliot continued to make much water, insomuch that she was in danger of sinking.

They remained in this condition until dawn, when the wind changed, and became fair for the land of Turkey. The yard was, therefore, turned round; but there were few to assist in working the sail, as the greater part of the crew were more dead than alive, so that if death had really come, they would not have cared much. Thus sail was made; and the people of the carrack, who had escaped to an island, fully believed that the galliot had gone down, and that all on board had perished; and they were astonished when they saw the galliot under sail, as they afterwards related, saying that they thought the galliot had sunk after she parted from the carrack; and they added that, before they saw her, they had prayed to God our Lord to deliver the galliot and her crew, and, if she had gone on shore, that the people might be saved.

The ambassadors, after they had landed, set about diligently to get the presents, sent by the king, taken out of the galliot and landed. They were all taken on shore, nothing being lost, but this was done with great trouble and danger; for, the galliot being aground, the sea swept into her, and at intervals the swell caused by the tempest broke over her; and in the lulls the men carried the things to the land, and thus all the king's property was saved. In a very short time, however, the galliot was broken up, and her cargo was piled up in a heap. The boatswain of the galliot then said to the ambassadors that, as all these things were now on shore, the Turks would come and take possession of them for their king.

In this state of things, some Turks came and asked who they were; and they replied that they were Genoese of Pera, and that they had come in the carrack which was lost in that harbour the night before, and that they wished to convey the property piled on the beach to the other carrack which was at Carpi, and that, if they could procure horses, they would pay for them. The Turks said that they could have horses from the neighbouring villages; and, accordingly, a number of people came with horses on the following Sunday, which conveyed the ambassadors and their property to Carpi, where the other carrack was. The said ambassadors found the carrack in port, and they went to speak with Master Ambrosio, the captain of her, and to relate the disaster which had befallen them, and how the other carrack was wrecked. The captain said that, for the service of the king of Castille, they might use the said carrack as if she was their own, and that they might put all their things on board. He also said that he would tell the Turks of the place, that they were people belonging to the other carrack. So they dressed the ambassador of Timour Beg, who was with them, like a Christian, and said that he came from the city of Pera; for if the Turks had recognized him, they would have killed him. When everything was put on board the carrack, they all understood that God our Lord had performed many miracles for them, in many ways.

The first, in the escape from so great and destructive a tempest, for the captain and mariners who were there, said that they had navigated that sea for twelve years, and had never seen one equal to it; the second miracle of our Lord God was displayed in saving the people, and the property of our lord the king, and in their not being robbed by the Turks, or by the mariners; and the third, in the discovery of that other carrack, which, the captain said, was also nearly lost. They remained in that port until the following Tuesday, hoping for a fair wind; and on that day a Turk who was chief of a village, came to the ambassadors, and said to them, that they had taken clothes and other things through the territory of his master, on which they ought to pay duty. He demanded payment; and this was because the Turks had found out that they were not Genoese, nor of the city of Pera; and if they had caught them on shore, they would have detained them. In the afternoon of the same day they made sail, to return to the city of Pera.

Early on Thursday morning, the 22nd of November, they reached the city of Pera, and the ambassadors caused all their things to be taken to the city; and all their acquaintances said that, considering the tempest, and the place where they were wrecked, it was a wonder they had escaped. The ambassadors desired to find some way of continuing their voyage, but they could not find a ship to enter and navigate the great sea, as winter had already set in, and the ships which were bound for Trebizond, had either not started, or had returned to winter at Pera, and wait until the month of March.

The reason why this sea is so dangerous is that it is round, and three thousand miles in circuit, and it has only one entrance, namely the strait near the city of Pera. It is surrounded by very high mountains, and many great rivers fall into it. The sea boils and rises into great waves, when the wind springs up. This sea is also dangerous because, when ships approach the strait, it is very difficult to know it, and if they miss it, they go on shore and are lost, as has happened many times; also, if when the strait is made out, and the vessel is near it, any of the gales arise, she is in danger of being driven on shore, and in this manner a vessel was lately lost which was coming from Caffa.[1]

At this time six Venetian galleys arrived at the great city of Constantinople, to meet the ships which were coming from Tana. The emperor ordered them to be brought close to the city, and said to the captains that the harbour was his, that he was at peace both with them and with the Genoese; and that they must not attack each other. The Genoese and Venetians, therefore, made a truce, for a certain period, and the Venetian ships passed.

[1] "Of one thousand Turkish vessels which skim over the waters of this sea every year, five hundred are said to be wrecked as a matter of course. The winds sometimes will blow from all the four quarters of heaven within two hours time, agitating the waters like a boiling cauldron. Dense fogs obscure the air during the winter, by the assistance of which the Turkish vessels continually mistake the entrance of a valley, called the false Bogaz, for the entrance of the Bosphorus, and are wrecked perpetually."—Curzon's *Armenia*.

The ambassadors were obliged to remain in the city of Pera all the winter, as they could not find a ship. At length they secured a galliot of nineteen pairs of oars, and they caused her to be armed, which cost a large sum of money; and she was armed and ready by the month of March. The owners of this galliot were Master Nicholas Pisano, and Master Lorenzo Veneciano. The ambassadors secured this galliot, so as to reach the winter quarters of Timour Beg, before he left them; and the first vessel which entered the great sea, during that year, was the above mentioned galliot.

On Thursday, the 20th day of March, in the year of our Lord 1404, the galliot was ready, and the ambassadors started in the afternoon, at the hour of vespers; the ambassador, whom Timour Beg had sent to our lord the king, accompanying them. On that day they did not go beyond the columns, about a mile from Pera, as they had to take in water there. On Friday they started again, and entered the great sea, with a fair wind, at the hour of mass. At vespers they reached the castle of Sequel, and remained there until midnight, when they again made sail. At vespers they were off Finogia, where the other galliot was lost, but, as they had no wish to stop there, they went on, and at night they were off a river in Turkey, and it fell calm, so they remained outside the port.

On the following Sunday, at vespers, they were in a port, which is near a Turkish town called Pontoraquia, belonging to Mizal Mathalabi, the eldest son of the Turk.

On Monday they still remained, on account of the contrary winds. The town of Pontoraquia is built on some rocks near the sea, and on the highest there is a castle, which is very strong. The town is thinly populated, the people being all Greeks, except a few Turks; and it used to belong to the empire of Constantinople. They say that, about thirty years ago (more or less), the emperor of Constantinople sold it to the Turk, who was father of Mizal Mathalabi, for so many thousand ducats. This town was very famous for its good harbour, and it takes its name from the emperor who built it, whose name was Ponto, and from the land, which they call Raquia.[1]

In the evening, on Tuesday, the 25th of March, they again started, and were off a castle of the land of Turkey, near the sea, called Rio. It is uninhabited, and at the foot of it there is a harbour. They could not land, because there were large bodies of Turks there, who had come to the coast, where they were seen from the galliot. At midnight the galliot went on, and at dawn she was off the mouth of a river called Parten.[2] They entered it, to procure water, and at the entrance there were some very high rocks, on the top of one of which there was a tower, built to guard the entrance, that galliots might not be able to anchor. Presently they departed from this place, and at noon they were off a town called Samastro.[3]

This town of Samastro belongs to the Genoese, and is near the sea, in the land of Turkey, on a very high hill. Opposite this hill, but more inland, there is another on which the town is built, and both are surrounded by a wall; and from one hill to the other there is a great arch, like a bridge, by which people pass, and it has two gates, one at each end. The town is small, and the houses are small, but outside the walls there are ruins of great edifices, churches, palaces, and houses; and it seemed that in former days the best part of the town was outside the walls.

They remained that day, and Thursday, and on good Friday they got under weigh, and reached a port called "the two castles", at the hour of vespers. On Saturday they went on, and there was a dense fog. Afterwards there was a fresh breeze, and the sea rose, and made great waves; and they knew not whether they were near or far from land.

[1] Heracleia Pontica ? [2] Bartan, the ancient Parthenius.
[3] Amastris, the modern Amasera ?

After mid-day they were off a castle in Turkey, called Ninopoli,[1] but there was no anchorage, so they went on. At vespers the fog returned, so that they could not see the land, and night came on, while they knew not where they were. The sea rose, and some said that they had passed the harbour, others that they had not come abreast of it yet; and while they were thus consulting, they heard the bark of a dog, so those in the galliot shouted, and those in the castle heard them, and showed a light, so that the galliot reached the port. Outside there were rocks, over which the sea broke, and, not knowing the entrance, they were in danger; but a sailor swam on shore, and took a lantern, lighting up the entrance, so that the galliot entered in safety.

On Easter Sunday they were in this harbour. On the top of a rock there was a very strong castle called Quinoli,[2] belonging to a Moorish knight called Espandiar, who is lord of much land, and tributary to Timour Beg, whose money is used in this land. The lord was not there, but his lieutenant, when he knew that the ambassadors were on board, came to see them, with a sheep, fowls, bread, and wine, as presents. In the forests near the castle of Quinoli, there is the best wood for cross bows in all Romania.

On Monday, the 31st of March, they sailed, and at vespers they arrived in the port of a city, which is called Sinope, and anchored there. This city belongs to Espandiar, and when the ambassadors arrived there, they found that he was not there, but in another city, three days journey distant, called Castamea,[3] with forty thousand men, fighting against the son of the Turk, who hated him, because he paid tribute to Timour Beg. The ambassadors desired much to go there, that they might obtain intelligence of Timour, and they held counsel together, about going on shore. The reason why the lord of this land pays tribute to

[1] Ionopolis, now Ainabol? [2] Cinolis.

[3] Kastamuni or Castamon.

Timour, is that the Turk Bayazid, whom Timour conquered, killed his father and deprived him of his land; but when Timour Beg was victorious, he restored all the land to this knight, named Espandiar.

Early on Saturday, the 5th of April, the ambassadors left this port; but it fell calm, and the galliot remained out at sea, during the night. On Sunday they were off a town, near the sea, called Simiso,[1] which has two castles, one belonging to the Genoese, and the other, with the town, to a Mussulman named Chalabi; but they did not wish to touch there, so they were out at sea during that night also, when there was a calm. On Monday, at noon, they reached a harbour, where there was a castle called Hinio,[2] where they anchored, because the wind was foul. Near the port, on some high rocks, there was a small town, inhabited by Greeks; and on a very high hill, near the town, there was a castle, in which, they say, live three hundred Turks. This castle and town belongs to a Greek lord named Melaseno, who pays tribute to Timour Beg. Close to the sea there were some small blacksmiths' shops, for in that place the sea threw up a fine black sand, from which they made iron.

On Tuesday they departed from this place; but there was a foul wind, so they took shelter in a harbour of the land of Turkey, called Leona, where there was a castle on some rocks near the sea, which was uninhabited, and they said that it was pillaged by the Genoese, four years ago. This land belonged to a Turkish lord called Arzamir. Leaving this place, they passed a small castle, on the top of a rock, near the sea, called Santo Nicio; and, owing to the foul wind, they anchored off the mouth of a river, and there were several villages in sight, belonging to the said Arzamir, who was said to possess as many as ten thousand or more cavalry, and he paid tribute to Timour Beg.

On Wednesday there was a fair wind, but much rain, and

[1] Samsun ?

[2] Unieh.

they were off a town near the sea, called Guirifonda, on the top of a high rock, with a great wall surrounding it, within which there were many fruit trees. At noon they were off a great town, on the sea shore, called Tripil,[1] which is in the territory of the emperor of Trebizond, and soon after they passed a castle, near the sea, called Corila, but they did not desire to touch at these places, because there was a fair wind. At the hour of vespers they were off a castle called Viopoli, where they anchored for the night. On Thursday there was a foul wind, with a heavy sea, and they anchored off a castle called Sanfoca, to refresh the people. Leaving this place, they came to a port called Platana, at the hour of vespers; and as the wind was still contrary, they did not attempt to reach Trebizond that night, though it was not more than twelve miles distant. During the night the wind was very strong, and the waves rose, so that they were in some danger.

On Friday, the 11th of April, at the hour of vespers, they reached the city of Trebizond; and from the city of Pera, whence they came in this galliot, to this city of Trebizond the distance is nine hundred and sixty miles.[2] The Genoese resided in a fine castle, outside the walls of the city, and the ambassadors went to lodge there, as their guests, and were honorably received.

[1] Tereboli.

[2] The distance is six hundred miles.

IV.

TREBIZOND

AND THE

JOURNEY THROUGH ARMENIA.

On Saturday, the 12th of April, the Emperor of Trebizond sent for the ambassadors, and when they arrived at his palace, they found him in a saloon, which was in an upper story; and he received them very well. After they had spoken with him, they returned to their lodging. With the emperor was his son, who was about twenty-five years of age; and the emperor was tall and handsome. The emperor and his son were dressed in imperial robes. They wore, on their heads, tall hats surmounted by golden cords, on the top of which were cranes' feathers; and the hats were bound with the skins of martens. They call the emperor Germanoli,[1] and his son Quelex;[2] and they call the son emperor as well as the father, because it is the custom to call the eldest legitimate son emperor, although his father may be alive; and the Greek name for emperor, is Basileus. This emperor pays tribute to Timour Beg, and to other Turks, who are his neighbours. He is married to a relation of the Emperor of Constantinople, and his son is married to the daughter of a knight of Constantinople, and has two little daughters.[3]

[1] Manuel II. [2] Alexis.

[3] The empire of Trebizond was founded by the Comneni, when they

On Sunday afternoon, the ambassadors being in their lodging, two knights came to see them, the most honored and confidential of the emperor's household. The first was named Horchi, which means the page who bears the bow before the emperor; and the other Protovestati, which means the same as treasurer. The latter was very intimate with the emperor, who did nothing in the empire against his advice, and they say that he was of base lineage, the son of a baker. They also say that the young emperor, seeing that his father made so much of this knight, and that he took no notice of the nobles of the empire, was enraged, and rose against his father, saying that he must dismiss this man. He made war, and besieged the city for three months, being assisted by the greatest men of the empire; but afterwards they came to an agreement, through Horchi, who was a friend of the young emperor, and of the others who had risen; nevertheless there afterwards succeeded dishonour, trouble, and injury to the said emperor, through his friendship for this cavalier.

The city of Trebizond is built near the sea, and its wall rises up over some rocks, and on the highest part there is a very strong castle, which has another wall round it. A small river passes by the castle, and dashes over the rocks, and on this side the city is very strong, but on the other side it is on open ground. Outside the city walls there are suburbs, and the most beautiful part is a street near the sea, which is in one of these suburbs, where they sell all the things required in the city. On the shore there are two castles, with strong walls and towers, one belonging to the

fled from the cruelty of Isaac Angelus, at Constantinople, in 1186. Alexis Comnenus assumed the title of Emperor of Trebizond. His descendants retained the title, and ruled over this small territory, until David Comnenus was deposed by Mohammed II in 1461.

The Emperor of Trebizond, at the time when Clavijo passed through the city, was Manuel II, who paid tribute to Timour. He died in 1412, and was succeeded by his son Alexis IV.

Venetians and the other to the Genoese, and they hold them with the consent of the emperor.

Outside the city, there are many churches and monasteries. In this city the Armenians have a church and a bishop, and they consecrate the body of God in the same way as the Catholics; but the priest, when he dresses, does not put the stole with the cross on his breast, and when he reads the gospel, he turns his face to the people. When they consecrate, they do not put water in the chalice. They confess, and fast during Lent, and eat meat on Saturdays, and at Easter. During Lent their fast consists in not eating fish, nor oil, nor suet; and the common people eat fish, but do not drink wine. From Easter to Pentecost they eat meat every day, as well on Fridays as on other days in the week. They say that Jesus Christ was baptized on the day he was born, and they have other errors in their faith, but they are very religious, and hear mass very devoutly.

The Greeks are also a very devout people, but they have several errors in the articles of their faith. In the first place they consecrate bread which contains leaven; and make it in this way—they take a loaf, about the size of a man's hand, and in the middle they make an impression, with certain letters, the size of a *dobla*,[1] which they consecrate. The priest who says mass, wears an ornament before him; and when he has consecrated the bread, he puts it on his head, in a white cloth, and, singing, goes forth to the people, who all put their faces to the ground, crying, and smiting their bosoms, and saying they are not worthy to see it. The priest then returns to the altar, and consumes the impression which is in the middle of the bread. When mass is said, he takes the remainder of the bread, breaks it, as if it was consecrated, and gives it to the people. When the priests officiate at mass, they do not have either books or

[1] An old Spanish coin.

bells in the churches (except in St. Sophia, at Constantinople). The clergy are married, but they do not marry more than once, and with a virgin. When their wives die, they do not marry again, but remain widowers, and they are very unhappy for the rest of their lives. They only say mass twice a week, on Saturdays and Wednesdays; and when they have to say mass, they remain in the church all the week, and do not go out, or to their houses. They have six fasts in the year, in which they do not drink wine, nor eat fish which has blood, nor oil; and the clergy do not go to their houses, during these fasts; which occur as follows: —the first is from 1st of August to St. Mary's day in the middle of August; the second, from St. Catherine's day to the Nativity; the third is the forty days of Lent, which we also keep; the fourth is for twenty-four days, in honour of the twelve Apostles; the fifth is for fifteen days, in honour of a saint, whom they call Saint Demetrius; and throughout the year, they do not eat meat, neither on Wednesdays nor on Fridays; but they eat meat on Saturdays. They keep Wednesdays very strictly, and would rather eat meat on Fridays, than on Wednesdays: for they do eat meat on the following four Fridays in the year, namely, the Friday before Christmas day, the Friday in Carnival week, the Friday after Easter, and the Friday before Pentecost. They err in their doctrine of baptism, and in other things; and when any one dies, who has done evil in this life, and is a great sinner, they dress him in cloths, and change his name, that the devil may not know him. They hold these, and other erroneous opinions, yet they are very devout, and say long prayers.

The Greeks are armed with bows and swords, and other arms like the Turks, and they have cavalry.

The ambassadors were in this city of Trebizond from the Friday on which they arrived, being the 11th of April, until Saturday the 26th of the same month; preparing harness for their horses, and other things necessary for a journey by land. On Sunday, the 27th of April, the ambassadors set out accompanied by a guard which was provided for them, by order of the emperor, to guide them through his territory. On the same day they slept near a river called Pexic, in a ruined church. The road led over high hills, which were inhabited, and covered with corn, and mills; and many streams flowed from these hills.

On Monday they left this halting place, and the guard which the emperor had given them turned back, and said that they could not go any further, for fear of the enemies of the emperor; but the ambassadors went on their way. At the hour of vespers they came to a castle belonging to the emperor, called Pilomazuca, built on a very high rock. The entrance to it is by steps; and there were a few houses in the face of the rock. The road, on this day, was very good for travelling, and led through very beautiful mountains; but they found that a great piece of rock had fallen, which blocked up the road, and a river, so that the ambassadors could not pass without trouble; and on that day they did not travel far, and encamped in the open plain.

On Tuesday they travelled on a very bad road, over very high mountains, covered with snow, and traversed by many streams; and at night they encamped near a castle called Sigana, which is on the top of a high rock, the only entrance to which was by a wooden bridge, leading from a rock to the gate of the castle. The owner of the castle was a Greek knight, named Quirileo Arbosita.

On Wednesday they came to a castle, on a high rock near the road, called Cadaca, on one side of which there was a river, and on the other a precipice, and the road led through a very narrow pass, between the river and the foot of the castle rock, so that only one man could pass at a time. A few men in the castle might defend this pass against an army, and in all this country there is no other pass. Men came forth from

9

the castle, and demanded a toll from the ambassadors, for their effects. This castle always contains thieves and bad men; and the lord of it is also a thief; and this road is not used, except when many merchants travel together, and give a great present to the lord of this land, and to his men. Three leagues beyond this castle there was a tower, on the top of a high rock, in a narrow pass; and at the hour of vespers they approached a castle, on a high hill, called Dorile, which looked very beautiful, and the road came close to it. The ambassadors understood that the lord of the country lived in that castle, so they sent an interpreter to let him know who they were; and when they approached the foot of the castle, a man on horseback came out to them, and said that the lord of the castle desired that they should stop, and they put their luggage in a church close by. The man then told them that it was the custom for those who travelled on that road, to pay a certain duty to the lord of the castle, and that they were expected to do so. He said that his master had people in the mountains, who were making war on the Turks; and that he lived by the dues taken from travellers who used that road, and by the spoils taken from his enemies. When the ambassadors wished to visit the lord of the castle, to show him such courtesy as he might desire, his men would not consent, and said that they should not go to him, but that next morning he would come to them.

On Thursday, the 1st of May, Cabasica, the lord of the castle, came to the place where the ambassadors were encamped, with thirty men on horseback, armed with bows and arrows. They all got off their horses, and sat down, and Cabasica made the ambassadors sit down near him, and said to them that his country was barren and craggy, as they might see, that he was always at war with the Turks, who were his neighbours, that he and his people had nothing to live upon, except what was given them by those who passed that way, and what they robbed from their neighbours. He, therefore, desired that they would help him, with some clothing and money.

The ambassadors replied that they were not merchants, but ambassadors, whom their lord the king of Spain had sent to the lord Timour Beg, and that they had nothing but what they were taking to the said Timour; and the ambassador from Timour Beg said that he knew well that the emperor of Trebizond was lord of that land, and that he was a vassal of Timour Beg; adding that the things they had with them belonged to Timour, and that they ought to be allowed to pass safely through that land. They of the castle replied that what he had said was true, but that they had nothing to live on, except what they had already described, and that, at all events, they must give them what they demanded. The ambassadors, seeing their determination, produced a piece of scarlet, and a silver cup; and Timour Beg's ambassador gave a scarlet cloth made in Florence, and a piece of fine linen; but they were not satisfied with all this, and asked for more. Notwithstanding all the courteous speeches that were made to them, they cared nothing for them, but continued to insist upon being given what they demanded, and declared that words were worth nothing. The ambassadors therefore bought a piece of camlet from a merchant who was with them, and gave it to the people of the castle. At last they were satisfied, and the lord of the castle said that the ambassadors should be guarded on their road, as far as the land of Arsinga, which then belonged to Timour Beg.

The ambassadors desired to depart at once, but they could not. They, however, hired horses to carry them as far as the land of Arsinga, and men to guard them. On Friday they set out, accompanied by ten men on horseback, and at the hour of mass they came to a castle, on the top of a high rock, which also belonged to Cabasica, where they found men in the road, who took a toll from them. At noon they came to a valley where they were told that there was a castle belonging to the Turks of a lineage called Chapenies, who were at war with Cabasica, and that in the valley there was a guard, which waited for passengers. At the hour of vespers they came to a town of Arsinga, called Alangogaza, and Cabasica's ten men took leave of them. On this day the road was very mountainous; and in this town there was a Turkish cavalier, who held the place for the lord of Arsinga. He received the ambassadors very well, and gave them good lodging and food, and everything they required; and they learned from this cavalier that Timour Beg had departed from Carabaqui,[1] where he had wintered, and had gone to the land of Sultanieh.

On Saturday, the 3rd of May, they set out again, and reached a town where they were treated well, and given food and fresh horses; and at night they came to another town, where they were given plenty of food and horses, and everything they required. The custom of the country was that, at each town where they arrived, small carpets were brought from each house, for them to sit upon, and afterwards they placed a piece of printed leather in front, on which they had their meals. The bread of these towns was very bad, and was made in this way:—they knead a little flour, and make very thin cakes, which they put on a pan, over the fire, and when they are hot, they take them out; and this is the bread which they bring on these pieces of leather. They also bring out plenty of meat, and milk, and cream, and eggs, and honey. This is the best food they have, and they bring it from each house; and if the ambassadors had to remain, the people brought them plenty of meat, and all that they required. When the ambassadors came to any place, an officer went on before, and the ambassador from Timour Beg ordered food, and horses, and men for them; and if they did not come, the people received such a number of blows with sticks and whips, that it was quite

[1] Karabagh.

wonderful. Thus the people of these towns were so severely punished that they fled, when they saw a Zagatay coming. A Zagatay is a man[1] in the host of Timour Beg, of noble lineage. In these towns, some Armenian christians resided.

On Sunday, the 4th of May, they arrived at the city of Arsinga,[2] at the hour of vespers; and the road they had traversed that day was very rugged, and passed over high ridges of mountains; and near the city they found much snow in the road. Many people came out from the city, to receive and to see the ambassadors, and they were conducted to the lodgings which had been prepared for them. That night the lord of the city sent them boiled and dressed meat, and much fruit, and bread, and wine.

Next day the lord of the city sent them a certain sum of money, to maintain them while they were there; and at noon he sent horses to convey them to visit him, and men to guard them, to a plain outside the city. They found him seated in a saloon, under the shade of a silken canopy, supported by two poles, with cords to draw it out, and there were many people with him. When the ambassadors arrived, some cavaliers came forward to receive them; and when they came to the lord, he rose up, and gave them his hand, making them sit down near him, and treating them very well. He was dressed in a robe of blue silk, embroidered with gold, and he had a tall hat on his head, with precious stones in it, and on the top of the hat he had a crest of gold, from which descended two tresses of red hair, reaching to the shoulders, and this hair, thus worn, is the device of Timour Beg. The lord seemed about forty years of age, and he was a well made man, with a black beard.

After he had asked the ambassadors concerning the state

[1] The Zagatays took their name from the son of Zengis Khan; just as the Uzbegs derived their name from another famous descendant of the great Mongol conqueror.

[2] Erzingan.

of the king our lord, the first honour he did them was to take a silver cup full of wine, and give it, with his own hands, to the ambassadors, to drink, and afterwards to all their followers. He who thus drinks, must take the cup in both hands, it being disrespectful to take it in one; for they say that a man ought to take a cup in one hand, from his equal, and not from a lord; and when he has taken the cup from the hand of his lord, he raises it, and walks a little backwards, and does not turn his back to the lord. When he has drunk, he raises his finger in the air three times; and it is the custom to drink all that is in the cup. After he had given them to drink, with his own hand, they brought some mules, on which were wooden boxes, containing plenty of copper pots for cooking, and many chopping knives, of hard iron, and a hundred small iron porringers; and all the utensils were round and deep, like a trooper's head piece. They then put meat into these pots, and pickled mutton, and balls of forced meat into the porringers, with rice and other victuals; and over each pot and each porringer they placed a thin cake. Before the lord and the ambassadors they placed a silken cloth, on the ground; and on it they placed the pots and porringers of meat; and every one began to eat. Each person had his knife to cut, and his wooden spoon to eat with. But a man cut up the food, before the lord, and two cavaliers sat and ate with him; and when they had to eat the rice, and other dishes, they ate out of one porringer, with one spoon; when one had done with it, the other took it up, and so they went on eating.

While they were at this meal, a Turkish boy, about seven years old, arrived with about ten mounted attendants; and the lord received him, and made him sit down by his side. This boy was a nephew of Espandiar, the lord of Sinopoli, who was a great lord in Turkey; and he came from Timour Beg, with an order to Espandiar, to give the half of his land to this boy, because he was the son of his sister. Presently two other cavaliers arrived, who came from Timour Beg, and they were natives of this city of Arsinga. They said that Timour Beg had detained them for some time, but that now he had released them, and the reason he had imprisoned them was this :—

Zaratan, a great noble, was lord of this city of Arsinga, and of its land, which is a great territory; and when he died, he did not leave children by his wife, who was daughter of the emperor of Trebizond. Some time before he died, he declared that he who is now lord of Arsinga was his son, but when he died, they did not wish to receive this man as lord. A cavalier, who was the son of a sister of Zaratan, named Xevali, seized the land, saying that Zaratan died without children, and that he ought to inherit, as his nephew; and the two cavaliers who arrived at the meal, assisted him. When Timour Beg conquered the Turk, he came to this city, and seized the said Xevali, and the two cavaliers, making him, who is now in possession, and whom Zaratan had said was his son, lord of Arsinga. Timour Beg had now released these two cavaliers, but had taken Xevali to Samarcand.

The reason why Timour Beg and the Turk made war upon each other, was owing to Zaratan, the lord of this land, as will be related to you presently; it was a beautiful reason.

When they had finished eating, the ambassadors returned to their lodging, and the lord remained with his cavaliers; and at night the lord sent the ambassadors many things, such as pots of boiled meat, with the cooks who dressed it, and attendants to serve it up: and he gave them money for their expenses, as much as they required.

On Wednesday, after dinner, he sent for the ambassadors, and they went to him, and found him at his lodging. He was in a porch, before a fountain, with many cavaliers, attendants, and also buffoons, who were performing before him. As the ambassadors entered, he bowed to them, and made them sit near him, and gave them many pieces of sugar. He said that he and the knight who did not drink wine (which was Ruy Gonzalez) should that day be drinking companions, and they brought a great crystal vase, full of water with sugar. He drank first, and then gave it to Ruy Gonzalez, with his own hand, but they gave wine to all the others. Afterwards they brought much meat, and rice, and various other dishes, and they ate in the same way as they did the day before. When the meat was eaten, they brought porringers of honey, and peaches cut in vinegar, and grapes, and capers; and they ate very dirtily. All this time the wine did not stop, and when this had lasted some time, they brought a cup, which the lord took, and gave it to certain of his knights, who drank all the wine, so that none was left, for this is their unseemly custom. These cavaliers then took the great cup, and gave it to each other, to drink, until most of them were drunk; but on that day the lord did not drink wine, to keep company with Ruy Gonzalez, and the lord's name was Pitalibet. At night the ambassadors returned to their lodging.

This city of Arsinga was built on a plain, near a river which is called Euphrates,[1] which is one of the rivers that come from Paradise. This plain is entirely surrounded by very high mountains, and on the top of the highest of these mountains there is much snow. There are many towns, and fruit gardens in the plain, which is covered with corn fields and vineyards, and very beautiful gardens. The city was not very large, and the walls and towers which surrounded it, were built of stone. It was built by the Armenians, and the sign of the cross is cut on many parts of the walls. The houses all have terraces, and the people walk along the terraces, as if they were streets. The city is very populous, and contains many fine streets, and it is very rich, and has much

[1] The Kara-sou, or Western Euphrates.

trade, and many beautiful mosques and temples. It is inhabited by many christians, Greeks, and Armenians. They say that when Timour Beg took and destroyed a Turkish city called Sabastria,[1] that the Turk came against this city of Arsinga, and entered it; but when Timour Beg conquered the Turk, he came to this city, and took it for himself.

While Timour Beg was at Arsinga, the Moors of the city quarrelled with the christians who were there, saying that Zaratan, their lord, allowed them to have churches which were better than the mosques; and Timour Beg sent for Zaratan, and told him what the Moors had said. Zaratan answered that he allowed the christians to be in the land, that he might take advantage of their industry. Timour Beg then sent for a Greek priest who lived there, and when he came before him, he, on account of the great hatred he had for the people of Constantinople, and for the Genoese of the city of Pera, ordered him to apostatize; and, because the priest did not wish to do so, Timour Beg commanded all the christians in the city to be put to death.

Zaratan interceded with Timour Beg, for them, and ransomed them for nine thousand *esperas*, each *espera* being worth half a silver rial; but Timour Beg caused all the churches of the christians to be destroyed, and he took a castle of that city, called Camag, and gave it to one of his Zagatays. He did this because the castle was very strong, and guarded all that country. From this city much merchandize goes to Syria, and to Turkey.

The reasons why the Turk and Timour Beg came to know of each other, and why Timour Beg came to Turkey, to fight the Turk Bayazid, are as follows:—This cavalier Zaratan, lord of this city of Arsinga, held a territory which bordered on the dominions of the Turk. The Turk, being desirous of possessing the land of this Zaratan, and especially the castle of Camag, sent to demand tribute from him, and that he

[1] Sebaste or Sivas.

should give up the said castle of Camag. Zaratan replied that he would pay tribute, but that he would not give up the castle; and the Turk declared that if he did not, he should be deprived of all his land.

Zaratan, having heard of the great power of Timour Beg, and that he was then waging war in Persia, sent an embassy to him, with presents and letters, beseeching him to defend him from the Turk, and protesting that he was ready to obey him. Timour Beg, therefore, sent his ambassador to the Turk, with letters, in which he declared that Zaratan was his subject, and that the Turk must not molest him, threatening, if he did, to do as much for him.

The Turk, never having heard of Timour Beg, until that time, and believing that there was no man in the world equal to himself, got into such a passion that it was quite wonderful, and sent back letters to Timour Beg, in which he said that he was astonished that there could be a man so mad and insolent as to write such great folly; that he would do what he chose against Zaratan, and against every other man in the whole universe. He further promised to come and seek for Timour Beg, and that he could not escape from falling into his hands. He also swore that he would disgrace him, by dishonoring his principal wife.

Timour Beg, being possessed of great confidence, determined to show his power, and marched from the beautiful plains of Carabaque,[1] in Persia, where he had wintered that year, with a great army, straight to the city of Arsinga. Thence he advanced into the land of Turkey, and besieged the city of Sabastria. The people of Sabastria sent to the Turk, their lord, for help; and when he heard that Timour Beg was in his territory, he got into a great passion, and collected a force, which he sent against him, under his eldest son Muzulman Chalabi. The force consisted of two hundred thousand

[1] Karabagh.

cavalry, and he intended to follow himself, with a larger army; but before the Turks could arrive, Timour had entered the city; and he did so in this manner: he fought the besieged very fiercely, so that at last they came to speak with him, and he agreed that certain men of the city should come to him; that he would cause no blood to be shed; and that they should give him a certain quantity of gold and silver.

When Timour Beg had received the tribute which he demanded, he said that he desired to tell those of the city certain things, which were much to their advantage; and that, for this purpose, the chief men should come to him. These, trusting in the safe conduct he had given them, came to him; and Timour Beg, as soon as he had got them outside the city, caused great holes to be made; and said to them that he had certainly promised not to shed their blood, but that he would stifle them in those holes; and he ordered his troops to enter the city. He buried all who had come out to him, alive, and ordered the city to be pillaged, pulled down, and destroyed.

When this was done, he marched away, and on the day that he departed the son of the Turk arrived, with his two hundred thousand cavalry; and when he found that the city of Sabastria was destroyed, and Timour Beg gone, he waited there for his father; and Timour Beg marched straight to the land of the Sultan of Babylon.

Before he arrived there, he met with a race, called the white Tartars, who always wander over the plains; and he fought and conquered them, and took their lord prisoner; and took away as many as fifty thousand men and women with him.

He then marched to Damascus; against the people of which city he was much enraged, because they did not pay tribute; and he imprisoned their ambassadors, and entered their city, and destroyed it. All those who understood any art, he took with him to the city of Samarcand, together with the white Tartars, and the people of Sabastria, amongst whom were many Armenian Christians.

After this, he returned to the land of Persia; and passed the summer in a land called Alara, in Upper Armenia.

Meanwhile the Turk marched to the city of Arsinga; and, on account of the rage and fury which he felt against Zaratan, because he had been the cause of this insult, he attacked the city and entered it by force, capturing the wife of Zaratan. But he ordered her to be released, and that no harm should be done to the city. He then returned to his own land. They say that he thus displayed very little courage, in not destroying that city, as Timour Beg had destroyed the city of Sabastria.

After these two lords had returned to their own territories, they sent ambassadors to each other; but they were unable to come to any reconciliation.

At this time the emperor of the great city of Constantinople, and the Genoese of Pera sent to Timour Beg, to say that if he was going to make war upon the Turk, they would be able to assist him with troops and galleys; and it should be in this way: that they would arm certain galleys, in a short time, to prevent the Turks who were in Greece, from passing back into Turkey; and they also offered to assist him with a certain quantity of money.

When the Turk would not come to any terms with the city of Constantinople, or with Timour Beg, they each began to collect their forces; but Timour Beg, who could do this with great rapidity, because he was astute and sagacious in war, marched quickly from Persia into Turkey, by the same road as he had taken before, passing through the cities of Arsinga and Sabastria. When the Turk knew that Timour Beg was in his territory, he marched, with his army, to a strong castle called Angora. As soon as Timour Beg heard of this sagacious movement of the Turk, he left the road by which he was marching, and led his army over a high mountain. When the Turk, therefore, found that Timour Beg had left the road, he thought that he had fled, and marched after him as fast as he could.

Timour Beg, after marching through the mountains for eight days, returned to the plain, and came to the castle of Angora, where the Turk had left all his baggage, and he pillaged it. When the Turk heard this, he came back as fast as he could, and when he arrived, his men were tired.

Timour Beg had made this movement, to throw his enemy into disorder; and they fought, and the Turk was taken prisoner. But the Emperor of Constantinople, and the Genoese of Pera, instead of doing what they had promised, allowed the Turks to pass from Greece into Turkey; and when they were defeated, they assisted them to escape; and this bad faith made Timour Beg very furious against the Christians.

The name of this Turk, who was conquered by Timour Beg, was Ilderim Bayazid, which means "lightning." The name of his father was Amurath, a very good knight, who was killed by a christian count, called Lazaro, on the field of battle, by two thrusts is his breast, which came out at his back. Afterwards this Ilderim Bayazid avenged the death of his father, by killing Count Lazaro in battle, with his own hand. The son of this Lazaro marched with Bayazid, and he now lives with Muzulman Chalabi, the son of this Ilderim Bayazid.

I have written this, that it may be understood whom they call Murate; because all the lords of Turkey are known by the name of Murate. Also Timour Beg is the proper name of that lord, and not Tamerlane, as we call him; for Timour Beg is as much as to say, in his language, the same as the *lord of iron;* because *Beg* means *lord*, and *Timour* is *iron.* Tamerlane, on the contrary, is an insulting name; and means *lame*, because he became lame on the left side, and was wounded in the two small fingers of the right hand, from blows which were given him when he was stealing some sheep one night, as will be more fully related to you presently.

The ambassadors were in this city of Arsinga until Thursday, the 15th day of May, when they departed. The road that day led over high mountains, without vegetation, and the snow fell, so that it was very cold. They passed the night in a town called Xabega, which had a small castle, and a river flowed near it; and they passed many corn fields and villages that day.

On Saturday they passed the night in a town called Pagarrix, which had a lofty castle on the top of a rock; and in this town there were two wards, one inhabited by Armenians, and the other by Turks; and they said that it was a year since Timour Beg passed through it, when he ordered the churches of the Armenians to be pulled down; and the Armenians gave three thousand *asperas*, each *aspera* being half a rial, to ransom their churches; but he ordered the money to be taken, and the churches to be destroyed also.

On Sunday, the day of Pentecost, they set out, and reached a town, where there was a castle on the top of a rock, which belonged to Arsinga.

On Monday they passed the night in the open air; and the road they travelled over that day passed over high mountains, without vegetation, from which many streams descended; but there was much pasture, both above and below; and this land belonged to the Turcomans, who wander as far as this, and they are a nation of Moors, allied to the Turks. On Tuesday they departed, and travelled over a plain, with much pasture, and plenty of water.

At noon they came to a town called Aseron,[1] which belonged to Timour Beg. It was in a plain, and was surrounded by a strong stone wall with towers, and it is very

[1] Erzeroum.

large. It also had a castle, but it is not very populous. In it there is a handsome church, for this city used to belong to the christians of Armenia, and many Armenians lived in it. Formerly it was the largest and the richest city in all this country. The lord of the city was a Turcoman named Subail.

On Thursday, the 22nd of May, they departed from this place, and passed the night in a town called Patir Juan, in the territory of a very strong city called Auniqui; and the lord of this land was a Zagatay knight, named Toladaybeque.

On Friday they arrived at a town called Ischu, and they remained there until Sunday. In this town there were many Armenians.

On Sunday they slept in a town called Delularquente, which means "the town of the mad men;" and the town was inhabited by Moorish hermits, called Caxixes; and many people came to them on pilgrimage, and they healed many diseases. Among them there was a chief whom they treat with great respect, and say that he is a saint, and that when Timour Beg passed by, he went to visit this Caxic. These hermits received many alms from the people, and their chief was lord of the town. Those who desire to be thought religious, shave their beards, and their heads, and take off their clothes, and go through the streets in heat and cold, dressed in the most tattered clothes they can find. They go about singing, day and night, with timbrels. On the top of the gate of their hermitage there was a pennon of black woollen threads, with a moon figured above them; and at the foot of the pennon were fixed many horns of deer, goats, and rams; and this is the custom of these Caxixes, to have these horns on the tops of their houses, and they carry them in their hands, when they walk in the streets.

On Monday, the 26th of May, the ambassadors departed,

and passed the night in a plain, near a great river called Corras,[1] which traverses the whole of Armenia; and the road passed over snowy mountains, whence descended many streams.

On Tuesday they passed the night in a town called Naujua; and the road, on that day, was along the banks of this river, being very rugged, and dangerous to pass. In this place there was a Caxic for governor, who received the ambassadors very well; and there were many Armenians.

On Wednesday they passed the night in a town, which had a high castle on the top of a rock; which rock was of salt, and any one may take this salt, who wants it.

THE CITY OF CALMARIN,[2] WHICH WAS THE FIRST IN THE WORLD, AFTER THE FLOOD.

On Thursday, the 29th of May, at noon, they reached a great city called Calmarin, and from it, distant about six leagues, they saw the great mountain on which the ark of Noah rested, after the flood. This city was in a plain, and on one side flowed the great river called Corras; and on the other there was a very deep and rocky valley, as broad as the flight of an arrow; and it encircled the city, until it united with the river. The valley and river made the city very strong, so that it could only be attacked where the river commenced; but at this place there was a very strong castle, with great towers, and it had two gates, one in front of the other. This city of Calmarin was the first city that was built in the world, after the flood, and it was built by the lineage of Noah. The people of the city said that, eight years ago, Tetani, Emperor of Tartary, besieged

[1] Kur, or Cyrus. [2] Etchmiazin?

the city, and that they fought day and night for two days, and on the third there was a parley. They gave up the city, on condition that neither he, nor his people should enter it, but that the citizens should pay to him a certain annual tribute; with which the emperor was satisfied, but he demanded that half the people of the city should be given up to him, to go with him to the land of Jugania,[1] where he was going to make war on the king Sorso. When the citizens had given up these men, the emperor attacked the city, entered it by force, pillaged and burnt it, making breaches in the walls, and killing many people.

The greater part of the inhabitants were Armenians; but the land of Armenia has been taken from the Christians by the Moors, as I will relate to you, presently. In this city there are very great edifices; and throughout all this country, they gave the ambassadors and their people lodging, and food, and horses; for all the land belonged to Timour Beg.

On Friday they departed, and passed the night at a castle, which was on the top of a rock, and belonged to a widow lady, who paid tribute to Timour Beg for this castle, as well as for other land which she held. In this castle there used to be robbers, and men who came out to plunder travellers on the road. Timour Beg marched against this castle, entered it by force, and killed the lord of it, who was the husband of this lady; and he ordered that malefactors should never be allowed to assemble in it again: and, that they might not be able to defend themselves, he caused the doors to be taken away, and ordered that they should never be replaced. He then gave it to this lady. The castle was, therefore, without doors, and was called Egida. This castle was at the foot of the lofty mountain of the ark of Noah; and all these mountain ranges, after leaving the land of Trebizond, were without woods. The lady received the ambassadors very well, and gave them all they required.

[1] Georgia.

On Saturday, the 13th of May, the road led along the foot of the mountain of the ark of Noah. It was very high, and the summit was covered with snow, and it was without woods; but there was much herbage upon it, and many streams. Near the road there were many edifices, and foundations of houses, of stone; and great quantities of rye was growing, as if it had been sown by man, but it was useless, and did not come to grain; and there was also plenty of water cresses. At the foot of this mountain they came to the ruins of a town long since deserted, which was a league in length; and the people of the country said that it was the first town that was built in the world, after the flood, and that it was founded by Noah and his sons.

After leaving these ruins, they came to a great plain, in which there were many streams of water, and trees, and rose gardens, and fountains. The mountain had a very sharp peak, which was covered with snow, and they say that the snow never leaves this peak all the year round, either in winter or summer, and this is on account of its great height.

On this day the ambassadors took their siesta by a beautiful fountain, near a stone arch; and while they were there, the clouds moved away, and the peak of the mountain appeared, but they suddenly returned, and the people said that it was very seldom visible.

Next to this mountain, there was another, which also had a sharp peak, but not so high as the first, and between these two peaks there is one like a saddle, and they were all very high, and their summits were all covered with snow.

This night they slept at a castle called Vasit-calaside, which was on the top of a high rock, and was wonderfully strong. On another rock there was a large town, joined to the castle by a great wall, with towers; and from this wall, a flight of steps led to the castle gate. The rock was very high, and within the castle, there was a spring of water. This castle was besieged by Timour Beg; and the lord of it agreed to pay tribute, on condition that the troops should not enter it.

On Sunday, the first of June, at the hour of vespers, they came to a castle called Maca, belonging to a catholic christian named Noradin, and the people who lived in it were catholic christians, though they were by birth and language Armenians, and they also knew the Tartar and Persian tongues. In this place there was a monastery of Dominican friars. The castle was in a valley, at the foot of a very high rock, and there was a village on a hill above, and on the top of the hill there was a wall of stone and mortar, with towers, and against the wall there were houses. There was also another wall with towers, and the entrance to it was by a great tower, built to guard it, along steps cut in the rock. Near the second wall there were houses cut in the rock, and in the centre were some towers and houses, where the lord lived, and here all the people in the village kept their provisions. The rock was very high, and rose above the walls and houses; and from the rock, an overhanging part stretches out, which covers the castle, walls, and houses, like the heaven that is above them; so that when it rains, the water does not fall upon the castle, for the rock covers it; and thus the castle cannot either be attacked from the land, or from the sky. Inside the castle a spring rises up, which supplies all the people, and irrigates many fruit gardens. At the foot of this castle there is a beautiful valley, full of vineyards, and corn fields, through which a river flows.

Timour Beg besieged this castle, and could not take it; but he negotiated with the lord of it, that he should supply him with twenty mounted soldiers, when he called for them. Soon afterwards Timour Beg marched away, with his army; and the lord of the castle sent his son, who was about twenty years old, with three richly caparisoned horses, as presents to Timour Beg, who received them; and the lord's son asked him not to damage the lands belonging to the castle.

Timour replied that the lord of the castle had so fine a son that he must accompany him, and he took him, and afterwards ordered him to live with his grandson, Omar Meerza, who was governor of Persia, and of that land. He still lives with him, and marches in his army; and that governor made the son of this lord turn Moor, by force, and named him Sorgart-mix, and made him one of his guards; but, though he became a Moor by force, he is not one willingly, or by his acts.

The ambassadors were well received by the lord of this castle, and he was much comforted by their being christians, and was very hospitable; and told them that it was about fifteen days since Janza Meerza, the nephew and favourite of Timour Beg, sent to him to say that he wished to use the castle as a deposit for his treasure; and he answered that he could not admit it. The ambassadors remained during the day on which they arrived, and afterwards they saw the son of the lord of the castle, who was in the host of the ruler of Persia, and spoke with him. The lord of the castle also had another son, smaller than this, and he told the ambassadors that that son was learned, and a good grammarian; and that when God willed that they should return, he should go with them to the lord their king, that he might be recommended to the pope, to be made bishop of that land. It is very wonderful that this castle should hold out, amidst so many Moors, with a garrison of christians, and of Armenians turned catholics, which is a very great service to God.

On Monday, the 2nd of June, they departed, and slept in the open air, as they could not reach any village; and on that day they were shown a castle, on the left hand side of the road, called Alinga, which was on a high mountain, and surrounded by a wall with towers; within which there were many vineyards, and fruit gardens, and corn fields, and streams, and pastures for sheep, and on the highest part of the mountain there was a castle. When Timour Beg conquered the Sultan of Persia, who was called Sultan Ahmed, he besieged this castle of Alinga for three years, and Ahmed fled from it, and went to the Sultan of Babylonia, where he is now.

On Tuesday they slept in a plain, where there were about a hundred tents of Zagatays, who were wandering over that land with their flocks.

On Wednesday they passed the night near some other tents of Zagatays, and in these tents they gave meat and horses to the ambassadors, in the same way as they did in the towns and villages. The road by which they had passed went over hills, in which there was plenty of water and herbage, and there were many of these Zagatays, who belonged to the host in the city of Khoi.

On Thursday, the 5th of June, at noon, they arrived at a city which is called Khoi, and is situated in a plain, and is surrounded by many fruit gardens and corn fields, and near the city there are plains of very great extent, through which, and through the city, flow many streams of water. The city is surrounded by a brick wall, with towers and barbicans. At the city of Khoi the land of upper Armenia ends, and the land of Persia commences.

V.

THE JOURNEY

THROUGH

AZERBIJAN, IRAK, AND KHORASSAN.

When the ambassadors arrived in the city of Khoi,[1] they found in it an ambassador, whom the Sultan of Babylon had sent to Timour Beg; who had with him as many as twenty horses and fifteen camels, laden with presents, which the Sultan of Babylon[2] sent to Timour Beg. He also had six rare birds, and a beast called *jornufa*,[3] which creature is made with a body as large as that of a horse, a very long neck, and the fore legs much longer than the hind ones. Its hoofs are like those of a bullock. From the nail of the hoof to the shoulders it measured sixteen *palmos*; and when it wished to stretch its head, it raised it so high that it was wonderful; and its neck was slender, like that of a stag. The hind legs were so short, in comparison with the fore legs, that a man who had never seen it before, might well believe that it was seated, although it was standing up; and the buttocks were worn, like those of a buffalo. The belly

[1] In the Persian province of Azerbijan. Khoi is still the chief town of a rich and fertile district, and the emporium of the trade between Turkey and Persia.

[2] Probably an ambassador from Cairo.

[3] Giraffe.

was white, and the body was of a golden colour, surrounded by large white rings. The face was like that of a stag, and on the forehead it had a high sharp projection, the eyes were large and round, and the ears like those of a horse. Near the ears it had two small round horns, covered with hair, which looked like those of a very young stag. The neck was long, and could be raised so high, that it could reach up to eat from the top of a very high wall; and it could reach up to eat the leaves from the top of a very lofty tree, which it did plenteously.

To a man who had never seen such an animal before, it was a wonderful sight. The ambassadors were at Khoi from the Thursday on which they arrived, until the following Sunday, the 8th of June, when they departed. From Trebizond to this place, the ambassadors had always seen snow on the tops of the mountains, but after leaving this place the country was warmer, and they saw none. On this night they slept on a plain.

On Monday, at noon, they came to a place called Caza, which was large and populous. It was situated in a plain, with many fruit gardens, and streams flowing from all parts. Before reaching this place, there is a lake of salt water, a hundred miles round, and in it are three islands, one of which is inhabited.[1] They passed the night at a place called Cusacana, which was a large town, but half destroyed. They say that Toktamish, Emperor of Tartary, destroyed it; who was afterwards conquered by Timour Beg, and driven out of his dominions, and is now deprived of them; as will be related to you presently. In this place there were many Armenians.

On Tuesday they slept at a place called Chauscad, in a plain covered with many orchards, vineyards, and fruit trees; and many streams descended from a mountain, which rose up above the plain, and irrigated the gardens. They

[1] Lake Urumiyeh.

take quantities of fruit from this town to the city of Tabreez, and other places.

They passed that night in a plain, and most of the road they traversed that day, passed through gardens and vineyards; and the road was level, and it seemed very pleasant to pass through these gardens.

On Wednesday, the 11th of June, at the hour of vespers, they arrived at the great city of Tabreez. This city is in a plain, between two high ranges of hills. It is not walled, and the hills on the left hand are very near the city, and are very hot, and the water which descends from them is not wholesome; but those on the right hand are more distant, and they are very cold and capped with snow, and the water which descends from them is very good. These streams come down to the city, and flow through it in various directions.

In the range of hills, opposite the city, there are two high rocks, which used to be united, but every year they move further from each other. In the range on the left hand side there is a high hill, which, they say, was once bought by the Genoese, from a ruler whose name was Sultan Veis,[1] for the purpose of building a castle upon it. They add, that after it was sold, he changed his mind, and, when the Genoese wished to build the castle, he sent for them, and told them that it was not the custom for merchants to build castles in his country. He said that they might take their merchandize away, and that if they wanted to build a castle, they

[1] Sultan Weis was the son of Hosein Boozoorg, a grandson of Arghoun, a ruler of Persia, of the house of Zengis. Hosein founded a dynasty called the "Eelkhanees of Irak," with his capital at Bagdad. Sultan Weis succeeded him in 1356, and invaded Azerbijan; and then it was that the hard bargain was struck with the Genoese, which Clavijo describes. Sultan Weis died in 1374, and was succeeded by his son Ahmed, who passed his life in a fruitless attempt to check the progress of Timour, and was at last obliged to take refuge in Egypt. He was eventually killed by a Toorkish chief in 1419.

might move the hill out of his territory. When they answered him, he ordered their heads to be cut off.

From the range of hills on the right hand, a great river descends towards the city, and is divided into many channels, which flow through the streets. In this city there are many well ordered streets and lanes, where they sell many things. In some of the streets there are very large buildings, with many doors, within which are shops, and there are officers who keep order. From these buildings there are gateways leading to certain streets, where they sell many things, such as cloth, silk, cotton, tafeta, and other stuffs; and this city has a great trade.

In one place, in these buildings, there are certain men who sell many kinds of scents and pigments for women; and the women come themselves to buy them, and they paint and anoint themselves. These women go about, covered all over with a white sheet, with a net, made of black horse hair, before their eyes, and thus they are concealed, so that no one can recognize them.

In this city there are many grand edifices, especially mosques, which are ornamented very skilfully with mosaics, and blue and gold work, made in Greece. They say that these great works were made by very rich men, who were jealous of each other, and each strove to erect the most wonderful work, and in this way they spent their wealth. Amongst these edifices there was a great house, which was surrounded by a wall, very beautiful and rich, in which there are twenty thousand chambers and apartments; and they say that this house was built by a ruler of Persia, named Sultan Veis; with the treasure that was paid him, as tribute, by the Sultan of Babylon. He called this house *Tolbatgana*,[1] which means "the house of fortune." This house is well built.

The city of Tabreez is very large and rich, owing to the

[1] Dowlat-khanah?

quantity of merchandize that passes through it, every day. They say that in former days it was more populous; but even now there are more than two hundred thousand inhabited houses. There are also many market places, in which they sell very clean and well dressed meat, cooked in a variety of ways, and plenty of fruit. In this city, near an open space, there is a tree quite dry; and they say that, at one time, a christian bishop came to this city, with a great many christians, with a cross in his hand, to convert the people to the faith of Jesus Christ, and this was what a Moor, who was a hermit, related. The people of the city saw this with great indignation, and went to cut down this tree; and they gave it three blows with an axe, and those who struck the blows, broke their arms. It is not long since the Moor died, who told this story, and they say that he told many other stories; they even add that when Timour Beg was in the city, he sent for this Moor, who told him this, and many other things. This tree is now in the street, where it stood before, so that no one can remove it.

In the streets and squares of this city there are many fountains, and in summer they fill them with pieces of ice, and put many brass and copper jugs near them, so that the people can come and drink.

The magistrate of this city, called the *Darogah*, received the ambassadors very honorably. In this city there are many very rich and beautiful mosques, and the finest baths that, I believe, can be seen in the whole world. The ambassadors remained in the city for nine days, and when they wished to depart, horses were provided for themselves and their retinue. From this place the ruler of the country had horses in readiness, that those who were coming to him, might ride them, and travel day and night, in relays; and thus the post is arranged, all along the road as far as the city of Samarcand. From Tabreez to Babylon is ten days journey, and Baldac is on the right hand side of the road.

On Friday, the 20th of June, the ambassadors departed from Tabreez, and passed the night at a castle called Zaydana.[1]

On Saturday they dined at a village called Hujan,[2] and passed the night in the open air.

On Sunday morning they reached a village called Santguelana, and dined at another village called Tucelar, inhabited by a people called Turcomans; and the country was more level than any they had yet passed through, and very hot. At each village the people brought out plenty of meat, and gave it to the ambassadors, and the custom was as follows:—when the ambassadors arrived, they had to dismount, and sit upon small carpets, which were placed in the open air, under the shade. Then from each house came something to eat, either bread, or cream, or other dishes of the country; and if they wished to remain, they received much more food. When night came on they continued their journey, for they could not travel in the day time, on account of the great heat, and the number of insects, which kill both men and beasts. Although, when they arrived at the village of Tucelar, the sun was not very powerful, the insects were such that the beasts could not endure it, so that there came from them so much blood, that it was quite wonderful.

On Monday they came to a place called Miana, which means "half way," and they stayed there all day, and departed at night, on good horses which had been provided for them, travelling all night.

On Tuesday, being St. John's day, at dawn, they found themselves near some large buildings, which were erected for the use of merchants and other travellers; and they remained there until the hour of vespers. While they were there a messenger arrived from Miran Meerza, eldest son of the lord,[3] who said that his master desired them to ride as fast

[1] Sirdarud? [2] Gogan?

[3] Timour Beg. From this place, Clavijo usually calls Timour *the lord.*

as they could, to a plain where he was encamped with his army, which was not far off, where they would be provided with fresh horses. At night they set out, and at dawn they met another messenger from Miran Meerza, who said that his master had gone to Sultanieh, and wished them to ride on as fast as possible, that he might see them. At noon they came to a house, near the banks of a river, where they took their siesta, starting again in the afternoon.

At night they came to a city called Sanga,[1] which was almost deserted. They were told that it was formerly one of the greatest cities in Persia. It was situated on a plain, between two ranges of mountains, without woods, and the city wall had fallen down. Inside there were large houses and mosques, and streams of water flowed through the streets. This was the chief city of the dominions of Darius, and the one which he liked best, and in which he resided most; and from this place he marched forth, to fight Alexander. They remained during the night, and were provided with fresh horses, and plenty of meat and fruit, and were very well treated.

On Thursday, the 22nd of June, at noon, they arrived at the great city of Sultanieh,[2] where they found Miran Meerza, the eldest son of Timour Beg. On Friday morning they went to see the said Miran Meerza; and as it is the custom for every one who goes to see him, to give him some-

[1] Zengan ?

[2] The city of Sultanieh was founded by Mohammed Khodah Bundah, a ruler of Persia, of the house of Zengis, in 1303. He was the first Persian ruler of the sect of Ali, and is consequently much venerated by the modern Persians. Sultanieh was situated in a pleasant and fertile plain, seventy miles from the present town of Kazveen. It is now a mere mass of ruins, but the splendid tomb of Khodah Bundah is still standing, with a dome one hundred feet in diameter, and one hundred and twenty feet high, covered with green tiles. The building is of an octagonal form, and once had a minaret at each angle, but there is only one left entire. The plain is a favourite place of encampment, for the modern shahs of Persia.

thing, the ambassadors brought some cloth, and other things. They found him in a palace, where there was a large fruit garden, full of armed men; and he received them very well, and invited them into a tent where he was sitting, asking them after the health of the lord our king.

After they had talked for a long time, they were asked to eat, and the ambassadors ate according to their custom, and, when they wished to go away, they were given some robes to dress in.

This city of Sultanieh is in a plain, and has no wall; but it has a castle with strong walls, and handsome towers, and all the towers and walls were ornamented with patterns, and each tower had a small catapult on the top.

This city is very populous, but it is not so large as Tabreez, though it possesses more trade. Every year, especially in the months of June, July, and August, very large caravans of camels arrive, with great quantities of merchandize. They mean the same as we do by the word *caravan*, namely, a drove of beasts. This city has a great traffic, and yields a large revenue to the lord. Every year many merchants come here from India, with spices, such as cloves, nutmegs, cinnamon, manna, mace, and other precious articles, which do not go to Alexandria. Also all the silk which is made in Gheelan comes here, and Gheelan is a province near the sea of Bakou, where much silk is made every year.[1] This silk of Gheelan is sent to Damascas, and Syria, and Turkey, and many other countries. Also there arrives all the silk which is made in the province of Xamahi, and merchants come here for silk, even Venetians and Genoese.

This land is so hot that when any foreign merchant is struck by the sun, he is killed; and they say that when the sun strikes any one, it presently penetrates to his heart and

[1] The raw silk of Gheelan is still the most important Persian article of export. In 1844 the quantity of silk produced in Gheelan weighed more than one million pounds, and was worth £450,000.—*Sir J. Sheil.*

kills him, burning his back very much; and those who escape, almost always remain quite yellow, and never return to their proper colour.

There also arrive in this city many silken cloths, cottons, tafetas, and other stuffs from a land called Shiraz, which is near India, and from Yesen, and Serpi; and from Khorassan there come cotton threads, and cotton cloths, woven in many colours. This land of Khorassan is a great territory, which extends from Tartary to India. Many precious stones also arrive in this city of Sultanieh. From Cathay vessels come within sixty days journey of this city, having navigated the western sea, which is the sea which bounds this land; and they come to a river, which is ten days journey from the city of Ormuz.[1] The ships and boats which navigate this sea have no iron; but their timbers are joined with cords and wooden pegs; for if they were united with iron, they would soon be torn to pieces by the loadstones, of which there are many in that sea.[2] These ships bring many pearls, and some of them bring rubies, (which are very fine in Cathay), and much spice; and from Ormuz these things are sent to all parts of the world.

Most of the pearls are found in that sea of China, and they bring them to the city of Ormuz, to be pierced and cut; and the Moorish and Christian merchants say that they know of no place where the pearls can be pierced, except this city of Ormuz. The city of Sultanieh is sixty days journey from the city of Ormuz. They also say that these pearls are formed in large shells, which they call *jacares*; and those who come from Cathay, and from Ormuz, say that the pearl is formed in the shells, which are large, and as white as paper. They

[1] The river Minav, opposite the island of Ormuz, is navigable for small vessels, for a few miles; but Clavijo obtained all this interesting information respecting the great mart of the Persian gulf, from hearsay.

[2] This corroborates the story of Sindbad the Sailor. See the introduction to "India in the Fifteenth Century," published by the Hakluyt Society.

bring them to this city of Sultanieh, and to Tabreez, where they make girdles and rings of them.

All the merchants who come from the land of the Christians, from Caffa, and Trebizond, and the merchants of Turkey and Syria, come every year, at this time, to the city of Sultanieh, to make their purchases. This city is situated in a plain, and many channels of water pass through it, and in it there are many well ordered streets, where the people sell their merchandize. In this city there are several large inns, where the merchants lodge. The city is surrounded by very extensive and populous plains; and on the right hand there are some mountains, and beyond them is a land called Koordistan. These mountains are very wild, and there is snow upon them all the year round. On the left hand there is another range of hills, which are very hot, and behind them is the province of Gheelan, and the sea of Bakou,[1] which is surrounded by land, and is not connected with any other sea whatever; and it is six days journey from Sultanieh to the sea of Bakou. Diamonds are found, on some islands in the sea of Bakou. Snow never falls in the land of Gheelan, because it is so hot; and it produces many citrons, lemons, and oranges.

The city of Sultanieh has a great traffic, and yields a large yearly revenue to the lord; and this city, with Tabreez, and the empire of Persia, was formerly governed by Miran Meerza, the eldest son of Timour Beg, but he has been deprived, for the following reasons:—Miran Meerza, being the ruler of this land, had many knights with him, and a large army, which his father had given him. Being in the city of Tabreez, he ordered a great number of houses, mosques, and fine buildings to be destroyed, and many were pulled down. He then went to Sultanieh, ordered the same to be done there, took his father's treasure out of the castle, and divided it amongst his followers. Outside the city, a little apart, there

[1] The Caspian.

was a very fine edifice, built by a great knight, who lies interred within it.[1] Miran Meerza ordered this also to be destroyed, and the body of the great knight to be cast out. He is said to have done these things in a fit of madness, and to have said,—" I am the son of the greatest man in the world. What deed shall I perform in these cities, that I may be remembered after I am dead?" and when he saw that he could perform no deed, equal to those which had been done before, he said, " How shall I be had in remembrance, when I am gone?" and he ordered all these edifices to be destroyed; that men might say " Miran Meerza did nothing himself, but he caused the grandest works in the world to be destroyed."

When his father, who was then in Samarcand, heard this, he set out for the country which his son governed; and when his son heard that he was coming, he put a rope round his neck, and came to his father, and asked for pardon. His father would have killed him, but his relations asked him to shew mercy, and prayed so hard, that he pardoned him; but he deprived him of his government, and of his army. He then sent for one of his grandsons, a son of this Miran Meerza, named Abubeker Meerza, and said to him,—" Thy father hath erred, take thou his land, and his government." The grandson answered, " Sire, it is not the will of God that I should take the possession of my father, for you will repent of your anger, and restore him." Timour Beg then called for another son of Miran Meerza, who took the government from his father. This prince is now in opposition to his father and brother, and they wish to kill him, as you will presently hear.[1]

After this transaction, Timour Beg took the cities of

[1] Probably the tomb of Khodah Bundah.

[2] Ali of Yezd says that Miran Meerza, the ruler of Azerbijan, having lost his senses from a fall from his horse, committed all kinds of enormities, and passed his time in drinking and revels; and that this conduct obliged Timour to take the field in A.D. 1399.

Babylon, Aleppo, and Baldac from the sultan of Babylon, and gave them to his grandson, who refused to take the government from his father. This son, and his father live in these cities, and have done so since the father was deprived of his government, for Abubeker Meerza is very obedient to his father.

When Miran Meerza did these things, he had a woman with him, named Gansada. She left him in disguise, and travelled day and night until she came to Timour Beg, whom she informed of what his son had done; for which he deprived his son of the government, as you have heard. This Gansada remained with Timour, and he treated her honourably, not allowing her to return to her husband; but Miran Meerza has a son by her, named Khulleel Sultan.[1]

This Miran Meerza is forty years of age, a large, corpulent, and gouty man. The ambassadors were in this city of Sultanieh for three days.

On Sunday, the 29th of June, the said ambassadors departed from Sultanieh, on good horses, and passed the night at a village called Atengale. Next day, at noon, they came to another large village called Huar, and at night they came to a village called Cequesana, where there were many streams and fruit gardens.

On the following Wednesday they spent the night in a castle, which had been abandoned a few days before; and they said that the lord had passed by, with his army, about a month since; and as he did not find either barley or straw in that place, and, besides, as there was no grass in the neighbourhood for the horses and flocks of the army, he ordered that they should eat the wheat which was sown; and the rear guard of his army plundered everything they found in the place, and for this reason it was abandoned. But there were men here, with a hundred post horses of the lord; and

[1] The successor of Timour, at Samarcand.

from Sultanieh to this place, there were only two villages without post horses.

On Thursday, the 3rd of July, they provided horses for the ambassadors, who departed from this place, and reached a city called Xaharcan,[1] where they were well received, and provided with all that they required. While they were in this city, a message came from a knight named Baba Sheikh, to say that the great lord had ordered them to be treated with honour, and to ask whether they desired to visit him. They remained in this city from the Thursday, on which they arrived, to Saturday.

On Saturday they were provided with post horses, and set out at night. On Sunday, the 6th of July, at noon, they came to a city called Teheran, where they found Baba Sheikh, who came out to receive them, and conducted them to a lodging, which was used by the lord when he was there, and which was the largest in the city.

On Monday the said knight sent for the ambassadors, and, when they were near his house, he came out to meet them, and sat down in a room with them. Presently he sent for the ambassador of the Sultan of Babylon, who had arrived with presents for Timour Beg, and gave him many dishes of meat to eat, which had been prepared; amongst which was a horse roasted with its head. After they had eaten, the knight said to them that, on another day, they should go and visit a great Meerza, who was son-in-law to the lord. When the ambassadors were going to depart, he gave Ruy Gonzalez a dress, and a hat, and said that he was to accept them as a token of the friendship which Timour Beg felt for his king.

This city of Teheran was very large, but it had no walls, and it was a very delightful place, well supplied with everything; but it was an unhealthy place, according to the natives, and fevers were very prevalent. The territory in

[1] Kazveen ?

which it stands is called Rei, which is a great and extensive lordship, possessed by the son-in-law of the lord.

The road from Sultanieh to Teheran is very level, and the country is populous, and very hot.

On Tuesday, in the afternoon, they departed, and, at a distance of two leagues, they came in sight of a great city, all in ruins,[1] on the right hand side of the road; but there appeared towers and mosques, and the name of the place was Xahariprey. This was once the largest city in all that land, though it is now uninhabited.

On Wednesday they came to a village; and the road had now left the plains, and entered mountains, through which they had to go to visit that knight. In the night they left the village, which is called Lanaza, and that night they slept in the open air.[2]

On Thursday, the 10th of July, at the hour of mass, they met some men on horseback, who said, that the knight was in an adjacent plain with his horde, and that he had sent to say that he intended to wait for the ambassadors of the Sultan, and that he would see all the ambassadors together. When the ambassadors from Cairo arrived, they all went on until they were near the horde, when they stopped. In a short time the knight sent for them, and they found him sitting under a shade, before his tent. He made them sit near him, caused food to be set before them, and received them well. He then ordered them to return to their tents, and said that, on another day, they should eat with him. When they reached their tents he sent them much food, live sheep, and bread, and flour. On another day they went to eat with him; and they had plenty of dishes, dressed according to the custom of the

[1] The ruins of the ancient city of Rhé (the Rhages of the Apocrypha), are a few miles south of the city of Teheran. They cover a vast extent of ground, and have supplied materials for the modern capital of Persia.

[2] They seem to have turned up towards the mountain passes leading into Mazanderan.

country, horses roasted, and their tripes boiled; and there was a great number of people at this feast. After they had eaten, he said that he was ordered by the lord to examine the presents which they brought. When he had seen them, he ordered that horses and camels should be provided, to convey them to where the lord then was; and when the ambassadors departed, he gave them robes, and he gave a tall ambling horse to Ruy Gonzalez, for they set a high value on those which amble; but it was not provided with a very good saddle or bridle. On another day he gave him a shirt, and a hat.

This knight was named Solyman Meerza, and he was a favourite of the lord; and the place where they found him was a small plain, watered by rivers, and surrounded by mountains. It was a very pleasant place, and the mountains were called the mountains of Lar, and there were as many as three thousand tents on the plain. This knight was married to a daughter of Timour Beg, and with him there was a grandson of Timour Beg, named Sultan Ahmed Meerza, who was sick. When he heard of the ger falcons which the king had sent to Timour Beg, he sent to Solyman, to say that he wished for one of the falcons, and that the lord would not resent his having taken one. Solyman, thinking that the gift of a falcon to the grandson would please Timour Beg, ordered one to be given to him. The ambassadors said that it was wonderful that he should venture to take any of the presents which they were taking to the lord; but they were told that this grandson was one of the most valiant Bahadoors in the family of the lord, that he was sick, and that, therefore, they might venture to give him one, as the lord would not resent it. They also said that, when Timour Beg was in battle with the Turk, this grandson commanded the body guard, and that, during the battle, the lord ordered certain guards who were with him, to go and fight; and this grandson said to him, that on such a day he ought not to be left behind, but should be ordered to go and fight also; and the lord did not answer him; they added that, in his hurry, his head piece fell off, and that he went into the battle, and fought, on that day, with nothing on his head.

On Saturday, the 12th of July, they departed. The master of theology, and Gomez de Salazar, were sick, but Ruy Gonzalez felt a little better, and some of the retinue were also sick. Solyman Meerza, therefore, sent to say that, as these people were sick, they must remain behind, that they might not perish in the long journey. Seven men were left behind; and there were among them two esquires of Ruy Gonzalez, and another of the master of theology, and a lad of Gomez. These sick people returned to the city of Teheran, and remained there until the ambassadors returned, but two of them died. On the day of their departure they encamped near a river.

On Sunday they encamped on the banks of another river; and at noon, on Monday, the 14th of July, they reached a castle called Perescote. Timour Beg had left this place, about twelve days before, on his road to Samarcand; and he had left orders that the ambassadors should follow him as fast as possible, such was his desire that they should see Samarcand. This city was the first which he conquered, and the one which he honours more than any other, and here he has deposited his treasure.

The lord had been besieging this castle of Perescote, and had entered it by force, about fifteen days before the ambassadors arrived, and the reason why he besieged it was this:—the lord of this castle was a servant to whom he had shown great kindness, and he had given him this castle and much land; but he was now enraged against him, and ordered him to be taken prisoner to Samarcand; but when the knight arrived to execute these orders, the people seized him.

When the lord knew this, he besieged this castle for thirty days, at the end of which time the people yielded, and the lord of the castle fled by night. This castle is so strong, that no one could ever enter it, if the defenders did not yield. It is built on a very high rock, which stands by itself, on a plain; and is surrounded by a wall, with towers, and at the foot of it there is a village. Above the first wall, there is a second higher one, and above that, there is another with towers; and between the walls there is a village, above which there is a very strong castle, with walls, and many towers; so that there are three fortresses, one above the other. Within there is a spring of water, which supplies the garrison, besides which a river flows by the rock on which the castle stands; and the gates of the town open upon the draw bridges, below which the river flows.

On Tuesday, the 15th of July, before dawn, they departed, and passed the night in the open air; and on Wednesday they also slept in the open air, as they came to no village during those two days. The road was very rugged, and passed over very hot mountains, and there was no water, or at least very little. On Thursday they reached a great city, on the banks of a river, and two deserted castles.

On Thursday, the 17th of July, in the night, they arrived at a city which is called Damghan,[1] situated in a plain, and surrounded by an earthen wall, with a castle at one end. This city is in the province of Media. On this day it was so hot, with a hot fierce wind, that it was quite wonderful. The wind was so hot, that it seemed as if it came out of hell; and on this day a ger falcon escaped, and flew away.

Outside the city there were two towers, so high that a man could scarcely throw a stone to the top of them. They were made of mud, and the heads of men; and there were

[1] Damghan, a town in Khorassan, is described by modern travellers as a mass of desolate ruins, in a vast gravelly plain, with a wretched vaulted lane of mud-built huts for a bazar.

two other towers, fallen to the ground. These towers, which are made of heads, are built of the heads of a race of people called "white Tartars," natives of a country between Turkey and Syria. When Timour Beg departed from Sebastria, and marched towards Damascus, he encountered these people, fought, and conquered them; taking many prisoners, and sending them to settle at Damghan, which was thinly populated. When they arrived there, they collected together, and lived in the plains, as was their custom. When they were all assembled, they desired to return to their native land, and they set out on their journey, robbing every one they met. When they were near this city, the army of the lord met them, defeated them, and killed them without mercy. The lord then ordered that these four towers should be built, of their heads, plastered together with mud. He also ordered that every white Tartar, wherever he might be found, should be put to death, and so it was done. The army, when they received this order, killed every white Tartar they could find; so that along the roads, in one place ten, in another twenty dead bodies might be seen, and they say that sixty thousand of these Tartars were killed. The people of the city say, that they often see lights burning on the top of these towers in the night.

On Friday they were supplied with post horses, and travelled all night. On Saturday morning they came to a small town, and remained there until night, on account of the great heat; when they again set out, and travelled all night.

On Sunday, the 20th of July, they reached the city of Vascal; and when the ambassadors arrived there, they found a great knight called Ennacora, who was waiting for them by order of the lord, to do them honour. He came to see them at their lodging, and, as they were too unwell to dine with him, he sent them much meat and fruit. After they had dined, he sent to say that they should come to him, to a great palace, and that they should be clothed in the robes of the great lord. They replied that they could not walk, and that they trusted he would excuse them; but he sent again to ask them to come, and at last the master of theology went to him, and he dressed him in a robe, according to the custom; and it was usual when these robes were presented, to have a grand feast, and afterwards to put on the robes; and then to touch the ground three times, with the knee, out of reverence for the great lord. This was done, and afterwards the knight sent horses to the ambassadors, and to their retinue. He also sent to say that they should proceed on their journey, as it was the command of the lord that they should follow him, as quickly as possible, both by day and night. They answered that they would prefer to rest for two days; but he replied that they must not stay any longer, for that, if the lord should know of it, it would cost him his life. The ambassadors were so ill, that they were more dead than alive; so the knight caused soft pillows to be placed on the bows of their saddles, and so they departed. They travelled all night, and rested in a plain, near a deserted village.

On Monday they slept in some large buildings, which were erected by the road side, for travellers, as no people live in the country, for a distance of two days journey, on account of the great heat, and the want of water. The water in the buildings was brought from a great distance, by pipes under ground.

On Tuesday, the 22nd of July, they slept at a city called Jagaro, and the day was very hot. This city was in a plain, at the foot of a mountain, without trees, and large pipes lead water from the mountain to the city. In the middle of the city there is a castle, on the top of a mound of earth, and the city had no wall of any kind. In the previous winter there was much snow, and when the summer came, it melted; and so much water came down the pipes that it ruined the castle, and several houses. The road was very level, and there was not a single stone to be found on it; and the country was very hot, and with little water.

When they arrived, they were given plenty of meat, and fresh horses; and they set out again with the knight whom the great lord had sent, who provided them with food, and with all that they required; and gave them fresh horses every day, that they might travel faster. The lord had horses waiting at the end of each day's journey, at some places one hundred, and at others two hundred; and thus the posts were arranged, on the road, as far as Samarcand. Those whom the lord sent in any direction, or who were sent to him, went on these horses as fast as they could, day and night. He also had horses placed in deserts, and uninhabited districts, as well as in places that were populous; and he caused great houses to be built in uninhabited places, where horses and provisions were supplied by the nearest towns and villages. Men were appointed to take care of these horses, who were called *Anchos*. Thus, when ambassadors or messengers arrive, these men take their horses, take off their saddles, and place them on fresh horses, and one or two of these *Anchos* go with them, to take care of the horses; and when they reach another post, they return with these horses. If any of the horses become tired on the road, and they meet another at any place, belonging to any other man, they take it in exchange for the tired horse. The custom is that when any one rides on a road, if he is a lord, or merchant, or ambassador, he must give up his horse for the service of any one who is going to the great lord, and if any one refuses, it costs him his head, for such are the commands of Timour Beg. They even take horses from the troops, and the ambassadors often took horses from the troops, for themselves and their men; and, not only can those, who are going to the great lord, take the horses of such people, but they can even demand them from the son or the wife of the great lord himself. They told the ambassadors that even the eldest son of Timour Beg had been obliged to give up his horse to ambassadors who were going to the great lord.

Not only was this road thus supplied with post horses, but there were messengers on all the roads; so that news could come from every province, in a few days. The lord is better pleased with him who travels a day and night for fifty leagues, and kills two horses, than with him who does the distance in three days.

The great lord, considering that the leagues were very long, in his empire of Samarcand, divided each league into two, and placed small pillars on the roads, to mark each league; ordering all his Zagatays to march twelve, or at least ten of these leagues, in each day's journey. They call these leagues *moles*, because these turrets, which he caused to be built at the end of each league, and these leagues, the length of which he regulated, are in a country which is called Mogolia. The ambassadors travelled in the country, and saw the pillars, and each of the leagues was equal to two leagues of Castille.

In truth it would scarcely be believed, unless it was actually seen, the distances which these fellows travel, each day and night; for they ride as far as their horses can carry them; and they do not only travel the distance which the lord has ordered, but they sometimes go over fifteen and twenty leagues in a day and night, without any consideration for the toil of their horses. When their horses are knocked up, they kill and sell them, if they are in an inhabited country; but we found many dead horses on the road, which had been killed by hard riding.

The ambassadors left this city, on the day they arrived; and travelled all night, for, though they wished to rest, they were not permitted; and, although it was night, the heat was so great that it was quite wonderful, and there was a hot and burning wind.

On this night Gomez de Salazar, who had been ill, was

nearly dying. There was no water on the road, during this day's journey, and they did not stop all night, except to give barley to the horses.

On Tuesday they travelled all day, without seeing any habitation whatever, until night, when they arrived at a city called Zabrain. This city is very large, and contains many fine houses and mosques; but most of them were deserted. When they had dined, they departed with fresh horses, and travelled all night. On Friday, near noon, they reached a deserted village; but the people brought them food, and all they required, from another village, distant about half a league. At the hour of vespers they set out again, and travelled all night, along a very level road.

On Saturday, the 26th of July, they arrived at a great city, which is called Nishapore; and before they reached it, at a distance of about a league, they crossed some great plains, where many streams of water were conducted to numerous fruit gardens, and in these plains they found as many as four hundred tents pitched. These tents were not made in the usual way, but they were long, and of black cloth, and a people called Alabares lived in them.

These people do not possess anything but their tents, and they do not live in cities or villages, but in the open plains, as well in winter as in summer. They have large flocks of sheep, and herds of cattle, besides twenty thousand camels. They wander, with their flocks and herds, over all the territory of the lord, and pay a yearly tribute of three thousand camels and fifteen thousand sheep to him, for the right of grazing in his territory. When the ambassadors came to their tents, the chief came out, and led them to a tent, and gave them much milk and cream, according to their custom.

They departed from the tents, and set out for the city, but Gomez de Salazar was left behind in a village, very ill, as he could not travel any longer.

The city of Nishapore is in a plain, and is surrounded by

gardens, and very handsome houses. The ambassadors were conducted to very fine lodgings, and the chiefs of the city came to them with meat, and fruit, amongst which were very large and good melons, and also they sent them much wine. After they had eaten, they were presented with a robe, as it was the order of the lord that, whenever they arrived at a city, they should either be presented with a robe or a horse.

Five leagues before they reached the city, they met a knight who was marshal of the army of the lord, named Melialiorga.[1] He was sent to them, by the lord. He said that the lord had sent him, to do them honour, and to provide them with all that they required. When he heard that Gomez de Salazar was left behind sick, he went back for him, and found him so weak that he could not stand. On the same night he caused a litter to be made, and, placing Gomez upon it, caused him to be carried on men's shoulders, to the city of Nishapore, where he was lodged in a good house, and attended by the best doctors; but it pleased God that the said Gomez should end his days at this place.

This city is very large, and well supplied with all things. It is the chief city of Media, and here they find torquoises, and, though they are met with in other places, those of Nishapore are the best that are known.[2] They are found in the earth, near a river which descends from a mountain, above the city. The neighbourhood is very populous, and fertile. Here the land of Media ends, and the land of Khorassan commences, which is a great empire.

On Sunday, the 27th of July, the ambassadors departed from this city, and slept near a deserted village. On Monday they slept at a large place, called Ferrior, and most of the inhabitants fled, from fear of the soldiers of the lord; for he had passed by, about twelve days before, and the troops

[1] Malek Ali Oghlou-?

[2] The torquoise mines are in a mountain glen, about thirty miles from Nishapore.

which followed him, had done much damage. They gave robes to the ambassadors at this place, which is very flat, and very hot.

On Tuesday they slept in a great city called Hasegur, and departed again in the night. On Wednesday, the 30th of July, they came to a great city called Ojajan, where they were received with much honour, and were given food, and all that they required. In this city an order arrived from Shah Rokh Meerza, a son of Timour Beg, to invite the ambassadors to visit him at a city called Herat, which was a good thirty leagues off the road, on the right hand side, in the direction of India. He said that they should be received with great honour, and be supplied with all that they required. They consulted with the officer who accompanied them, and answered that the great lord had ordered that they should follow him as fast as possible, and that they trusted that he would, therefore, excuse them. This Shah Rokh Meerza was lord and emperor of this land of Khorassan.[1]

On the same day, the ambassadors reached the great city of Meshed, where the grandson of the prophet Mohammed lies interrred. He was the son of his daughter, and they say he is a saint.[2] He lies buried in a great mosque, in a

[1] Shah Rokh, Timour's youngest son, was so called from Timour having received news of his birth, while playing at chess. He had just made the move which the Persians called *Shah Rokh*, checking the king with the castle. In 1397 his father gave him the government of Khorassan, which he retained until his death in 1446. Shah Rokh was not more celebrated for his piety and liberality, than for his courage and military virtues. As regards this message to Clavijo, Shah Rokh seems to have been particularly fond of sending and receiving embassies. The curious account of the embassy he sent to a rajah of Southern India, written by the envoy himself, Abdul Rizak, has been already printed in one of the volumes of the Hakluyt Society—"India in the Fifteenth Century;" and translations of the letters which passed between Shah Rokh and the emperor of China, were published in the "Asiatic Miscellany," in 1785.

[2] Ali Riza, the eighth Imaum, is the Meshed saint. He was eighth in descent from Ali, the son-in-law of the prophet.

large tomb, which is covered with silver gilt. On account of this tomb, the city is crowded with pilgrims, who come here in great numbers every year. When the pilgrims arrive, they dismount, and kiss the ground, saying that they have reached a holy place. The ambassadors went to see the mosque; and, afterwards, when, in other lands, people heard them say that they had been to this tomb, they kissed their clothes, saying that they had been near the holy Horazan.[1] This nephew of Mohammed was named Sultan Horazan, and thence, perhaps, the land derives its name of Khorassan.[2]

On Thursday, the last day of August, they came to a great city called Buelo, in the land of Khorassan. This city is in a very healthy situation, and was better peopled than any place between it and Sultanieh. They remained here a short time, to obtain barley and provisions, because they were about to cross a desert, fifty leagues in breadth. When they had eaten, they mounted fresh horses to cross the desert, and, departing in the evening, travelled all night.

On Friday they travelled all day and night, but could not reach any inhabited place. On Saturday, the 10th of August, at night, they reached a valley, covered with corn fields. A river ran through it, on the banks of which many Zagatay tents were pitched, belonging to the host of Timour Beg, with many sheep, horses, and camels, as in this valley there was much grass.

When the ambassadors arrived, they found a knight, who had been sent by the great lord, to do them honour, and provide them with provisions, and to hurry them on their journey, as much as possible. The name of this knight was Mirabozar. He came to the ambassadors, and said that he was sent to guide and assist them; and at this place the ambassadors exchanged the attendance of the first knight whom the lord had sent, for that of this Mirabozar; but the

[1] Hosein ?

[2] *Khorassan* means the province of the sun, or of the east.

former still continued in their company, with his men, for the sake of food, and fodder for his beasts. The custom was that at any place where they arrived, whether it was a city or a village, they were supplied with much food, fruits, and fodder for horses, being three times as much as they wanted; and men were made to watch the property and horses of the ambassadors day and night, and if any were missing, the people of the place had to make up the loss. If the people, when they arrived, did not bring what was required, they immediately received such a number of blows, with sticks and whips, that it was wonderful. The chiefs of the place were then sent for, and brought before these knights, the first thing they heard of being about blows and whippings. They received a wonderful number, and were told that they knew it to be the command of the great lord that, when ambassadors were on their way to him, they were to receive honour, and everything they required: that the said knights had arrived with these Frank ambassadors, and that they had not found anything ready for them: that the people should pay dearly for such neglect of the orders of the great lord; and that they would know, in future, what to expect when ambassadors arrived, if everything was not ready.

When they arrived at any city or village, the first thing which the followers of the knights, who accompanied the ambassadors, did, was to ask for the *reis* or chief of the place; and they took the first man they met in the street, and, with many blows, forced him to show them the house of the *reis*. The people who saw them coming, and knew they were troops of Timour Beg, ran away as if the devil was after them, and those who were behind their shops, selling merchandize, shut them up, and fled into their houses; and they said one to another, "*Elchee*," which means ambassador, and that, with the ambassadors, there would come a black day for them.

When they arrived at a village, the people brought out all the things that the ambassadors required. You must know that, from the time that they took leave of the son-in-law of the lord, the ambassadors and the ambassador of the Sultan of Babylon travelled in company; and these things were not only done for the ambassadors, but for every one who travelled with orders from the lord. They were to kill any one who impeded the execution of his orders, and thus it was that the people were in marvellous terror of the lord, and of his servants.

In these tents, the knights caused much cooked meat to be placed before the ambassadors, together with rice, milk, cream, and melons, which are good and plentiful in this country.

The people of these tents have no other dwelling place, and they wander over the plains, during both winter and summer. In summer they go to the banks of the rivers, and sow their corn, cotton, and melons, which I believe to be the best that can be found in the world. They also sow much millet, which they boil with their milk. In the winter they go to the warm districts. The lord, with all his host, wanders in the same way over the plains, winter and summer. His people do not march all together, but the lord, with his knights and friends, servants and women, go by one road, and the rest of the army by another, and so they pass their lives.

These people have many sheep, camels, and horses, and but few cows; and when the lord orders them to march with his army, they go with all that belongs to them, flocks and herds, women and children; and so they supply the host with flocks, especially with sheep, camels, and horses.

With these people the lord has performed many deeds, and conquered in many battles; for they are a people of great valour, excellent horsemen, expert with the bow, and enured to hardships. If they have food, they eat; and if not, they suffer cold and heat, hunger and thirst, better than any people in the world. When they have no meat, they feed on milk and water boiled together, and they make their food in this manner :—they fill a great cauldron with water, and, when it is hot, they pour in sour milk, and make a sort of cheese, which is as sour as vinegar. They then take thin cakes of flour, cut them very small, and put them in the cauldron. When this mess is cooked, they take it out, and they go without other food very well, and this is the food upon which they live.

They have no wood to cook their food, but they use the dung of the horses and camels; and this food, which has been described to you, is called *hax*.

At dawn the ambassadors departed, with the knight who had been sent by the great lord, and travelled all night, and all next day, without seeing any habitation, except a large deserted building, where they rested, and procured barley for the horses. They were told that they were twelve leagues from any inhabited place. They departed, in the night, with good fresh horses, and travelled in the night, on account of the great heat, and during all this time they came to no water. The journey was so long that the horses were tired, and unable to move, being ready to perish of heat and thirst; the country was a sandy desert, and they were all in danger of dying of thirst.

A lad, belonging to the knight, had a horse which was a little fresher than the rest, and he went on as fast as he could, and arrived at a river, where he wet some shirts and other clothes, and returned with all haste; and those who could get a chance, drank the water, for they were ready to faint from heat and thirst. A little before sunset they reached a valley where there were some tents of the Zagatays, near a river they call Morghan.[1] The journey which they made, during

[1] The Moorghab? a deep stream of very pure water, with precipitous banks, fringed with tamarisks and a few reeds. On the east banks there

the last day and night, was twenty good leagues of Castille, and more; and they rested here all night. On Tuesday they departed, and, after two leagues, arrived at a large building, which they call *caravanserai*, where there were Zagatays, guarding the horses of the lord.

They slept here, and, at the hour of vespers, departed with good horses, and travelled over great plains, where there were tents of the Zagatays; and they remained there all Wednesday.

On Thursday they departed, and took their siesta near a village, passing the night on the plain, near the banks of this river. On Friday they again started, and rested, at noon, by the tents of some Zagatays, departing, in the afternoon, on fresh horses, and sleeping in the open air.

On Saturday, the 9th of August, they dined at a place called Salugar-sujassa, which once belonged to a great Caxis, whom they look upon as a saint. It was in a valley, near a river, and many channels of water passed through the place, which was well peopled, and full of gardens, and beautiful vineyards.

This Caxis, the lord of this place, was dead, and he left two children. When Timour Beg passed through the place, about ten days before, he took these children with him, to bring them up, as the Caxis was of a noble family. The place was governed by the mother of these children, who received the ambassadors with much honour, and gave them plenty of food, and all that they required, and dined with them. At night they departed on good horses, and travelled all night.

On Sunday they dined, and took their siesta, amongst some tents of the Zagatays, remaining there all day. On Monday they started very early, and slept in the plain; and, at these

are sloping sand hills, on the west a desert sandy plain, overrun with camel thorn, and extending to the mountain barrier of Khorassan. The valley abounds in pheasants and rock pigeons. The ancient city of Merve is in a plain, watered by the Moorghab.—Abbott's *Khiva*.

tents, they gave them meat, and fruit, and all they required; and, notwithstanding that they belonged to the lord's army, they were obliged to provide all that the ambassador wanted, and men to watch their horses day and night; and they had to give up their tents to the ambassadors. When they crossed any desert, these people had to supply meat, fodder, and water, at their own cost, though they wanted them for their own use.

On Tuesday, the 12th of August, they dined and took their siesta on a great plain, where there was a large building, and men watching the horses of the lord; and they mounted, and rode away from that place, at the hour of vespers.

At the hour of vespers they departed, and reached a city called Anchoy, of which one of the attendants of the ambassadors was a native. This city was beyond the land of Media, in a land called Tagiguinia, and the language of the people differed from the Persian. The men of the city received the ambassadors with much honour, and they remained there until Thursday, the 14th of August. They were well supplied with plenty of meat and wine; and were presented with a robe, and a horse. This city is in a plain, and is surrounded, for two leagues, by many gardens, vineyards, and houses, with numerous channels of water.

On Thursday afternoon they departed, and slept amongst some tents of the Zagatays, in a plain, near the banks of a river. These Zagatays have received the privilege from the lord, to go where they like for pasture for their flocks and herds, as well in summer as in winter; and they serve the lord in his wars, whenever they are called for. They do not leave their women, children, and flocks behind, when they go to the wars, but take them all with them. The women, who have little children, when they travel, carry them in small cradles before them, on their horses, and they tie these cradles with broad bands, which they fasten round their waists; and thus they travel with their children, and ride as light as if they were without them. The poor people carry their children and tents on camels, and this way of travelling is very wearisome for the children, as the camels go very uneasily. Not only do these people, whom we met on the road, live in these plains; but there are a vast number of others, for, when we found some in any place, many others also appeared, in one part or another, and so we travelled amongst them. Near towns, and places where there was water and pasture, we met many of them, and they were so burnt by the sun, that they looked as if they had come out of hell.[1]

This country was very flat, and very hot, and most of the troops who followed the lord, travelled by night; and the ambassadors remained amongst these tents of the Zagatays,

[1] The inhabitants of these deserts, who formed part of the host of Timour, have ever since been famous for their terrible inroads into the Persian province of Khorassan. They are Toorkmans of the Sooni creed, a cruel and rapacious race, and so far cowardly as always to prefer flight to facing a superior force. They are divided into three tribes, namely, the *Yamoots, Goklans*, and *Tuckehs*.

The Yamoots consist of about twenty-five thousand families, and are settled between Khiva and the river Attruck; they are the least ugly of the Toorkman tribes. The Goklans, of twelve thousand families, live between Astrabad and the Attruck; and the Tuckehs, of thirty-five thousand families, wander between the sources of the Attruck and the town of Merve.

The arms of the Toorkmans are a spear ten feet long, and a sword. They are excellent horsemen, and pass their lives in pillage and rapine. Their raids into Khorassan are called *chapows*. When a chief determines upon making one, a month is given to his followers, to get their horses into proper condition. Spies are sent out, and news being brought, the whole party gallops swiftly on the prey, whether caravan or village. In a few minutes all is over, the people carried off into slavery, and the village burnt. The prisoners are tied to the saddle bows of the captors, and are treated with horrible cruelty, until they are finally sold in the slave markets of Khiva. The horses of the Toorkmans have been known to go over six hundred miles in six days.

The tents of these Toorkmans are of a conical form, the framework being of wood, and folding up. Thick felts are stretched over this frame, and the tent may be made very warm, so as to protect its inmates from the severe winters.—*Fraser; Ferier.*

until night. On Friday, at noon, they came to a village, where they dined, and took their siesta. In the night they arrived at a great city, the name of which I have forgotten, but it was very large, and formerly it was walled, but now the wall is fallen, and most of the city is deserted, and in this city there were great edifices and mosques. The ambassadors were here presented with robes, and received with great honour.

On Saturday they departed on fresh horses, and slept amongst some tents of the Zagatays. On Sunday there was such a high wind that the men were obliged to dismount, and it was so hot, that it felt like fire. The road led through sandy deserts, and the wind raised the sand in clouds, and concealed the road, so that they lost it many times during the day.[1] The knight sent for a man from the tents, to guide them, and it pleased God that they should find their way to a village called Alibed, where they took their siesta, and remained until the wind went down. In the night they slept at another village called Ux; but, as soon as the horses had eaten their barley, they set out again, and travelled all night, amongst small villages, and fruit gardens.

On Monday, the 18th of August, they arrived at a city called Vaeq, which is very large, and surrounded by a broad earthen wall, thirty paces across, but it is breached in many parts. This city had three divisions, and the first, between the first and second wall, was quite uninhabited, and much cotton was sown there. The second was inhabited; and the third was well peopled; and, though the other cities we had seen were without walls, this one was well provided with them. In this city the ambassadors were received with much honour, and were given meat and wine, and robes, and horses. On Tuesday they departed, and slept near a

[1] This is the desert between Khiva and Merve. It is a broken and irregular surface of deep sand, with a small growth of brushwood, affording excellent fuel, and of the thorny herb which the camel loves.

village, and on Wednesday they dined and took their siesta in a village, and passed the night in the open air.

On Thursday, the 21st of August, they reached a great river called the Viadme,[1] which is another of the rivers which flow from Paradise. It is a league in width, and flows through a very flat country, with great and wonderful force, and it is very muddy. It is lowest in winter, because the waters are frozen in the mountains, and the snow does not melt: but in the month of April it begins to increase, and goes on increasing continually for four months; and this is because the summer melts the ice and snow. Last summer they said that it had swollen much more than usual; for it increased so much that the water reached a village, near the banks, and destroyed many houses, doing great damage.[2]

This river descends from the mountains, flows through the plains of the territory of Samarcand, and the land of Tartary, and falls into the sea of Bakou.[3] It separates the government of Samarcand from that of Khorassan.

[1] Oxus.

[2] The famous river Oxus rises in the lake of Sirikol, which is fifteen thousand six hundred feet above the sea. It is a sheet of water, fourteen miles long and one broad, on the high table land, called by the natives *Bami-i-duniah.* After watering the valley of Badakshan, passing through a mountainous region, thirty miles south of the old city of Balk, the Oxus enters the desert, and flows past Khiva into the sea of Aral, fertilizing a tract of land, about a mile broad, on either side. It formerly had another outlet into the Caspian, but that channel is now dried up. It is navigable, and free from rocks, as far as Koondooz, a distance of six hundred miles; but there are vast swamps at its mouth. Its average depth is nine feet, and the current runs at the rate of four knots an hour. The inundations commence in May and end in October, and the river is often frozen over in the winter. Large flat-bottomed boats are used on the river, fifty feet long by eighteen, with the gunwale three feet above the water, when loaded. They are made of logs of wood clamped together with iron, and one hundred and fifty men might be embarked on one of them. A bridge of these boats has usually been used by conquerors, in all ages, to transport their invading armies across the Oxus.—*Burnes; Abbott; Fraser.*

[3] The Caspian.

VI.

JOURNEY

FROM THE

OXUS TO SAMARCAND.

FESTIVITIES AT THE COURT OF TIMOUR BEG.

THE lord Timour Beg, as soon as he had gained the government of Samarcand, desired to pass over this great river, to conquer the land of Khorassan. He therefore caused a great bridge of timber to be made, supported by boats; and when his army had crossed, the bridge was destroyed; but, on his return to Samarcand, he ordered it to be made again, for the passage of himself and his host; and the ambassadors crossed over on this bridge; and they said that the lord had given an order to destroy the bridge, as soon as all his host had passed over. Near this great river Alexander fought a battle with Porus, king of India, and defeated him.[1]

On the Thursday that the ambassadors reached this great river, they crossed to the other side, and, in the afternoon, they arrived at a great city called Termit, which once belonged to India the Less, but is now in the territory of Samarcand, having been conquered by Timour Beg, and from this place the empire of Samarcand begins. The territory of this empire of Samarcand is called Mongolia, and

[1] The good knight's informant must have been a bad geographer.

the language of the people is Mongol, so that those on the other side of the river do not know it, as they speak Persian: and the handwriting which they use on the Samarcand side of the river, is not understood by those on the other side. The lord has certain scribes who read and write this Mongol writing. The land of Samarcand is very populous, and very rich and fertile.

The custom which the lord causes to be observed at this great river is, that when he has passed from one side to the other, the people have to break the bridge, and afterwards no one can cross over; but there are boats in this river, which convey people from one side to the other, and no one is permitted to pass over in these boats, without showing a letter stating whence he comes, and whither he goes, even when he is a native of the land. When, however, any one wishes to enter the land of Samarcand, this letter is not required. The lord has a great guard placed at these boats, who take heavy tolls from those who use them. This guard is also placed, because the lord has brought many captives into Samarcand, from the countries which he has conquered, to people the land, and enrich and ennoble it; so as to prevent them from escaping, and returning to their own land. Though, when the ambassadors passed, they found orphans, and women without support, in the land of Persia and Khorassan; yet the men had been taken by force, to people the land of Samarcand. One brought a cow, another an ass, another a sheep or goat; and they were fed, by the officers of the lord, on the road; and in this way the lord conveyed above one hundred thousand persons to the land of Samarcand.

This city of Termit, which the ambassadors had reached, was very large and populous, and it was without any wall. The city was surrounded by many gardens and streams of water. I cannot tell you more of this city, because we were very tired when we reached our lodging, except that we passed through populous streets and squares, where they sold many things. The ambassadors were received with much honour, and supplied with all that they required, and were presented with a silken robe. In this city a messenger arrived from the lord, who came to the ambassadors, and said that the lord saluted them, and desired to know how they had borne the journey, and how they had been treated, and whether they would soon arrive. When this messenger departed, they gave him a robe, and they also gave a Florentine robe to the knight who had been sent first, and who had come with them, the ambassador from the Sultan of Babylon doing the same. They also gave a horse to the second knight, whom the lord had sent; for such is the custom of all who come to the lord, to give something, and thus respect the custom of giving and taking presents. Their greatness is considered according to the number of presents they give, in honour of the lord, and such is the measure of the praise they receive.

On Friday, the 22nd of August, after dinner, the ambassadors departed, and slept on the plain, near some large houses. On Saturday, they travelled over extensive plains, amongst many well peopled villages, and reached a village where they were supplied with all that they required. On Sunday, they dined at some large buildings, where the lord is accustomed to stop, when he passes this way, and they were given much fruit and meat, wine and melons, and the melons were very good, and large, and abundant. The custom is to place the fruit before the ambassadors, on the ground.

On that day they departed, and slept on a plain, near the banks of a river. On Monday they dined at the foot of a high hill, where there was a handsome house, ornamented with very fine brick work, and in it there were many ornamental patterns, painted in many colours. This hill is very high, and there is a pass leading up by a ravine, which looks as if it had been artificially cut, and the hills rise to a great height on either side, and the pass is smooth, and very deep. In the centre of the pass there is a village, and the mountain rises to a great height behind. This pass is called "the *gates of iron*," and in all the mountain range there is no other pass, so that it guards the land of Samarcand, in the direction of India. These "*gates of iron*" produce a large revenue to the lord Timour Beg, for all merchants, who come from India, pass this way.

Timour Beg is also lord of the other "*gates of iron*," which are near Derbent, leading to the province of Tartary, and the city of Caffa, which are also in very lofty mountains, between Tartary and the land of Derbent, facing the sea of Bakou; and the people of Tartary are obliged to use that pass, when they go to Persia. The distance from the "gates of iron" at Derbent, to those in the land of Samarcand, is fifteen hundred leagues.

Say if a great lord, who is master of these "*gates of iron*," and of all the land that is between them, such as Timour Beg, is not a mighty Prince! Derbent is a very large city, with a large territory. They call the "*gates of iron*" by the names of Derbent and of Termit. At this house they made the ambassadors a present of a horse; and the horses of this country are much praised for their great spirit. These mountains of the "*gates of iron*" are without woods; and in former times, they say that there were great gates, covered with iron, placed across the pass, so that no one could pass without an order.

On this day they departed, and slept in the open air, on the top of a hill. On the next day they dined and took their siesta near some tents of the Zagatays, on the banks of a river. In the afternoon they rode on, and slept on the top of a range of hills. They started again in the middle of the night, and dined next day at a village; and here an attendant of the Master Fray Alfonzo Paez, who had been ill, departed this life.

On Thursday, the 28th of August, at the hour of mass, they arrived at the great city of Kesh,[1] which is situated in a plain, traversed in every direction by channels of water, which irrigate many gardens. The surrounding country was flat, and they saw many villages, well watered pastures, and a very beautiful, bright, and well peopled country. In these plains there were many corn fields, vineyards, cotton plantations, melon grounds, and groves of fruit trees. The city was surrounded by a wall of earth, with a deep ditch, and drawbridges leading to the gates.

The lord Timour Beg, and his father, were both natives of this city of Kesh.

In this city there are great mosques, and other edifices, especially a grand mosque which the lord Timour Beg has ordered to be built, for as yet it is not finished; within which the body of his father is interred. There is also another great chapel, which Timour Beg has ordered to be built, for his own body, and it was not finished. They say that when he was here, a month ago, he did not like this chapel, saying that the door was low, and ordering it to be raised, and they are now working at it. The firstborn son of Timour Beg is also interred in this mosque, named Jehanghir.[2] This mosque, with its chapels, was very rich, and beautifully ornamented in blue and gold, and within it there was a large court, with trees, and ponds of water. In this mosque the lord gives twenty boiled sheep every day, for the souls of his father and son, who lie buried there.

[1] The town of Kesh is thirty-six miles south of Samarcand. Timour's famous descendant Baber, the first Great Mogul, tells us that in spring the walls and terraces of the houses at Kesh are always green and cheerful. Timour and Baber both mention Kesh as *Sheher Subz*, or the "verdant city."

[2] Timour's eldest son Jehanghir died in 1372, when his father was just commencing his career of conquest. Timour's grief was very great, for he loved his son. The body was taken to Kesh, and interred in a superb tomb. He was only twenty years old, and left two sons, Mohammed, and Peer Mohammed, the latter having been born forty days after the death of his father.—*Ali of Yezd.*

When the ambassadors arrived, they were conducted to this mosque, and provided with much meat and fruit; and, when they had dined, they were taken to their lodging, in a great palace.

On Friday they were taken to see some great palaces, which the lord has ordered to be built, and they say that they have been working at them every day, for twenty years, and many workmen are still employed on them. These palaces had a long entrance, and a very high gateway. On each side there were arches of brick, covered with glazed tiles, and many patterns in various colours. These arches formed small recesses, without doors, and the ground was paved with glazed tiles. They are made for the attendants to sit in, when the lord is here.

In front of the first entrance there was another gateway, leading to a great court yard paved with white stones, and surrounded by doorways of very rich workmanship. In the centre of the court there was a great pool of water, and this court was three hundred paces wide. The court led to the body of the building, by a very broad and lofty doorway, ornamented with gold and blue patterns on glazed tiles, richly and beautifully worked. On the top of this doorway there was the figure of a lion and a sun, which are the arms of the lord of Samarcand; and, though they say that Timour Beg ordered these palaces to be built, I believe that the former lord of Samarcand gave the order; because the sun and lion, which are here represented, are the arms of the lords of Samarcand; and those which Timour Beg bears, are three circles like O's, drawn in this manner ○○○ and this is to signify that he is lord of the three parts of the world. He ordered this device to be stamped on the coins, and on everything he had; and for this reason I think that some other lord must have commenced this palace, before the time of Timour Beg. The lord has these three O's on his seals, and he has ordered that those who are tributary to him shall have it stamped on the coins of their countries.

This doorway led to a reception room, the walls of which were covered with polished glazed tiles, in gold and blue patterns, and the ceiling was gilded all over. Thence the ambassadors were taken to so many chambers, that it would take a long time to describe them all, in which there were ornamental works in gold and blue, and many other colours, executed with wonderful skill. They were also shown the apartments which the lord has caused to be made for his women, which were covered with strange and rich ornaments, both on the walls, ceilings, and floors; and many skilled workmen were employed in this palace.

Afterwards the ambassadors went to see a chamber, which the lord had set apart for feasting, and for the company of his women. In front of it there was a great garden, in which there were many shady trees, and all kinds of fruit trees, with channels of water flowing amongst them. The garden was so large, that great numbers of people might enjoy themselves there in summer with great delight, near the fountains, and under the shade of the trees. The workmanship of this palace was so rich that it would be impossible to describe it, without gazing and walking over everything, with slow steps. The mosque and palace are amongst the magnificent edifices which the lord has ordered to be built, in honour of his father, who lies interred there, and was a native of this city. But though he was a native of this city, he did not belong to the races of this land, but was of a lineage called Zagatay, which came from the land of Tartary when this country was conquered, as will presently be related to you.

The father of Timour Beg[1] was a man of good family, but

[1] Timour was the son of Teragay Nevian. He gives the following account of his lineage, in his memoirs :—" My father told me that we were descendants from Abu-al-Atrak (father of the Turks) the son of Japhet. His fifth son, Aljeh Khan, had twin sons, Tatar and Mogul, who placed their feet on the paths of infidelity. Tumene Khan had a son Kabul, whose son, Munga Bahadur, was the father of Temugin,

small estate, with not more than three or four mounted attendants. He lived in a village, near this city of Kesh, for the men of this land prefer living in the villages, and in the plains, to living in cities. His son, also, had not more than four or five horses. I will now tell you, what was told to the ambassadors, as certain truth in this city, and in other parts. It is said that Timour, having four or five servants, went out one day to steal a sheep, and on another day a cow, by force, from the people of the country. When he had got them, he ate them with his followers; and some because of the plunder, others because he was a brave and good hearted man, joined him, until he had a force of three hundred mounted followers. From that time he traversed the country, to rob and steal all he could lay hands on, for himself and his companions, and he also frequented the roads, and plundered the merchants.[1]

News of these doings reached the emperor of Samar-

called Zengis Khan. Zengis Khan abandoned the duty of a conqueror by slaughtering the people, and plundering the dominions of God, and he put many thousands of Moslems to death. He bestowed Mawur-ul-naher on his son Zagatai, and appointed my ancestor, Karachar Nevian, to be his minister.

"Karacher appointed the plain of Kesh for the residence of the tribe of Berlas (his own tribe), and he subdued the countries of Kashgar, Badakshan, and Andecan. He was succeeded by his son Ayettekuz as *Sepah Salar* (general). Then followed my grandfather, the Ameer Burkul, who retired from office, and contented himself with the government of his own tribe of Berlas. He possessed an incalculable number of sheep and goats, cattle and servants. On his death my father succeeded, but he also preferred seclusion, and the society of learned men." —*Timour's Memoirs.*

[1] In the year 1355, when he was twenty years of age, Timour's father made over to him a number of tents, sheep, camels, and servants. In 1356 he wished to unite the tribe of Berlas and rebel, and the death of his mother made him very melancholy, and induced him to give up ambitious projects for a short time; but in the following year he was engaged in a fight with some invaders. From this time he was constantly engaged in war, and soon became famous for his enterprise and daring, amongst the Zagatayan chiefs.—*Timour's Memoirs.*

cand, who was lord of that land, and he ordered the robber to be killed, wherever he could be found. But there were Zagatay knights at the court of the emperor, of Timour's lineage, who obtained his pardon, and brought him to live at court. Of these knights, who obtained his pardon, two still live with Timour; and the one is called Omar Tobar, and the other Caladay Sheikh.

They say that, when Timour lived with the emperor of Samarcand, he became so enraged against him, that he ordered him to be killed; but Timour was informed of it, and fled with his followers, returning to his life of robbery. One day, when he had plundered a caravan of merchants, he obtained great wealth, and went to a land called Seistan, where he stole sheep and horses, for that land is very rich in flocks: and he had as many as five hundred followers. When the people of Seistan knew this, they assembled together; and, one night, when he had fallen upon a great flock of sheep, they attacked him, killed many of his men, knocked him off his horse, and wounded him in the right leg, which lamed him. They also wounded him in the right hand, and cut off two of the fingers, leaving him for dead.[1] As soon as he was able, he got up, and went to the tents of some people who were encamped in a plain, whence he returned to collect his followers again.

The emperor of Samarcand was not liked by his subjects, especially by the common people, and some of the nobles also wished him ill. They proposed to Timour to kill the emperor, and declared that they would raise him to power in his place. The conspiracy went so far that the emperor, being in a city near Samarcand, was attacked and defeated by Timour. He fled to the mountains, and called to a man

[1] Timour's own account is that the Wali of Seistan, named Jelal-ud-Deen Mohammed, asked for his assistance; but that in a battle he was wounded in the arm and the foot, but, he adds, "I did not feel it at the time."

to hide and protect him, promising to make him rich, and giving him some valuable jewels. This man, instead of hiding him, betrayed him to Timour, who presently came and killed him, and took the city of Samarcand. Timour married the wife of the late emperor, named Caño,[1] which means "great empress," and she is still his chief wife. Afterwards he conquered the land of Khorassan, taking advantage of a quarrel between two brothers, lords of that land. Thus it was that he gained these two empires of Khorassan and Samarcand, and such was his origin.

One of those who was a companion of Timour Beg from the first, was a Zagatay of his own lineage, and was amongst those whom he trusted most. He married one of his sisters, and was made a great lord, over many people. He had a son named Janza Meerza, who is now the most confidential friend of the lord, and is captain and constable of the army, so that, besides the lord, no one commands in the army but him, and all the army and people are content with him.[2]

The reason why the Tartars came to this land, and took this name of Zagatays, was as follows:—a long time ago there was an emperor of Tartary, who was native of a city called Dorgancho, which is as much as to say "the treasure of the world." This emperor ruled over a vast territory, which he had conquered, and, when he died, he left four sons named Gabuy, Zagatay, Esbeque, and Charcas,[3] all sons of one mother. When the father died, he divided the land amongst his sons, and Zagatay received this land of Samarcand, with other territory. The father told his four sons to be as one, for that on the day in which discord arose amongst

[1] Mulk Khanum, the daughter of Kazan, Sultan of Samarcand, and mother of Shah Rokh. *Khanum* means "lady."

[2] Janza Meerza's death is described in the last chapter.

[3] The sons of Zengis Khan were Jojy Khan, Tuli Khan, Octai Khan, and Zagatai Khan. Authors differ as to the proper way of spelling their names. Jojy Khan's name is spelt in five different ways. (See *Asiatic Miscellany*).

them, they would be lost. This Zagatay was a man of great bravery and generosity; but there rose up envy amongst the brothers, and they made war upon each other. When the people of Samarcand saw this, they rose against Zagatay, killed him, with many of his followers, and made one of their own countrymen, emperor.[1]

Many followers of Zagatay remained in the land, in possession of property on which to live; and, when their master was killed, all the people of the country called them Zagatays, and that is the origin of the name. Timour Beg, and the other Zagatays who follow him, are descended from these Zagatay Tartars; and many people of the land of Samarcand have now taken this name of Zagatay, that they may share in the great name which the Zagatays have now attained.

The ambassadors were in this city of Kesh during the Thursday on which they arrived; and, having departed on Friday afternoon, they passed the night in a village. On Saturday, the 30th of August, they dined at a great house, which the lord had built, in a plain near the banks of a river, and in the midst of a large and very beautiful garden. They passed the night in a large village, which was a league from Samarcand, called Mecer. The knight who conducted them, now left the ambassadors, as on that day they could easily reach the city of Samarcand; he said that he would announce their approach to the great lord, and that he would send a man to report their arrival; and that night the man was sent to report it to the great lord.

Next day, at dawn, he returned with an order from the great lord to the knight, that the ambassadors, and the ambassador of the Sultan of Babylon, who travelled with them,

[1] This is a mistake. Zagatai was his father's chief justice; and on the death of Zengis Khan in 1227, he became ruler of Samarcand. His descendants ruled in Samarcand until Timour was crowned in 1363; and, indeed, during the whole reign of Timour, a puppet descendant of Zagatai was treated with outward reverence.

should be taken to a garden near the village, and remain there until he gave further orders. On Sunday, the 31st of August, at dawn, the ambassadors were taken to this garden, which was surrounded by a mud wall, and might be about a league round. It contained a great number of fruit trees of all kinds, except citrons and limes ; it was traversed by many channels of water, and a large stream flowed through the centre. These channels flowed amongst the trees, which were large and tall, and gave a pleasant shade. In the centre of the avenues formed by the trees, there were raised platforms, which traversed the whole garden. There was also a high mound of earth, made level on the top, and surrounded by wooden palings ; and on this hill there were palaces, with chambers very richly ornamented with gold and blue, upon polished tiles. This hill was surrounded by a very deep ditch, full of water, into which the water poured down from a large pipe.

To ascend the hill, there were two bridges, on opposite sides ; and after the bridges were crossed, there were two doors, which opened upon flights of stairs leading up to the summit of the hill, where the palace stood. In this garden there were deer, and many pheasants. Beyond the garden there was a great vineyard, as large as the garden, which was also surrounded by a mud wall, and all round the wall there were rows of tall trees, which looked very beautiful. They call this garden and palace *Talicia,* and in their own language *Calbet*: and, in this garden, the ambassadors were given much food, and all that they required. They had their tents pitched on the grass, near a stream of water, and there they remained.

On Thursday the 4th of September, a noble who was related to the lord, came to the garden, and told the ambassadors that the lord was occupied with the business of some ambassadors from the emperor Tokatmish, and that, therefore, he could not see them yet: but, that they might not be impatient, he had sent some refreshments to them, and to the ambassador of the Sultan, that they might make merry for that day. They brought many sheep, cooked and dressed, and a roasted horse, with rice served up in various ways, and much fruit. When they had eaten, they were presented with two horses, a robe, and a hat. The ambassadors were in this garden from Sunday, the 31st of August, to Monday the 8th of September, when the lord sent for them; for it is the custom not to see any ambassador until five or six days are passed, and the more important the ambassador may be, the longer he has to wait.

On Monday, the 8th of September, the ambassadors departed from the garden where they had been lodged, and went to the city of Samarcand. The road went over a plain covered with gardens, and houses, and markets where they sold many things; and at three in the afternoon they came to a large garden and palace, outside the city, where the lord then was. When they arrived, they dismounted, and entered a building outside; where two knights came to them, and said that they were to give up those presents, which they brought for the lord, to certain men who would lay them before him, for such were the orders of the private Meerzas of the lord; so the ambassadors gave the presents to the two knights. They placed the presents in the arms of men who were to carry them respectfully before the lord, and the ambassador from the Sultan did the same with the presents which he brought.

The entrance to this garden was very broad and high, and beautifully adorned with glazed tiles, in blue and gold. At this gate there were many porters, who guarded it, with maces in their hands. When the ambassadors entered, they came to six elephants, with wooden castles on their backs, each of which had two banners, and there were men on the top of them The ambassadors went forward, and found the men, who had the presents well arranged on their arms, and they advanced with them in company with the two knights, who held them by the arm pits, and the ambassador whom Timour Beg had sent to the king of Castille was with them; and those who saw him, laughed at him, because he was dressed in the costume and fashion of Castille.

They conducted them to an aged knight, who was seated in an ante-room. He was a son of the sister of Timour Beg, and they bowed reverentially before him. They were then brought before some small boys, grandsons of the lord, who were seated in a chamber, and they also bowed before them. Here the letter, which they brought from the King to Timour Beg, was demanded, and they presented it to one of these boys, who took it. He was a son of Miran Meerza, the eldest son of the lord. The three boys then got up, and carried the letter to the lord; who desired that the ambassadors should be brought before him.

Timour Beg was seated in a portal, in front of the entrance of a beautiful palace; and he was sitting on the ground. Before him there was a fountain, which threw up the water very high, and in it there were some red apples. The lord was seated cross-legged, on silken embroidered carpets, amongst round pillows. He was dressed in a robe of silk, with a high white hat on his head, on the top of which there was a spinal ruby, with pearls and precious stones round it.

As soon as the ambassadors saw the lord, they made a reverential bow, placing the knee on the ground, and crossing the arms on the breast; then they went forward and made another; and then a third, remaining with their knees on the ground. The lord ordered them to rise and come forward; and the knights, who had held them until then, let them go. Three Meerzas, who stood before the lord, and were his most intimate councillors, named Alodalmelec[1] Meerza, Borundo Meerza, and Noor Eddin[2] Meerza, then

[1] Abdulmalec—"Servant of the king."
[2] Noor-ud-deen—"Light of the faith."

came and took the ambassadors by the arms, and led them forward until they stood together before the lord. This was done that the lord might see them better; for his eyesight was bad, being so old that the eyelids had fallen down entirely. He did not give them his hand to kiss, for it was not the custom for any great lord to kiss his hand; but he asked after the king, saying, "How is my son the king? is he in good health?" When the ambassadors had answered, Timour Beg turned to the knights who were seated around him, amongst whom were one of the sons of Tokatmish, the former emperor of Tartary, several chiefs of the blood of the late emperor of Samarcand, and others of the family of the lord himself, and said, "Behold! here are the ambassadors sent by my son the king of Spain, who is the greatest king of the Franks, and lives at the end of the world. These Franks are truly a great people, and I will give my benediction to the king of Spain, my son. It would have sufficed if he had sent you to me with the letter, and without the presents, so well satisfied am I to hear of his health and prosperous state."

The letter which the king had sent was held before the lord, in the hand of his grandson; and the master of theology said, through his interpreter, that no one understood how to read the letter except himself, and that when his highness wished to hear it, he would read it. The lord then took the letter from the hand of his grandson and opened it, saying that he would hear it presently, and that he would send for the master, and see him in private, when he might read it, and say what he desired.

The ambassadors were then taken to a room, on the right hand side of the place where the lord sat; and the Meerzas, who held them by the arms, made them sit below an ambassador, whom the emperor Chayscan, lord of Cathay, had sent to Timour Beg to demand the yearly tribute which was formerly paid. When the lord saw the ambassadors seated below the ambassador from the lord of Cathay, he sent to order that they should sit above him, and he below them. As soon as they were seated, one of the Meerzas of the lord came and said to the ambassador of Cathay, that the lord had ordered that those who were ambassadors from the king of Spain, his son and friend, should sit above him; and that he who was the ambassador from a thief and a bad man, his enemy, should sit below them; and from that time, at the feasts and entertainments given by the lord, they always sat in that order. The Meerza then ordered the interpreter to tell the ambassadors what the lord had done for them.

This emperor of Cathay is called Chuyscan, which means nine empires; but the Zagatays called him Tangus, which means "pig emperor." He is the lord of a great country, and Timour Beg used to pay him tribute, but he refuses to do so now. As soon as these ambassadors, and many others, who had come from distant countries, were seated in order, they brought much meat, boiled, roasted, and dressed in other ways, and roasted horses; and they placed these sheep and horses on very large round pieces of stamped leather. When the lord called for meat, the people dragged it to him on these pieces of leather, so great was its weight; and as soon as it was within twenty paces of him, the carvers came, who cut it up, kneeling on the leather. They cut it in pieces, and put the pieces in basins of gold and silver, earthenware and glass, and porcelain, which is very scarce and precious. The most honorable piece was a haunch of the horse, with the loin, but without the leg, and they placed parts of it in ten cups of gold and silver. They also cut up the haunches of the sheep. They then put pieces of the tripes of the horses, about the size of a man's fist, into the cups, and entire sheep's heads, and in this way they made many dishes. When they had made sufficient, they placed them in rows. Then some men came with soup, and they sprinkled salt over it, and put a little into each dish, as sauce; and they took some very thin cakes of corn, doubled them four times, and placed one over each cup or basin of meat.

As soon as this was done, the Meerzas and courtiers of the lord took these basins, one holding each side, and one helping behind (for a single man could not lift them), and placed them before the lord, and the ambassadors, and the knights who were there; and the lord sent the ambassadors two basins, from those which were placed before him, as a mark of favour. When this food was taken away, more was brought; and it is the custom to take this food, which is given to them, to their lodgings, and if they do not do so, it is taken as an affront; and so much of this food was brought, that it was quite wonderful.

Another custom is, that when they take any food from before any of the ambassadors, they give it to their retinue; and so much food was placed before them, that, if they had taken it away, it would have lasted them for half a year. When the roast and boiled meats were done with, they brought meats dressed in various other ways, and balls of forced meat; and after that, there came fruit, melons, grapes, and nectarines; and they gave them drink out of silver and golden jugs, particularly sugar and cream, a pleasant beverage, which they make in the summer time.

When dinner was finished, the men who bore the presents on their arms passed before the lord, and the same was done with the presents sent by the Sultan of Babylon; and three hundred horses were also brought before the lord, which had been presented that day. After this was done the ambassadors rose, and a knight was appointed to attend upon them, and to see that they were provided with all that they required. This knight, who was the chief porter of the lord, conducted the ambassadors, and the ambassador from the Sultan of Babylon, to a lodging near the place where the lord abode, in which there was a garden, and plenty of water.

When the ambassadors took leave of the lord, he caused

the presents[1] which the king had sent, to be brought, and received them with much complacency. He divided the scarlet cloth amongst his women, giving the largest share to his chief wife, named Caño,[2] who was in this garden with him. The other presents, brought by the ambassador from the Sultan, were not received, but returned to the men who had charge of them, who received them, and kept them for three days, when the lord ordered them to be brought again: because it is the custom not to receive a present until the third day. This house and garden, where the lord received the ambassadors, was called Dilkoosha,[3] and in it there were many silken tents, and the lord remained there until the following Friday, when he went to another garden, where there was a very rich palace, which he had lately ordered to be built, called Bayginar.[4]

On Monday, the 15th of September, the lord went from that palace and garden to another, which was very beautiful. This garden had a very lofty and handsome entrance, made of bricks, and adorned with tiles in blue and gold, arranged in various patterns. On this day the lord ordered a great feast to be prepared, and sent for the ambassadors, and many other people, both men and women. This garden is very large, and contains many fruit, and other trees, which give shade. Amongst them there were avenues, and wooden terraces, on which the people walked. In the garden there were many tents, and awnings of red cloth, and of various coloured silks, some embroidered in various ways, and others plain. In the centre of the garden there was a very beautiful house, built in the shape of a cross, and very richly adorned with ornaments. In the middle of it there were three chambers, for placing beds and carpets

[1] Amongst the presents there was a "suit of tapestry, which eclipsed the pencil of the oriental artists."—*Gibbon*, chap. lxv.

[2] *Mulk Khanum*. [3] *Dil-khushi*—"Heart's delight."

[4] *Bagh-e-chenar?*—"Plane-tree garden," mentioned by Baber.

in, and the walls were covered with glazed tiles. Opposite the entrance, in the largest of the chambers, there was a silver gilt table, as high as a man, and three arms broad, on the top of which there was a bed of silk cloths, embroidered with gold, placed one on the top of the other, and here the lord was seated. The walls were hung with rose-coloured silk cloths, ornamented with plates of silver gilt, set with emeralds, pearls, and other precious stones, tastefully arranged. Above these ornaments there were pieces of silk, a *palmo* broad, whence hung tassels of various colours, and the wind moved them backwards and forwards, which caused a very pretty effect. Before the great arch, which formed the entrance to the chamber, there were ornaments of the same kind, and silk cloths raised up by spear poles, and kept together by silken cords, with large tassels, which came down to the ground. The other chambers were furnished in the same way, and on the floors there were carpets and rush mats.

In the centre of the house, opposite the door, there were two gold tables, each standing on four legs, and the table and legs were all in one. They were each five *palmos* long, and *three* broad; and seven golden phials stood upon them, two of which were set with large pearls, emeralds, and torquoises, and each one had a ruby near the mouth. There were also six round golden cups, one of which was set with large round clear pearls, inside, and in the centre of it there was a ruby, two fingers broad, and of a brilliant colour.

The ambassadors were invited to this feast by the lord, but they had to wait for their interpreter, and when they arrived the lord had dined. The lord said that, on another day, when he sent for them, they were to come at once, and not to wait for the interpreter, but that this time he would forgive them. He had made this feast for them, that they might see the house, and the people. The lord was in a great rage with the Meerzas, because the ambassadors did not come in time for the feast, and because the interpreter was not with them. He sent for the interpreter, and said,—"How is it that you have caused me to be enraged, and put out? Why were you not with the Frank ambassadors? I order that a hole be bored through your nose, that a rope be passed through it, and that you be dragged through the army, as a punishment." He had scarcely finished speaking, when men took the interpreter by the nose, to bore a hole in it; and the knight, who attended upon the ambassadors by order of the lord, asked for mercy, and he was pardoned, escaping the infliction of his sentence.

The lord sent to the ambassadors, at their lodging, to say that as they had not been at the feast, they should have a part of it; and he sent them five sheep, and two great jars of wine. At this feast many people were assembled, as well ladies as great nobles, and many other people; but as the ambassadors did not see this house and garden, nor the chambers in it, they spoke to some of the people who had seen them.

On Monday the 22nd of September, the lord went to another house and garden, which was surrounded by a high wall, and at each corner was a high round tower. In the middle there was a house in the shape of a cross, with a great pond in front; and this house was larger than those in any of the gardens which they had yet seen, and the work in gold and blue was the richest. These houses and gardens were outside the city, and this house was called Bagino.

The lord ordered a great feast to be prepared, and the ambassadors were invited to it, and many people were assembled. In this feast, the lord gave an order that wine should be drunk, but the people are not allowed to drink wine publicly, nor in secret, without permission. The wine is given after dinner, and they serve it out in such quantities, and so often, that it makes the men drunk; and they do not consider that there is either pleasure or festivity without being drunk. The attendants serve the wine on their knees, and when one cup is finished, they give another; and these men have no other duty, except to give another cup, as soon as the first is finished. As soon as one attendant is tired of filling the cups, another takes his place; and you must not think that one attendant supplies all, but he confines himself to one or two, so as to make them drink more; and those who do not wish to drink the wine, are told that they insult the lord, at whose request they drink. They give the cups full, and they must not leave any wine in them; and if they leave any, the attendants will not take the cup from them, but make them drink it all. They drink from one cup, once or twice, and if they are called upon to drink by their love of the lord, or by the lord's head, they must drink it all at one pull, without leaving a drop.

They call the man who drinks the most wine *Bàhadur*, which is as much as to say "a valorous man"; and he who does not drink, is made to do so, although he does not wish it.[1]

On this day, before the ambassadors came to the lord, he sent one of his Meerzas, with a jug of wine, and a message, asking them to drink the wine before they came, so that they might arrive in a jovial mood. Before the lord arrived, they were seated according to the order observed at the previous interview; and the drinking lasted a long time. The food consisted of many roasted horses, boiled and roasted sheep, and rice cooked in their mode. After they had eaten, one of the Meerzas of the lord came with a silver basin, full of their silver coins, called *Tagaes*; and they scattered them over the ambassadors, and over the rest of the company, and when they had done this, they put what was left into the skirts of their clothes. The lord then caused the ambassadors to be

[1] In those days most of the Mohammedan sovereigns of Central Asia died of *delirium tremens;* so that tobacco was a fortunate discovery for these people. Baber, in his *Memoirs*, gives some idea of the drinking propensities of himself and kindred.

clothed in robes, and they bowed their knees to him three times, according to the custom; and he said that they should come and dine with him again, on another day.

On the next day, which was the 23rd of September, the lord went to another house and garden, near the former one, called Dilicaya; where he gave another feast, at which a great multitude of his followers were assembled, and the ambassadors also went.

This house and garden is very beautiful; and on this occasion the lord was very jovial, and he drank wine as well as those who were with him; and the food consisted of horses and sheep, according to their custom. When they had eaten, the lord ordered robes to be given to the ambassadors, and they returned to their lodgings, which were very near at hand. At these feasts such a multitude of people were assembled, that, when they came near to the lord, they could not get on, except by the help of the guards appointed to make way for the ambassadors; and the dust was such that people's faces and clothes were all one colour.

In front of these gardens there was a vast plain, through which a river flowed, and many smaller streams. On this plain the lord ordered many tents to be pitched for himself and his women; and that all his host, which was scattered in detachments over the land, should be assembled together, each man in his place, and that their tents should be pitched, and that they should come there, with their women, to be present at the festivals and marriages which he wished to celebrate.

When the tents of the lord were pitched, each man knew where his own tent should be pitched, and every one, high and low, knew his place, so that the work was done without confusion or noise. After three or four days, twenty thousand men were assembled round the tents of the lord, and a day did not pass without many arriving from all parts.

In this horde there are always butchers and cooks who sell cooked sheep, and others who sell fruit and barley, and bakers who sell bread. Every division of the horde is provided with all that the troops require, and they are arranged in streets. There are even baths and bath men in the horde, who pitch their tents and make their huts for hot baths, with boilers for heating the water, and all that they require; and as each man arrived, he was shown his station.

The lord ordered that the ambassadors should be conducted to a house and garden near the encampment.

On Monday, the 29th of September, the lord went to the city of Samarcand, and lodged in some houses near the entrance, which he had ordered to be built in honour of the mother of his wife Caño, who was interred in a chapel within these houses. These houses were very rich, and they were not yet finished, but every day there were men working at them. On this day the lord gave a great feast, and sent for the ambassadors. He gave this feast, at the reception of some ambassadors who had come to him, from a land which borders on the territory of Cathay, and which used to be within the dominions of the emperor of Cathay.

These ambassadors arrived on that day, and were dressed in the following manner:—the chief amongst them had on a dress of skins, with the hair outside, and these skins were the worse for wear. On his head he wore a small hat, with a cord to fasten it to his breast, and the hat was so small that his head would scarcely go into it. All those who came with him wore dresses of skin, some with the hair outside, and others with it turned inside, and they looked like a party of blacksmiths. They brought presents to the lord, of skins of martins and sables, white foxes, and falcons: and they were Christians, after the manner of those of Cathay.

The object of the embassy was to ask the lord, to give them a grandson of Tocatmish, who was formerly emperor of Tartary, to be their ruler. On this day the lord played at chess,[1] for a long time, with some Zaytes,[2] or men who were of the lineage of Mohammed. On this day he would not receive the presents from the ambassadors, but they were brought forward, and he saw them.

On Thursday the 2nd of October, the lord sent the ambassadors to a garden, where a knight lodged who was his chief porter; and the knight told them that the lord had ordered him to say that he knew well that the Franks drank wine every day, but that they did not drink at their ease before him. He had therefore sent them to this place, that they might eat and drink at their ease: and he sent them ten sheep and a horse to eat, and also a load of wine; and, when the food was eaten, and the wine drunk, they dressed the ambassadors in robes, and gave them shirts and hats, and horses.

On Monday, the 6th of October, the lord ordered a great feast to be given, at the place where his horde was encamped on the plain, and he ordered that his relations and women, all his sons and grandsons who were near, his councillors, and all the people who were scattered round, should assemble at this place. On this day the ambassadors were brought to the plain, and, when they arrived, they found many handsome tents pitched, most of them on the banks of the river, close together, and it was a very beautiful sight. The ambassadors went through some streets of tents, where they sold all that was required by this great host; and, when they were near the tents of the lord, they were placed under an awning, made of white linen cloth, ornamented with cloths of various colours, and it was long, and secured above by cords, to two poles, and there were many awnings of this kind on the plain, and they make them long and high, that the sun may be screened off, and that air may enter

[1] Timour was very fond of the game of chess. He increased the number of the men and squares, and made it much more complicated.

[2] *Syuds.*

freely. Near these awnings, there was a great and lofty pavilion, which was like a tent, only square, and three lances high. It was a hundred paces broad, and had four corners, and the ceiling was round, like a vault. It was pitched against twelve poles, each as large round as a man, measured round the chest. They were painted gold and blue, and other colours, and from corner to corner there were poles, three fastened together, and making one. When they pitched the tents, they used wheels, like those of a cart, which were turned by men, and they have ropes fixed in various directions, to assist them. From the vault of the ceiling of the pavilion silken cloths descended, between each of the poles, which were fastened to them, and when they were fastened, they made an arch from one side to the other. Outside this square pavilion, there were porticoes, joined above to the pavilion, and supported by twenty-four poles, not so large as the central ones, so that the whole pavilion was supported by thirty-six poles. From this pavilion at least five hundred red cords were extended, and inside there was a crimson carpet, beautifully ornamented with silken cloths of many colours, and embroidered with gold threads. In the centre of the ceiling there was the richest work of all; and in the four corners were the figures of four eagles, with their wings closed. The outside of thepavilion was lined with silk cloths, in black, white, and yellow stripes. At each corner there was a high pole, with a copper ball, and the figure of a crescent on the top; and in the centre, there was another tall pole, with a much larger copper ball and crescent; and, on the top of the pavilion, between these poles, there was a tower of silken cloths, with turrets, and an entrance door; and when the wind blew the pavilion about, or made the poles unsteady, men went on the top, and secured anything that was loose. This pavilion was so large and high that, from a distance, it looked like a castle; and it was a very wonderful thing to see, and possessed more beauty than it is possible to describe.

Within the pavilion there was, in one part, a chamber covered with carpets, for the use of the lord; and on the left hand there was another carpeted chamber, and another beyond that. Round this pavilion there was a wall, like that of any castle or city, made of silken cloths of many colours, ornamented in various ways, with turrets, and it had cords, inside and out, to draw it straight, and inside there were poles, which supported it. The wall was round, and encircled a space which was about three hundred paces across, and it was as high as a man on horseback. It had a broad gate, made like an arch, and on the top of it there was a tower with turrets; and the wall, as well as the tower and turrets, was ornamented with patterns and devices of very beautiful workmanship, and they call this wall *Zalaparda*.[1]

Within the wall there were many tents, and awnings pitched in various ways; amongst which was a high tent, not drawn out by cords. The walls were of poles, a little larger than a lance, which crossed each other like a net; and on the top of these poles, there were others forming a high capital. These poles were secured by broad girths to each other, and to stakes fixed near the walls of the tent. The tent was so high, that it was wonderful how it could be secured with these girths, and the top was covered with a crimson cloth, and the walls were lined with cotton, like a coverlid, so that the sun could not penetrate. It had no ornaments or figures whatever, except that there were some white stripes all round the outside. These stripes were covered with silver-gilt bezants, as broad as a man's hand, which were adorned with precious stones. Between these stripes there were others, which went all round the tent, folded in small folds like the skirts of a robe, and embroi-

[1] The encampments of old Futteh Ali, the Shah of Persia between 1798 and 1834, resembled these of Timour. He had a vast pavilion, surrounded by a canvass wall of bright coloured cloths, with numerous handsome tents within the inclosure. *Malcolm; Harford Jones; Fraser.*

dered with gold threads. When there was any wind, these folds moved backwards and forwards, and looked very beautiful. The tent had an entrance, with doors of very small canes, covered with red cloth.

Near this tent there was another, drawn out by cords of red velvet; and there were four other tents close to each other, so that there was a passage from one to the other, and the street between them was covered over. Within the wall there were many tents; and joined to the wall there was another as large, made of silk, with windows at intervals, but no man could enter through them, because silken nets were drawn across. In the centre of the space formed by this wall there was another very high tent, made like the former one, with the same red cloth and silver-gilt bezants; and these tents were higher than three lances. On the highest part of the latter tent there was a very large silver-gilt eagle, with wings displayed, and a little below it, above the door of the tent, were three silver-gilt falcons, with extended wings, and heads turned towards the eagle, which seemed to wish to attack them. These figures were very well made, and were so placed as to present a very beautiful effect. Above the door of the tent there was a silken awning of many colours, which made a shade before the door, and protected it from the sun; and it was made to move, so that the rays of the sun could never enter the tent.

The first wall and tents were for the use of the chief wife of the lord, who was called Caño; and the other was for his second wife, called Quinchicano, which means "the little lady." Near this wall there was another, with many tents and awnings within it; and in the centre there was a lofty tent, made in the same way as those I have already described to you; and these walls were joined to each other, and they are called *Zalaparda*. Each had its own colour, and in each there was one of those large tents, without cords, all covered with red cloth, and made in the same manner, and there were many tents and awnings in each. Between the walls there was only a narrow passage, and they were placed in rows, so as to look very beautiful. These enclosures were for the women of the lord and of his grandsons, and during the summer they were as good as houses. At noon the lord came out of one of these enclosures, and went to the great pavilion, and caused the ambassadors to be brought in, giving them a great dinner of roasted sheep and horses; and when the dinner was over, the ambassadors returned to their lodgings.

On Tuesday, the 7th of October, the lord ordered another great feast to be prepared, and the ambassadors were present. This feast was given in one of the enclosures, of which you have heard. He ordered the ambassadors to be brought to the great tent, where he gave them a feast, according to custom. After the eating was over, two of the most confidential friends of the lord, who regulated his household, named Xamelique Meerza, and Nooreddin Meerza, gave the lord a present, which consisted of many silver stands, with long legs, on which were sweetmeats, and sugar, and raisins, and almonds; and on some of the stands there was a piece of silk. These presents were brought in nines, and such is the custom when presents are brought to the lord, that they should be in nines, or consist of nine things. The lord divided this present amongst the knights who stood before him; and he ordered the ambassadors to be given two of those which contained the silk. When they rose, they scattered pieces of money, and small chaplets of thin gold, amongst the people; and when the eating was over, the company returned to their lodgings.

On Wednesday the lord ordered another great feast to be prepared, and invited the ambassadors; and on this day there was a great wind, so the lord did not come out to eat in the open air, but ordered that those who desired it, should be fed. The ambassadors did not want to eat, and returned to their lodgings.

On Thursday, the 9th of October, Hausada, the wife of Miran Meerza, the eldest son of the lord, gave a great feast, to which she invited the ambassadors, and it was given in the enclosure of tents which was set apart for her use, and which was very beautiful. When the ambassadors came near the tents, they found a very long row of jars of wine placed on the ground. The ambassadors were admitted into a tent, and ordered to sit down at the door, under an awning. The said Hausada, and many other ladies, were seated at the door of a large tent, under an awning.

On this day there was a marriage of one of her relations. Hausada herself was about forty years of age, fair and fat, and before her there were many jars of wine, and of a beverage of which they drink much, called *bosat,* made of cream and sugar.

There were also many knights and relations of Timour Beg, and jugglers, who were performing before her. When the ambassadors arrived, the ladies were drinking, and the way they drink is this:—an old knight, a relation of the lord, and two small boys, his relations, serve the cup, before Hausada, and before the other ladies, in this manner,—they hold white napkins in their hands, and those who pour out the wine, pour it into small golden cups, which they place on flat plates of gold. Those who serve the wine, then come forward, with the pourers-out behind, and when they have got half way, they touch the ground three times with their right knees. When they come near to the ladies, they take the cups, with their hands wrapped in the white napkins, so that they may not touch the cups, and present them kneeling, to the ladies who are going to drink. When the ladies have taken the cups, those who bring the wine, remain with the flat plates in their hands, and walk backwards, so as not to turn their backs to the ladies. As soon as they are at a little distance, they bend their right knees again, and remain there. When the ladies have finished drinking, the attendants go before them, and the ladies place the cups on the plates which they hold. You must not think that this drinking is of short duration, for it lasts a long time, without eating.

Sometimes, when these attendants are before the ladies, with their cups, the ladies order them to drink, and they kneel down, and drink all that is in the cups, turning them upside down, to shew that nothing is left; and on these occasions they describe their prowess in this respect, at which all the ladies laugh.

Caño, the wife of Timour Beg, came to this feast, and sometimes the company drank wine, and at others they drank cream and sugar. After the drinking had lasted a long time, Caño called the ambassadors before her, and gave them to drink with her own hand, and she importuned Ruy Gonzalez for a long time, to make him drink, for she would not believe that he never touched wine. The drinking was such that some of the men fell down drunk before her; and this was considered very jovial, for they think that there can be no pleasure without drunken men.

They also brought great quantities of roasted sheep and horses, and other dressed meats; and they eat all this with much noise, tearing the pieces away from each other, and making game over their food. They also brought rice, cooked in various ways, and tarts made with flour, sugar, and herbs; and besides the meat brought in basins, there were other pieces on skins, for those who wanted them.

This Hausada is the wife of Miran Meerza. She was of the lineage of the old emperors, and for this reason Timour Beg treats her with great respect. She has borne one son to Miran Meerza, named Khuleel Sultan, now about twenty years of age.

On Thursday, the 9th of October, the lord ordered a great feast to be prepared, to celebrate the marriage of one of his grandsons; to which the ambassadors were invited. It was given in a very beautifully ornamented enclosure, containing many tents, and Caño, the chief wife of the lord, Hausada, and many other ladies and knights, were present.

There was an enormous supply of cooked horses and sheep, according to their custom. Much wine was drunk, and they made very merry. The ladies drank their wine in the same way as they had done the day before. For the sake of more merriment, the lord sent orders to Samarcand, that all the traders in the city, the cooks and butchers, bakers and shoemakers, and all other people in the city, should come to the plain where the lord was encamped with his horde, pitch their tents, and sell their goods there, instead of in the city. He then ordered that each trade should play a game, and go through the camp, that his people might be amused. All the tradesmen, therefore, came out of the city, with all their goods, and peopled the plain, each trade in a different street of tents; and each trade played a game, and went through the horde, for the amusement of the people.[1] In the place where these traders had pitched their tents, the lord ordered a great number of gallows to be set up; and declared that, in this festival, he knew how to be merciful and kind to some, and how to be severe to others.

The first piece of justice was inflicted upon a chief magistrate, whom they call Dina, who was the greatest officer in all the land of Samarcand., Timour had left him in the city

[1] On this occasion Timour caused all sorts of amusements to be enjoyed. An amphitheatre was covered with carpets, where there were masquerades. The women were dressed like goats, others like sheep and fairies, and they ran after each other. The skinners and butchers appeared like lions and foxes, and all other tradesmen contributed specimens of their skill. At this time Ulugh Beg and Ibrahim, grandsons of Timour, were married; and a great feast was given to all the people, with abundance of wine and fruit.—*Ali of Yezd.*

as his magistrate, when he departed, for six years and eleven months; during which time this man had neglected his duties; so the lord ordered him to be hanged, and confiscated all his goods.[1] The justice inflicted upon this great man, caused terror amongst the people; and the same punishment was ordered to be inflicted upon another man, who had interceded for this magistrate. A councillor of the lord, named Burado Meerza, asked for his pardon, if he paid a sum of four hundred thousand bezants of silver, each bezant being equal to a silver rial. The lord approved of this, and when the man had given all he had, he was tormented to give more, and as he had no more, he was hung up by the feet until he was dead.

Another piece of justice was inflicted upon a great man, who had been left in charge of three thousand horses, when the lord departed; because he could not produce them all. He was hanged, although he pleaded that he would produce, not only three thousand, but six thousand horses, if the lord would give him time. In this, and other ways, the lord administered justice.

He also ordered justice to be executed upon certain traders, who had sold meat for more than it was worth, and upon shoemakers; and other traders were fined for selling their goods at a high price. The custom is, that, when a great man is put to death, he is hanged; but the meaner sort are beheaded.

On Monday, the 13th of October, Timour Beg gave a feast, and sent for the ambassadors. When they approached near the great pavilion where the lord was to dine, they found that two fresh enclosures were set up, with their tents; like the others which I have described to you, except that these tents were very rich, and more splendid than any that had been pitched before. One of the walls was of crimson cloth,

[1] Ali of Yezd mentions that two Wuzeers were hanged for committing injustice, on the return of Timour to Samarcand.

covered with embroidery of gold lace, in many figures and patterns, which was very beautiful to look upon. This wall was higher than any of the others, and the entrance was shaped like an arch, with a vaulted covering above it; and the whole was embroidered, in beautiful designs, with gold lace; and the doors were of carpeting, embroidered in the same way. On the top of the entrance there was a square tower with turrets, all made of cloth, embroidered with gold; and the wall had turrets of embroidered cloth, all round it, at intervals. There were windows in the walls, with lattices made of silken cords, and these windows also had cloth shutters. Within the enclosure the tents were pitched, and they were very rich and beautiful.

Close to this enclosure there was another, the walls of which were of white satin, with the entrance and windows the same as the former, and these enclosures had doors leading from one to the other.

The ambassadors did not go in to see these enclosures on this day, because the lord had the great feast under his own pavilion; but on another day they were shown these enclosures, and the tents.

In front of these enclosures a great pavilion was pitched, made of white silk; and it was ornamented, both inside and out, with many patterns, in various coloured silks. The ground, near the pavilion of the lord, was covered with jars of wine, which were placed in a row, a stone's throw in length. No man was allowed to pass beyond these jars towards the pavilion, and mounted guards were placed to watch the line, with bows and arrows, and maces in their hands. If any one passed the line, they shot arrows at him, and gave him such blows with their maces, that some men were taken outside the gates for dead; and a great assemblage of people was waiting in the camp, for the time when the lord should come forth, and go under the great pavilion.

Near this pavilion there were a great number of awnings, and under each awning there was a very large jar of wine, and these jars were so large, that they would hold fifteen ordinary jugs of wine. After the ambassadors had been waiting for a long time, they were told to go and pay their respects to a grandson of the lord, who had come from India the day before. Timour Beg had sent for him to see him, as it was seven years since they had met.

This grandson was a son of Timour's first born son, who was dead, whose name was Jehanghir. Timour loved him very much, and he was fond of this grandson, whose name was Peer Mohammed, for his father's sake. The ambassadors found him in a tent of red cloth, seated on the floor, with many knights standing round him. When the ambassadors approached the tent, two knights came and took them by the arms, and made them kneel on the ground, they then took them a little nearer, and made them kneel again. When they came into the tent, they made their reverence, which was this: to kneel with the right knee on the ground, cross the arms on the breast, and incline the head. The knights who conducted them then raised them, and led them out.

This grandson of the lord was very richly dressed, according to his custom. He had on a robe of blue satin, embroidered with golden wheels, some on the back, and others on the breast and sleeves. His hat was adorned with large pearls and precious stones, with a very brilliant ruby on the top; and the people who stood round him treated him with great reverence and ceremony. In front of him there were two wrestlers, dressed in leathern doublets, without sleeves; but they neither of them could throw the other. At last one of them threw the other, and held him down for a long time; for they all said that if he got up, the fall would not be counted.

On the same day all the ambassadors who were there went

to do reverence to this grandson of Timour Beg, who was about twenty-two years of age. He was dark and beardless, and they call him lord of India; but in this they do not speak the truth, for the present rightful lord of India is a Christian, named N.,[1] as the ambassadors were informed.

The chief city of India is called Delhi, and here Timour Beg fought a battle with the lord of India. The Indian collected a great force, and had fifty armed elephants; and in the first battle the lord of India defeated Timour Beg, by means of his elephants. On the following day they renewed the contest, and Timour took many camels, and loaded them with dry grass, placing them in front of the elephants. When the battle began, he caused the grass to be set on fire, and when the elephants saw the burning straw upon the camels, they fled. They say that the elephants are much afraid of fire, because they have small eyes; and thus the lord of India was defeated.

Timour Beg conquered all the plain country from this lord, which bordered on the empire of Samarcand; but most of the land is rugged and mountainous. They say that there are many great towns and cities, and that the country is very rich and populous. When the lord of India was defeated, he fled to the mountains, and collected another force, but he did not venture to attack his enemy. The plain country which was then conquered, is governed by this grandson of Timour Beg, from the great and rich city of Hormes; but the greater part of India is still held by the former lord. This battle took place about twelve years ago, and since that time, neither Timour Beg, nor his grandson, have attempted to advance further into India.

The people and the lord of India are Christians, of the Greek faith; but, among them, there are some who are distinguished by a brand in their faces, and who are

[1] The same in both editions.

despised by the others; and Moors and Jews live amongst them, but they are subject to the Christians.[1]

The ambassadors waited until noon, when the lord came forth from his tent, and went under the pavilion. The ambassadors, a great number of his relations, and other people sat with him, according to the order which had been previously arranged. On this day there were many games, played in various ways, and the elephants which the lord had, were painted green and red, with their castles, and they were made to exhibit their performances. The noise made by the drums, during these games, was so great that it was quite wonderful; and near the pavilion, where the lord sat, there were many performing jugglers.

There were three hundred jars of wine placed before the lord, on the ground; and there were also large skins full of cream, into which the attendants put loaves of sugar, and mixed it up; and this was what they drank on that day. When the people were all arranged in order round the wall which encircled the pavilion, Caño, the chief wife of the lord, came forth to be present at the feast. She had on a robe of red silk, trimmed with gold lace, which was long and flowing, but without sleeves, or any opening, except one to admit the head, and two arm holes. It had no waist, and fifteen ladies held up the skirts of it, to enable her to walk. She had so much white lead on her face, that it looked like paper; and this is put on to protect it from the sun, for when they travel in winter or summer, all great ladies put this on their faces. She had a thin veil over her face, and a crested head dress of red cloth, which hung some way down the back. This crest was very high, and was covered with large pearls, rubies, emeralds, and other precious stones, and it was embroidered with gold lace, on the top of which there was a circlet of gold, set with pearls. On the top of all there was a little castle,

[1] Perhaps Clavijo's Moslem informants looked upon Christianity and Brahminism as much the same thing.

on which were three very large and brilliant rubies, surmounted by a tall plume of white feathers. One of these feathers hung down as low as the eyes, and they were secured by golden threads; and, as she moved, they waved to and fro.

Her hair, which was very black, hung down over her shoulders, and they value black hair much more than any other colour. She was accompanied by three hundred ladies, and an awning was carried over Caño, supported by a lance which was borne by a man. It was made of white silk, in the form of the top of a round tent, and held over her, to protect her from the sun.

A number of eunuchs, who guard the women, walked before her, and in this way she came to the pavilion where the lord was, and sat down near him, with all her ladies, and three ladies held her head dress with their hands, that it might not fall on one side.

As soon as she was seated, another of the wives of the lord came out from another enclosure, with many ladies, dressed in the same way, and sat down in the pavilion, a little below Caño. She was the second wife, and was called Quinchicano. Then, from another enclosure, came another wife, and sat down a little below the second; and in this way nine wives came out, and sat round the lord, eight of them being his own, and one the wife of his grandson.

The wives of the lord had the following names. The chief wife was named Caño, which means "queen" or "great lady," and she was the daughter of a former emperor of Samarcand, named Ahincan,[1] who also reigned over Persia and Damascus. They knew the mother of this emperor, but not his father; and he was very brave in battle, and made many laws and ordinances, which still regulate the empire. The second wife was called Quinchicano, which means little lady, and she was a daughter of Tumanga, the king of a land called

[1] Kamil Khan?

Andricoja. The names of the others were Dileoltagna, Cholpamalaga, Mundagasa, Vengaraga, Ropa-arbaraga, and Yauguraga, which means "queen of the heart," and Timour Beg gave her that name last August.

When they were all seated in order, they began the drinking, which lasted a long time. They gave the women their wine, with the same ceremonies which have been described to you, when I told you of the entertainment given in the tents of Hausada. The lord called the ambassadors before him, and gave the master of theology a cup of wine with his own hand, for he now knew that Ruy Gonzalez never drank wine. Those who took drink from the hand of the lord, observed the following ceremonies. First they knelt down with their right knees, then they went forward a little, and knelt with both knees. They then took the cup, got up, and walked backwards a little, so as not to turn their backs, knelt down again, and drank so as not to leave a drop in the cup.

Each of the ambassadors was held under the armpits by two knights, who did not leave them, until they had returned to the place where they were before. Near the great pavilion there were many tents and awnings, for ambassadors who had come to the lord, and under each awning there was a jar of wine, for those to drink who sat there; and the lord ordered two of his own jars to be sent to the retinue of the ambassadors. Before the lord, there were certain poles and cords, on which men climbed and performed. The lord, also, had fourteen elephants,[1] and each one had a wooden castle, covered with silk, with four yellow and green banners; and in each castle there were five or six men, and on the neck of each there was a man with a goad, who made the elephants run, and perform tricks. These elephants were black, and had no hair except upon their tails, which were like those of

[1] Timour brought ninety captured elephants from India, and they were employed in carrying stones from the quarries, for his magnificent buildings at Samarcand.—*Price.*

camels. The animals were very large, equal in size to four or five great bulls, and their bodies were quite shapeless, like a full sack. Their legs were very thick, and the same size all the way down, and the foot round and without hoofs, but with five toes, each with a nail, like those of a black man. They had no neck whatever, and their heads were fixed, so that they could not touch the ground with them. Their ears were very long, round, and scolloped, and their eyes very small. A man sat across their ears, who guided them, with a goad in his hand, and made them go where he liked. Their heads were very large, and, instead of noses, trunks came out of their heads, and reached down to the ground. These trunks are pierced, and they drink through them. When an elephant wants to drink, he puts the trunk in the water, and brings it up to his mouth. He also browses with his trunk, as he cannot do so with his mouth. He takes the grass in this trunk, when he wants to eat, and, turning it up, tosses the food into his mouth. He is thus supported by this trunk, and he winds it about like a serpent, so that there is no part of his body that he cannot touch with it. Under this trunk, is the mouth; and he has jaws like a pig, and two tusks, as thick as a man's leg, and as long as an arm. When they make them fight, they bind their trunks with spikes of iron, and fasten swords upon them.

The elephant is a very intelligent animal, and obeys very readily what his guide wishes him to do. The man who guides him, sits on his neck, with his legs across the beast's ears. He carries a goad in his hand, with which he scratches its head, and makes it go where he wishes, for when he makes a sign with the goad, it goes in the direction pointed out. When it fights, the guide is armed, as well as the elephant. It walks like a bear, in jumps, and at each jump, it wounds with the swords. When they wish these elephants to fight, the guides hit them on the forehead with the goad, and make great wounds; and when they feel the wounds, they give loud grunts, like pigs, and, with open mouth, rush on in the direction pointed out by the guide. The wounds heal in the night, if they leave the beasts in the open air, but if they are put under a roof, they will die. When the guide orders the elephant to take anything off the ground, however heavy it may be, it raises it with its trunk, and gives it to the men who are in the castle on its back; and when those in the castle want to come down, they order it to stoop, and it stretches out its fore and hind legs in opposite directions, and touches the ground with its belly, while the men descend by cords which hang from the castle.

On this day they had much entertainment with these elephants, making them run with horses and with the people, which was very diverting; and when they all ran together, it seemed as if the earth trembled. I hold it to be true, from what I then saw, that one elephant is worth a thousand men in a battle; for when they are amongst men, they rush about wounding every one; and when they are themselves wounded, they become more fierce, rush about more wildly, and fight better. As the tusks are too high up for them to wound with them, they fasten swords to them, so that they may wound the people under them. They go a day or two without eating, and they are even able to go three days without food.

After the lord, and his women, had drunk a great deal, they began to eat many sheep and horses, roasted whole, which were served up on very large skins, like printed leather, which men carried round; and there was so much that it took three hundred men and more to bring it, and there was a great noise when they brought it before the lord. They then put it into the basins, and served it up without bread, according to the custom; and all this time cartloads of meat did not cease to arrive, and camels with panniers full of meat, which was placed on the ground, in great heaps, and eaten by the rest of the people. Afterwards they brought many tables, without cloths, on which were dishes of meat cooked with rice, and bread made with sugar. As night came on they placed many lighted lanterns before the lord; and they commenced eating and drinking again, as well the men as the ladies, so that the feast lasted all night; and during the night two relations of the lord were married. When the ambassadors saw that this would last all the night, and they had had as much as they wanted, they returned to their lodgings, while the lord and his ladies continued their revelry.[1]

On Thursday, the 26th of October, the lord gave a great feast, and invited the ambassadors. It was given in one of the richest enclosures of tents, in a tent without cords, very richly ornamented. The ambassadors entered with the lord, who drank wine with those who were with him; and, that they might get drunk sooner, he gave them spirits. The drinking was such that many men came out of the tent drunk. The lord remained in the tent, very jovial, and the ambassadors returned to their lodgings; but the eating and drinking lasted all night.

On Friday, the 27th of October, Caño, the chief wife of the lord, gave a great feast, and invited the ambassadors. The lady gave her entertainment in an enclosure of very rich tents, to which a great assembly of people came, as well ambassadors from various countries, as friends of her own, both knights and ladies. The enclosure was full of very rich tents, and the outer wall was made of white cloth, ornamented and embroidered with letters and figures, in a very beautiful design.

The ambassadors, when they came to the horde, were taken to the enclosure by certain knights, who were relations of the lord, and they entered a tent near the gateway of the enclosure. This tent was of crimson cloth, embroidered

[1] Ali of Yezd mentions that the Frank ambassadors were invited to this banquet, "for," says he, "even the *kasses*, the smallest of fish, have their places in the sea."

inside and out with white. Here they sat down, and much meat and drink was set before them. When they had eaten, Caño ordered that they should be shown the tents in her enclosure. Among them there was one tent very large and high, unsupported by cords, and covered with very beautiful red silk. There were bands of silver gilt plates all round it, and the tent was beautifully adorned inside and out, and it had two doors, one within the other. The first doors were made of thin red wands, close to each other, like a hurdle, and covered outside with rose coloured silk, beautifully woven. These doors were made in this way, in order that when they were shut, the air might enter freely, and that those inside might see the people outside, while those outside could not see the people inside. The second doors were so high, that a man might go through them on horseback, and they were covered with silver gilt, consisting of many square plates. They were ornamented very skilfully, and in a variety of patterns, amongst which were blue and gold knots, and the workmanship was so cunning and so excellent, that it could not be equalled, either in that country or in christendom. On one door was the figure of St. Peter, and on the other that of St. Paul, with books in their hands, which were covered with silver; and they say that Timour Beg found these gates at Bursa, when he pillaged the treasury of the Turk. Opposite these gates, in the middle of the tent, there was an ornamental cabinet or chest, containing silver. It was made of gold and very rich enamel work, and as high as a man's breast. The top was flat, and surrounded by small turrets, in green and blue enamel, with many precious stones and large pearls. In the centre of one of the sides, amongst these jewels, there was a stone as large as a small nut, and round, but not very bright. This cabinet had a small door, and within there was a shelf full of cups, above which there were six golden balls, covered with pearls and precious stones.

At the foot of this cabinet there was a small golden table, about two *palmos* high, round which were many precious stones, and on the top there was a very clear and brilliant emerald, which was flat, and four *palmos* long, and covered the whole table, being also a *palmo* and a half broad. In front of this small stand or table, there was a golden tree, made to resemble an oak; with the trunk as big as a man's leg, from which many branches spread out in all directions, with leaves like those of an oak; and it was as high as a man, and overshadowed the table, which stood near it. The fruit of this tree consisted of rubies, emeralds, torquoises, sapphires, and wonderfully large pearls, selected for their shape and beauty. On this tree there were many birds, made of enameled gold of various colours, which were seated on the leaves of the tree, with their wings spread out, and in the act of picking the fruit. In front of this tree, against the wall of the tent, there was a wooden table, inlaid with silver gilt, and near it there was a bed of rich silk, embroidered with golden leaves and flowers, and many other devices. On the opposite side of the tent there was a similar table and bed, and the ground was covered with rich silken carpets.

When the ambassadors had seen this tent, they were taken to the place where the lord was drinking wine with his Meerzas and knights. The feast was given because the lord had given one of his grandaughters in marriage to one of his grandsons, the night before. Entering the enclosure, on the right hand there was a tent of red cloth, embroidered and ornamented with white silk, and other colours. This tent was surrounded by doors and windows, covered with silken nets. The ambassadors entered by one of these doors, which was beautifully ornamented, and led to a vaulted passage, at the end of which there was another handsome door, which opened into the body of the tent. Beyond there was a door leading to another tent, which was embroidered with gold, and beyond this there was a great tent, where the lord sat drinking wine, and there was a great noise.

These tents and doors were all of red cloth, and they were so rich and so well made, that they cannot be described by writing, and they cannot be imagined without being seen.

The ambassadors were taken from this tent to a wooden house, which was in the enclosure. It was high, and was approached by a flight of steps. It was beautifully painted in gold and blue, and was made so that it could be set up and taken down at pleasure. This house was the mosque, in which the lord said his prayers, and he took it with him on his journeys. They were then taken to a tent, which was supported by green cords. It contained two beds. Thence they went to another tent, close to the former one, which was without cords. It was covered with red cloth outside, and ornamented in various ways inside. Part of the inside was lined with sables, which is the most precious skin in the world, and each skin is worth fourteen or fifteen ducats in that land, and in other countries its value is much greater. Above the entrance, there was an awning to prevent the sun from entering the tent.

The ambassadors went from these tents to some others, which were close at hand. They were covered with white satin, and near them there were many awnings of silk; and in this horde, there were not only these enclosures and tents belonging to the lord, but many others for the use of his Meerzas and courtiers, which were wonderful to behold; so that whichever way a man turned, he saw plenty of beautiful tents and silken walls.

In this horde, which the lord had assembled, there were as many as fourteen or fifteen thousand tents, which was a beautiful thing to see; and besides these tents there were many others in the gardens, meadows, and fields around the city. The lord caused all the Meerzas and nobles in the land of Samarcand to come to this festival; amongst whom was the lord of Balaxia,[1] which is a great city, where rubies are procured; and he came with a large troop of knights and followers.

The ambassadors went to this lord of Balaxia, and asked him how he got the rubies; and he replied that near the city, there was a mountain whence they brought them, and that every day they broke up a rock in search of them. He said that when they found a vein, they got out the rubies skilfully, by breaking the rock all round with chisels. During the work, a great guard was set by order of Timour Beg; and Balaxia is ten days journey from Samarcand, in the direction of India.[2]

Another lord also came to the festival, who held the city of Aquivi[3] for Timour Beg, whence they procure the blue mineral, and in the rock they find sapphires. This city is also ten days journey from Samarcand, in the direction of India.

On Thursday, the 23rd of October, the lord gave a feast in the horde, and invited the ambassadors. The feast was prepared under a pavilion, and a great assemblage of people were collected, and they drank wine. At this feast there was much merriment and many games, and the ladies also came to eat in the pavilion, dressed as they were on former occasions, and the feast lasted all night.

[1] Badakshan?

[2] Badakshan is a mountainous region, including the upper part of the valley of the Oxus. The people are of the Tajik race, and possessed the country before the inroads of the Turks and Uzbegs. They are a wild race, living in villages, surrounded by gardens, in the little mountain glens. In the remote mountains of Badakshan there are the richest known mines of rubies and lapis lazuli. Marco Polo mentions that the chief of Badakshan laid claim to a Grecian origin, Baber corroborates the story, and Elphinstone says that the chief of Durwaz, in the valley of the Oxus, was a Macedonian. Burnes also believed in the descent of many of the chiefs of Badakshan from the Greeks of Bactria.

[3] Akshi? in Fergana.

VII.

THE CITY OF SAMARCAND.

On Thursday, the 30th of October, the lord left the encampment, and went to the city of Samarcand, where he lodged at some houses and a mosque which he had ordered to be built for the burial of one of his grandsons, named Mohammed Sultan Meerza, who was killed in Turkey, when Timour Beg conquered the Turk; and this grandson had himself taken the Turk prisoner, but had died of his wounds. The lord loved this grandson very dearly, and had, therefore, ordered this mosque to be built in his honour. The lord went on that day to celebrate a vigil feast, and invited the ambassadors. When they came, they were shown the chapel and tomb. This chapel was square and very high, and was covered, both inside and out, with blue and gold ornaments. When this grandson died in Turkey, the lord sent the body to be interred in Samarcand, and ordered this mosque to be built. When the lord arrived, he said the chapel was too low, so he ordered it to be pulled down, and rebuilt in ten days. They worked day and night, and he himself came twice to the city, to watch the progress; and the chapel was finished in ten days. It is a wonder that so great a work could have been completed in so short a time.

In honour of his grandson the lord gave a feast on this

day, at which many people were present, and much food was brought in, according to custom. After they had eaten, a councillor of the lord named Xamelaque Meerza, took the ambassadors before the lord, and dressed them in robes of honour, and in furs, which they wear in cold weather, lined with silk. These robes had two marten skins, one on each side of the neck. They also put hats on their heads, and gave them a bag containing one thousand five hundred bits of silver, being money which they call *tangaes*, each piece worth two silver rials. They then made their obeisance to the lord, according to the custom; and the lord said that they should come to him on another day, when he would speak with them, and dismiss them, to return to his son the king. When the lord saw that this work was completed, he ordered another to be built in the city, being moved by a desire to ennoble the city of Samarcand, and this new work was built for the following purpose.

In this city of Samarcand there is much merchandize, which comes every year from Cathay, India, Tartary, and many other parts; and as there is not a place for the orderly and regular display of the merchandize for sale, the lord ordered that a street should be made in the city, with shops for the sale of merchandize. This street was commenced at one end of the city, and went through to the other. He entrusted this work to two of his Meerzas, and let them know that if they did not use all diligence to complete it, working day and night, their heads should answer for it. These Meerzas began to work, by pulling down such houses as stood in the line by which the lord desired the street to run, and as the houses came down, their masters fled with their clothes and all they had: then, as the houses came down in front, the work went on behind. They made the street very broad, and covered it with a vaulted roof, having windows at intervals to let in the light.[1]

[1] One of the peculiarities of Samarcand is that each trade has its own

As soon as the shops were finished, people were made to occupy them, and sell their goods; and at intervals in this street there were fountains. A great number of workmen came into the city, and those who worked in the daytime, were relieved by others who worked all night. Some pulled down houses, others levelled the ground, and others built the street; and day and night they made such a noise, that they seemed to be like so many devils.

This great work was finished in twenty days, which was very wonderful; and the owners of the houses which were pulled down went to certain Cayris,[1] who were friends of the lord; and one day, when they were playing at chess with the lord, they said that, as he had caused those houses to be destroyed, he ought to make some amends to the owners. Upon this he got into a rage, and said, "This city is mine, and I bought it with my money, and possess the letters for it, which I will show you to-morrow; and, if it is right, I will pay the people, as you desire." When he had spoken, the Cayris were afraid, and they were surprised that he did not order them to be killed, or punished for having thus spoken; and they replied that all that the lord did was right, and that all his commands ought to be obeyed.

The mosque which the lord caused to be built, in honour of the mother of his wife Caño, was the most respected in the city. When it was finished, he thought the entrance was too low, so he ordered the building to be pulled down; and that it might be sooner rebuilt, he took charge of one part himself, and ordered his Meerzas to watch over the other. At this time he was infirm, and could neither go about on foot, nor on horseback, but only in a litter, in which he came every day, and remained for some time. This work, as well as the work of the new street, was stopped when the snows began to fall.

bazaar. Very excellent paper is manufactured here, and another production of art is the *kermezi* (crimson velvet).—*Baber's Memoirs.*

[1] Syuds? Descendants of the prophet.

On Friday, the 1st of November, the ambassadors went to see the lord, according to his order, expecting that he would dismiss them, and they found him at the mosque, which was being built. They waited from morning until noon, when the lord came out of a tent, and sat down on a carpet, where they brought him much meat and fruit. He sent to the ambassadors to say that they must excuse him that day, as he could not speak with them, having much business with his grandson Peer Mohammed, who was called king of India; and who was about to return to his own territory, whence he had come. On that day the lord gave him many horses, and robes, and arms, and knights to accompany him on his return.

On the following Saturday the ambassadors returned to the lord, as he had commanded, but he did not come out of his tent, because he felt ill. The ambassadors waited until noon, when he came out; but some of his courtiers told the ambassadors to go away, as he would not see them, so they returned to their lodgings.

On Sunday the ambassadors again went to the lord, to see if he would order them to be dismissed, and they waited a long time. The three confidential Meerzas asked them what they wanted, and told them to return to their lodgings, as the lord would not see them. They then sent for the knight who had charge of them, asked him why he had let them come, and ordered his nose to be pierced through; but he proved that he did not send them, nor had he seen them that day, and he thus escaped, with only a sound flogging. The Meerzas did this, because the lord was very sick, and all his women and attendants were running about in a state of bewilderment: so the Meerzas told the ambassadors to return to their lodgings, and to remain there, until they were sent for.

The ambassadors returned there, and they neither went to the lord, nor did he send for them; but a Zagatay came and said that the Meerzas of the lord had sent him to say that they were to prepare to start on their journey the following day, in the morning, with the ambassadors from the Sultan of Babylon, from Turkey, and with Carvo Toman Oghlan, who was to accompany them as far as the city of Tabreez, and supply them with food, and all that they required. He added that, at Tabreez, Omar Meerza, the grandson of the lord, would dismiss them to their own land.

The ambassadors answered that the lord had not yet dismissed them, nor sent any compliments to the lord their king, and they desired to know how this could be; and he told them that he had nothing more to say, and that the Meerzas had ordered him to give this message to them, and to the other ambassadors. The ambassadors then went to the Meerzas, at the palace, and told them that they knew very well what the lord had said to them the Thursday before, with his own mouth, that they should come to him, and that he would speak to them, and dismiss them: but that now the Meerzas had sent a man to them, to tell them to prepare to start the next day, at which they were very much surprised. The Meerzas answered that they could not see the lord, and that they must prepare to start next day, as they were now dismissed.

The Meerzas did this because the lord was very ill, had lost the power of speech, and was at the point of death, as the ambassadors were told by those who knew it for certain; and this hurry arose, because the lord was dying,[1] and the Meerzas wished them to be gone, before his death became known, that they might not publish the news in their own countries. To the remonstrances which the ambassadors

[1] Timour did not die until February 17th, 1405, at Otrar, beyond the river Jaxartes, when he was marching to invade China. He was, however, subject to very severe attacks of illness, and Mirkhond mentions that he was seized by one of those attacks, which not unfrequently succeeded to any sudden change from violent motion in the field to perfect domestic repose, at this very time. He recovered in a week.—*Price.*

constantly urged upon the Meerzas, that they ought not to be dismissed in this way, without any message from the lord, to the lord their king; the Meerzas answered that they had nothing more to say, further than that the ambassadors were to go.

On the 18th of November, the Meerzas sent the Zagatay, who was to accompany the ambassadors, to say that they were to depart; and they replied that they would not go, without either seeing the lord, or receiving a letter from him; but he said that they must either go at once with all the supplies due to their rank, or stay, and go at another time without them. On that day, therefore, they left the place where they were lodging, and went to a garden near the city, with the ambassador from the sultan of Babylon, where they were ordered to wait for the ambassadors from Turkey. They remained in this garden until Friday the 21st of November, when they all assembled, and departed from Samarcand.

Now that I have related those things which befell the ambassadors in this city of Samarcand, I will give an account of that city and its territory, and of the things which the lord has done to ennoble it.

The city of Samarcand is situated in a plain, and surrounded by an earthen wall. It is a little larger than the city of Seville, but, outside the city, there are a great number of houses, joined together in many parts, so as to form suburbs. The city is surrounded on all sides by many gardens and vineyards, which extend in some directions a league and a half, in others two leagues, the city being in the middle. In these houses and gardens there is a large population, and there are people selling bread, meat, and many other things; so that the suburbs are much more thickly inhabited than the city within the walls. Amongst these gardens, which are outside the city, there are great and noble houses, and here the lord has several palaces.[1] The nobles of the city have

[1] On the south of Samarcand is the garden of paradise, and the plane

their houses amongst these gardens, and they are so extensive that, when a man approaches the city, he sees nothing but a mass of very high trees. Many streams of water flow through the city, and through these gardens, and among these gardens there are many cotton plantations, and melon grounds, and the melons of this land are good and plentiful; and at Christmas time there is a wonderful quantity of melons and grapes. Every day so many camels come in, laden with melons, that it is a wonder how the people can eat them all. They preserve them from year to year in the villages, in the same way as figs, taking off their skins, cutting them in large slices, and then drying them in the sun.

Outside the city there are great plains, which are covered with populous villages, peopled by the captives which the lord caused to be taken from the countries which he conquered. The land is very plentiful in all things, as well bread as wine, fruit, meat, and birds; and the sheep are very large, and have long tails, some weighing twenty pounds, and they are as much as a man can hold in his hand. These sheep are so abundant in the market that, even when the lord was there with all his host, a pair was worth only a ducat. Other things are so plentiful, that for a *meri*, which is half a rial, they sell a *fanega*[1] and a half of barley, and the quantity of bread and rice is infinite.

The city is so large, and so abundantly supplied, that it is wonderful; and the name of Samarcand or Cimes-quinte is derived from the two words *cimes* great, and *quinte* a town. The supplies of this city do not consist of food alone, but of silks, satins, gauzes, tafetas, velvets, and other things. The lord had so strong a desire to ennoble this city, that he

tree garden. On the east is the heart delighting garden, from which there is a public avenue planted with trees, all the way to the torquoise gate. In the garden of Dervish Khan there are elms, poplars, and cypresses. Another garden is named the miniature of the world.—*Baber's Memoirs.*

[1] A bushel.

brought captives to increase its population, from every land which he conquered, especially all those who were skilful in any art. From Damascus he brought weavers of silk, and men who made bows, glass, and earthenware, so that, of those articles, Samarcand produces the best in the world. From Turkey he brought archers, masons, and silversmiths. He also brought men skilled in making engines of war: and he sowed hemp and flax, which had never before been seen in the land.

There was so great a number of people brought to this city, from all parts, both men and women, that they are said to have amounted to one hundred and fifty thousand persons, of many nations, Turks, Arabs, and Moors, Christian Armenians, Greek Catholics, and Jacobites, and those who baptize with fire in the face,[1] who are Christians with peculiar opinions. There was such a multitude of these people that the city was not large enough to hold them, and it was wonderful what a number lived under trees, and in caves outside.

The city is also very rich in merchandize which comes from other parts. Russia and Tartary send linen and skins; China sends silks, which are the best in the world, (more especially the satins), and musk, which is found in no other part of the world, rubies and diamonds, pearls and rhubarb, and many other things. The merchandize which comes from China is the best and most precious which comes to this city, and they say that the people of China are the most skilful workmen in the world. They say themselves that they have two eyes, the Franks one, and that the Moors are blind, so that they have the advantage of every other nation in the world. From India come spices, such as nutmegs, cloves, mace, cinnamon, ginger, and many others which do not reach Alexandria.

In the city there are many open places, in which they sell

[1] Brahmins? or Parsees?

meat cooked in many ways, fowls and other birds very nicely dressed; and they are always selling, day and night, in these places. There are also many places for killing meat, fowls, pheasants, and partridges. At one end of the city there is a castle, which is defended on one side by a stream flowing through a deep ravine, and is very strong. The lord kept his treasure in that castle, and no man entered it except the magistrate and his officers. In this castle the lord had as many as a thousand captives, who were skilful workmen, and laboured all the year round at making head pieces, and bows and arrows.

When the lord departed from the city, to make war on the Turk, and to destroy Damascus, he ordered that all those who had to follow his host, should bring their women; and he did this because he intended to be absent from the city, fighting his enemies, for seven years, and he swore that he would not enter the castle, until that time was completed. When the lord returned to the city, the ambassadors from Cathay arrived, with orders to say that the lord held that land, subject to the emperor of Cathay, and to demand the payment of tribute every year, as it was seven years since any had been paid. The lord answered that this was true, but that he would not pay it. This tribute had not been paid for nearly eight years, nor had the emperor of Cathay sent for it, and the reason why he did not send for it, was this.

The emperor of Cathay died, leaving three sons, to whom he bequeathed his territories. The eldest son wished to take the shares of the other two. He killed the youngest, but the middle one fought with the eldest, and defeated him, and he, from despair at the consequences which he dreaded would follow his treatment of his youngest brother, set fire to his palace, and perished with many of his followers. The middle brother, therefore, reigned alone.[1] As soon as he was

[1] Choo-yuen-chang, the founder of the Ming Dynasty, was the son of

quietly established in his own empire, he sent these ambassadors to Timour Beg, to demand the tribute which was formerly paid to his father, but we did not hear whether he resented the answer which was given by Timour.

From Samarcand to the chief city of the empire of Cathay, called Cambalu, is a journey of six months,[1] two of which are passed in crossing an uninhabited land, never visited by any one but shepherds, who wander with their flocks, in search of pasture. In this year as many as eight hundred camels, laden with merchandize, came from Cambalu to this city of Samarcand, in the month of June. When Timour Beg heard what the ambassadors from Cathay had demanded, he ordered these camels to be detained, and we saw the men who came with the camels. They related wonderful things, concerning the great power of the lord of Cathay: we especially spoke to one of these men, who had been six

a common labourer, and served during his youth as scullion in a temple. He rose from a soldier to the command of a band of robbers, and thence to be the conqueror of provinces, and founder of a Dynasty. He drove the Mongols out of China, and in 1368, having expelled the Yuen Dynasty of the lineage of Zengis Khan, he became emperor of China, and is known in history as Hung-woo. He restored tranquillity to China, and drove the Mongols into their native deserts.

In 1399 Hung-woo was succeeded by his grandson Keen-wan, much against the wishes of his sons. This prince disgraced all his uncles but one, the prince of Yen, who advanced with a large army to avenge his brothers. He captured Nankin, degraded the young emperor, and committed many acts of cruelty.

The new emperor took the name of Yung-la in 1403, and transferred the capital from Nankin to Pekin; whence he carried his victorious arms far into the deserts of Tartary. He died in 1425. This is the passage in Chinese history, which is somewhat differently related in the text by the Spanish knight; and it was after these victories that Yung-la sent his insolent message to Timour. It would have been answered by the invasion of China, had not death cut short the career of the mighty conqueror.

[1] The town of Yarkand, on the extreme Western frontier of the Chinese dominions, is five months journey from Pekin. A telegraph, by means of beacons, can transmit a message in six days, and an extraordinary express can go over the distance in thirty-five days.

months in the city of Cambalu, which he said was near the sea, and twenty times as large as Tabreez. The city of Cambalu is the largest in the world, because Tabreez is a good league in length, so that Cambalu must be twenty leagues in extent. He also said that the lord of Cathay had so vast an army that, when he collected troops to march beyond his own territory, not counting those who thus departed with him, four hundred thousand cavalry and more were left to guard the land; he added that it was the custom of this lord of Cathay not to allow any man to mount a horse, unless he had a thousand followers; and he told many others wonders, concerning this city of Cambalu, and the land of Cathay.

This emperor of Cathay used to be a gentile, but he was converted to the faith of the Christians.[1]

While the ambassadors were in Samarcand, the seven years were completed, during which Timour Beg had sworn he would not enter the castle containing his treasure. He went to it, with much pomp and festivity, and all the arms which the captives had made since he departed, were carried before him, amongst which were three thousand pairs of breastplates, adorned with red cloth, well made, except that they are not strong, and that these people do not understand how to temper the iron. They also carried a great number of helmets; and on that day the lord divided the breastplates and helmets amongst his knights, and other followers. The helmets are round and high, and in front a plate, two fingers broad, descends as far down as the chin, which can be moved up and down, and is intended to protect the face from a sword cut. The breast plates are made like ours, except that long skirts of cloth hang from them, like shirts.

Fifteen days journey from the city of Samarcand, in the direction of China, there is a land inhabited by Amazons, and

[1] Yung-la is said to have promoted literature, and continued the universal toleration granted by his father Hung-woo, but his christianity may be doubted.

to this day they continue the custom of having no men with them, except at one time of the year; when they are permitted, by their leaders, to go with their daughters to the nearest settlements, and have communication with men, each taking the one who pleases her most, with whom they live, and eat, and drink, after which they return to their own land. If they bring forth daughters afterwards, they keep them; but they send the sons to their fathers. These women are subject to Timour Beg; they used to be under the emperor of Cathay, and they are Christians of the Greek Church. They are of the lineage of the Amazons who were at Troy, when it was destroyed by the Greeks.

The city of Samarcand is supplied with judges, and justice is maintained; for the people do not use force against each other, but refer their quarrels to the decision of the lord. Timour Beg always has judges with him, who administer justice in the following manner:—some of them judge the great quarrels which occur amongst these people, whilst others look after questions connected with the revenue of the lord. Three tents are pitched, at the court, where they hear the cases that are brought before them, and afterwards report them to the lord. When they order any letter to be written, their scribes presently write it in few words, and enter it in their registers, which they keep by them. They then deliver it to the judge, who puts four silver seals on it, with another seal of the lord in the middle, bearing an inscription which means "*the truth*"; and having three marks upon it, like this,—$\substack{\circ\circ\\\circ}$. Thus each judge has his clerk, and his register. When a letter bearing this seal reaches a Meerza, the orders it contains are complied with on that day, and that hour.

Now that I have written concerning the city of Samarcand, and of what happened to the ambassadors in it, I will relate, in this place, how Timour Beg conquered and destroyed Tokatmish, formerly emperor of Tartary, a powerful and valiant man, and a greater sovereign than the Turk himself. It is about eleven years since this emperor of Tartary, Tokatmish, being a great lord, and having a large army, sallied forth from Tartary with a powerful host, invaded Persia, and entered the province of Tabreez, devastating the land, and pillaging the towns and villages.[1] After he had committed this havock in the terrritory of Timour Beg, he returned into Tartary. This aggression came to the knowledge of Timour Beg, so he marched after the invader, with a smaller force, and overtook him on the banks of a great river called Tesina, which is near Tartary. Timour Beg marched, as fast he could, to secure a pass over the river, for in that part of the country there was no ford, except the one which Timour was intent upon reaching. When he arrived, the emperor Tokatmish had already crossed the river; and, as he knew that Timour Beg followed him, he turned round to defend the ford, and barricaded it with wood.

When Timour Beg reached the river, and found that Tokatmish guarded the ford, he sent to say that he did not come to fight, but that he was his friend. Notwithstanding this, the emperor continued to guard the ford; and next day Timour Beg marched up the river, Tokatmish keeping abreast of him, on the opposite side, and when Timour Beg halted on one side, Tokatmish encamped opposite. In this way they went on for three days, and on the third night Timour Beg ordered the women to put helmets on their heads, that they might look like men; and all the men rode on, with two horses a piece, leaving the royal encampment, the women who looked like men, the servants, and the prisoners. Timour then returned to the ford, and crossed the river. At midnight he fell upon the Tartar camp, routed the army, took all the spoils, and Tokatmish escaped by flight. This was a famous deed; for Tokatmish had a great army, and it was said to be one of the greatest victories of Timour Beg, for Tokatmish was more powerful than the Turk.

[1] In 1395.

Notwithstanding this disaster, Tokatmish assembled another army, but Timour Beg again defeated him, and he fled. Upon this the Tartars were disheartened, and they said that their lord had no luck, and there was discord amongst them. A knight, who was a servant of Timour Beg, named Ediguy, hearing that there was discord amongst the Tartars, proposed to fight against his master, and they chose him for their lord, so he rebelled against Timour Beg. Now this new lord of Tartary is a very powerful man, and there is much enmity between him and Timour Beg. The lord once marched against him, but Ediguy retreated; and this Ediguy has a horde of more than two hundred thousand cavalry.[1]

Tokatmish and Timour Beg then became friends, and worked together to entrap this Ediguy, to whom Timour Beg sent a message, saying that he loved him and pardoned him, and proposed that he should give one of his daughters in marriage to one of Timour's grandsons. The said Ediguy answered that he had lived with Timour for twenty years, and that he knew him well, and all his tricks, so that he could not deceive him; and that if they were to be friends, they must be friends with swords in their hands.

The emperor Tokatmish had a son who was also driven out of the land of Tartary by Ediguy; and Tokatmish fled to a land, bordering on Samarcand, and his son to Caffa, a city of the Genoese. Ediguy marched against Caffa, and did much damage to the surrounding country, so the people of the city made peace with him, and the son of Tokatmish fled to the court of Timour Beg. Tokatmish, and his sons, are now alive, and friends of Timour Beg. Ediguy converts some of the Tartars to the faith of Mohammed every day, for, a short time ago, they were not good believers in that faith.

The lord arranges the host which follows him every day, in this manner. He divides it into captaincies, and has captains over a hundred men, others over a thousand, others

[1] Kaverchik or Coiritchak Oglou, seems to have succeeded Tokatmish.

over ten thousand, and one over all, as constable: and when a force is ordered to march to any place, the orders are given through these captains.[1] The present captain general is called Janza Meerza, and he was one of those who assisted Timour Beg, at the death of the late emperor of Samarcand; for which he has received much land, and much favour, and been made a great lord. Timour Beg also gives his knights charge over the horses and sheep, some a thousand, others ten thousand; and if they do not produce them, when they are called for, or if any are wanting, they receive no other pay than the seizure of all they possess.

[1] When ten soldiers, men of proof, were collected together, I ordained that one distinguished for valour should, with the consent of the remaining nine, be commander over them, and be called *Oun-bashee.* When ten *Oun-bashees* were assembled one of them was leader, called *Euz-bashee.* When ten *Euz-bashees* were collected together, an officer of exalted lineage, son of a chief, of approved valour and knowledge, took the command, called *Ming-bashee.—Timour's Institutes.*

VIII.

THE RETURN OF THE AMBASSADORS.

Now that I have related the transactions which you have heard, I will write an account of the return of the ambassadors, and of what befell them on the road. They were accompanied by the ambassador from the Sultan of Babylon, and another knight who was brother to a great lord of Turkey, named Alaman Oglan, another from Sebaste, another from the city of Altologo, and another from the city which is called Palatia, and they all departed in company.

On Friday, which was the 21st of November, the ambassadors departed from Samarcand, and travelled along a level road, through a well peopled country, for six days, and they were supplied with all they required, as well lodging as food.

On Thursday, the 27th of November, they arrived at a great city called Boyar, which is in a great plain, and is surrounded by a wall of earth, at one end of which there is a castle, also built of earth, for in that land there are no stones for building a wall; and a river flowed close by the castle. In this city there was a quarter in which there were great edifices, and the place is well supplied with bread, meat, and wine, and there is much trade. The ambassadors were well supplied with horses, and all that they required. I will not write at any length respecting the events of this journey, because I have already written at large on the subject. They remained seven days in this city, and much snow fell, while they were there.

On Friday, the 5th of December, the ambassadors departed, and travelled for three days over plains covered with many populous villages, when they reached the great river of Biamo,[1] which I have already described. At a village near the banks they collected provisions of meat and barley, as they had to cross a desert which would take six days; and they remained in this village for two days.

On Wednesday, the 10th of December, they crossed the great river of Biamo in boats. On the banks there were great plains of sand, and the sand was moved from one part to another, by the wind, and thrown up in mounds. In this sandy waste there are great valleys and hills, and the wind blew the sand away from one hill to another, for it was very light; and on the ground, where the wind had blown away the sand, the marks of waves were left: and men could not keep their eyes on this sand, when the sun was shining. This road cannot be travelled over, without a guide who knows the marks and signs of the desert, and these guides are called *Anchies,* and the ambassadors had one of these guides. On this road there is no water, except a few wells sunk in the sand, with vaulted roofs, and surrounded by brick walls, for if they were not covered, the sand would fill them up. The water of these wells is either rain or snow water; and in the last day's journey, they found no water, and they travelled all night; but at the hour of mass they came to a well, and drank, and gave water to their beasts, and they all had much need of it.

On Sunday, the 14th of December, they reached a village, and stayed there until Wednesday, when they entered a desert, which was of great extent, being six days journey

[1] Amou or Oxus. He calls it *Viadme* in another place.

across, but having more water than the first. Along the road there were low shrubs,[1] growing in a sandy soil, and it was very hot. The three last journeys over this desert were very long, for they travelled day and night, and only stopped to feed the men and horses. On Sunday, the 21st of December, they arrived at a great city called Baubartel, belonging to the government of Khorassan, which is at the foot of snow peaked mountains, and is a very cold place, and the city was in a plain, and had no wall. Here they gave the ambassadors horses and food, and all that they required; and they remained until Wednesday.

On Thursday, the 25th of December, being Christmas day, which ended the year of our Lord 1405, they departed, and travelled over high snowy mountains for five days, and the land was thinly inhabited, and very cold.

On Thursday, the 1st of January, they came to a very large city, which was on a plain beyond these mountains, and was called Cabria, and it had no wall. They remained here until Saturday, and this city is in the land of Media.

On Saturday, the 3rd of January, they departed, and travelled over plains, in a hot country, without any ice or snow. On Monday, they came to a city called Jagaro, without any wall, and they were now on the same road that they had travelled over in coming.

On Wednesday, they again set out, and travelled over plains, without coming to any habitation during the whole day, and they passed the night in a large building, near a ruined castle, and the building was also deserted.

On Thursday, they departed, and travelled the whole day without seeing any inhabited place; but in the evening they came to a village; and the road, during the last two days, had traversed a hilly country, without snow, and very hot.

On Friday they travelled all day, without seeing any habitation; but on Saturday, at the hour of vespers, they

[1] Camel thorn.

came to a large city called Bostan. On Monday, they arrived at Damghan, and when they were about a league from that city, a strong cold wind sprung up, the day being clear, and the cold was so great, that it was very wonderful how the men and beasts could endure it. When they came to the city, they inquired concerning that strong wind; and they were told that in a hill above the city, there was a fountain, and that when any dirty thing fell into it, a fierce wind rose up, which did not cease until it was clean again. The following day some men were sent with staves and hooks to clean the fountain, upon which the wind went down. The ambassadors rested for two days.

On Wednesday, the 15th of January, they departed, and left the road to the castle of Perescote, by which they had come, because it went over snowy mountains. They took the left hand road, and travelled over a plain. In the night they slept at a large deserted building, and, travelling for two days without coming to any inhabited place, they reached a great city called Cenan,[1] on Saturday, at the hour of vespers. Here the land of Media ended, and Persia commenced.

This city is in a plain, at the foot of some high mountains. It is very populous, and has no wall. On Tuesday, they came to a small castle, and there was much snow on the road. They then travelled over hills, where there are many springs of brackish water; and on Friday, the 23rd of January, they came to a great city called Vatami, which was nearly depopulated, and without any wall, and they call this land, the land of Rei. In this land there was a great Meerza, who was son-in-law to Timour Beg, having married his daughter. He was with another great knight named

[1] Semnoon, the first town in Khorassan, coming from Teheran. Close round the walls there is a little cultivation, but the rest of the plain is brown and desolate up to the feet of the mountains, which frown in gloomy grandeur around it. It is a wretched poverty stricken place.—*Fraser; Ferier.*

Baxam Beg, and the son-in-law of Timour Beg was named Cumalexa Meerza. These were the people who took charge of the servants of the ambassadors, when they were sick, and they found them all there, except two who had died. Those who survived had been kindly treated by these lords, who always provided them with what they wanted. On Monday the ambassadors dined with the son-in-law of the lord, who gave them fresh horses, and on Tuesday they departed.

On Thursday, the 29th of January, they came to a city called Xaharica, and here they again joined the road which they had travelled over in coming. From Friday to Monday they rode on, and found much snow on the road; and on Tuesday, the 3rd of February, they reached a great city called Casmonil,[1] and most of it was in ruins; but it was once the largest city in those countries, except Tabreez and Samarcand. In this city we found much snow, so that we could not walk in the streets, and the snow that fell on the roofs of the houses was pushed off that it might not destroy them, and we could not leave this city, on account of the quantity of snow on the roads. The ambassadors were here supplied with food, and all that they required. On Saturday, they departed, and thirty men went before them, on foot, with poles in their hands, to open the road; and when they reached a village, these men returned, and others took their places. The snow was such that the ground was covered with it to a great depth, and no land could be seen. Both men and beasts were unable to see out of their eyes, on account of the snow; and when they approached a city or village, they could not see it for the quantity of snow, and in this way they arrived at the city of Sultanieh.

They reached Sultanieh on Friday, the 13th of February, and remained there until the following Saturday; but I will say no more concerning this city, because I have already described it, when the ambassadors passed through it

[1] Kazveen?

before; only that it is one of the largest and most noble cities of Persia, and that it has a beautiful castle, but no wall. They were eight days in this city, because they were forced to go and visit a grandson of the lord Timour Beg, named Omar Meërza, who was lord of Persia and other countries, and was wintering with his host in the plain which they call Karabagh. The most direct road to go there was by this city of Sultanieh, but as there was much snow on a range of mountains which they would have to cross, they waited until it became passable. Finally they were advised to go on to the city of Tabreez, whence they might more easily reach Karabagh, and they decided upon doing so.

On Saturday, the 21st of February, they left Sultanieh, and slept in a city called Sanga,[1] which they had passed through in coming; and on Sunday they slept in a great building near the road. On Tuesday they passed the night at a village called Miana, and on Wednesday they came to a village called Tunglar.

On Saturday, the last day of February, they arrived at the city of Tabreez, where they were lodged in the houses of Armenian Christians, and supplied with much food. On the 3rd of March, the ambassadors were presented with horses, and were told that Omar Meerza was at Karabagh, where he had wintered with his host. Karabagh consists of flat plains, with much pasture; and it is a very hot country, and if the snow ever falls it melts directly, and for this reason the lord of Persia goes every year to winter there.

On Thursday, the 5th of March, the ambassadors departed from the city of Tabreez, in company with the ambassadors from the Sultan of Babylon and from Turkey, to visit Omar Meerza on the plains of Karabagh. They were attended by the guide who had brought them from Samarcand, and had supplied them with all that they required, and they call these guides, *Xagave*. The ambassadors were

[1] Zenjan.

accompanied by a few men, but they left the rest of their retinue at Tabreez, as they were going to return thither. When they were two days journey from Tabreez, they met a messenger from Omar Meerza, who said that the lord desired they would return to Tabreez, and remain there until he should send for them. They therefore returned, and remained in that city until the 18th of March.

On Thursday, the 19th of March, they departed from Tabreez, and, passing a high hill near the city, entered a well-peopled valley, full of villages, gardens, and vineyards. The country was very hot, and very beautiful, and abounded in fruit; and a great river flowed through the centre of this valley. They travelled through this valley, amongst gardens and villages, for four days, at the end of which time they reached a great plain, also covered with villages, and on this plain much rice and millet was sown; and this country supplies many other lands with rice. They do not raise any wheat or barley, but there is so much rice, that they give it to the horses. On this plain many tribes were encamped, with their tents and flocks, which belonged to the host of the lord.

On Wednesday, the 25th of March, the said ambassadors, being now about ten or twelve leagues from the lord's encampment, met some men who said that there was a great tumult in the camp, and that they had better return. They inquired what was the cause of the tumult, and the men replied that Janza Meerza wished to kill Omar Meerza, but that the attendants and troops had seized him, and that the lord had ordered his head to be cut off. The people of Janza Meerza were, therefore, fighting with those of the lord, and men had been killed on both sides. The lord was about to cross over to the other side of the river, and break down the bridge; but the men knew no more, except that there was great confusion in the camp. The ambassadors consulted together, and determined to proceed.

On Thursday, the 26th of March, they reached the horde where the lord was, and dismounted, waiting to be sent for. There was great confusion in the horde, and every one was driving the flocks together. After waiting some time, a Zagatay came to them, and said that the lord was much engaged, and could not see them, and that they must return to Tabreez, and wait there for his commands.

This lord was encamped, with his host, on a plain near the banks of a river, and he had with him about forty thousand cavalry, but the whole of his army was not united, some divisions being detached in other places. As Timour Beg was accustomed to winter in these plains of Karabagh, he ordered a city to be built there, which contained twenty thousand houses and more.

This Janza Meerza, whose head Omar Meerza had just cut off, was the son of a sister of Timour Beg, and was the most valiant man of the family, and was the lord of much land, having a large army, which always marched with him. When Timour Beg made his grandson Omar Meerza lord of Persia, he appointed Janza Meerza to accompany him and regulate his household. The reasons why Janza Meerza was put to death, are related in two ways. Some say that it rose from jealousy, because Omar Meerza feared that, on the death of Timour Beg, Janza would rise against him with all his troops, and with all the Zagatays of his grandfather, who loved him very much; others say that, as soon as he heard of the death of Timour Beg, Janza armed himself, and some of his followers, and went to a tent, where the council used to meet. Here he met a Mollah, who was intimate with Omar Meerza. Janza had evil designs on a woman, whom Omar Meerza refused to give him in marriage, and he had given her to this Mollah; so Janza killed the Mollah, and then went to the tent of Omar Meerza, with his sword drawn, and followed by his men. When the guards saw this, they also went to the tent, and a rumour went through the camp that Ediguy, the emperor of Tartary, had attacked it, and that Janza, in the confusion, had gone to the tent of the lord to kill him. The troops ran to the tent, and a great knight rode up to Janza Meerza, and asked him what he was doing. Janza answered that Omar Meerza need have no fear, for that he was only doing this, to kill his enemy the Mollah. The knight found Omar in a state of great fear, with few troops, and he said to him,—"My lord, have no fear, for if it is your wish, I will kill this Janza Meerza": and he attacked him, and cut off his head.

When Janza was killed all his followers fled, and Omar Meerza ordered the head of Janza to be taken to his father Miran Meerza, and to his brother Abubeker Meerza, who were in Baldat, with a message that he had sent them the head of his enemy; and that, as his grandfather was now dead, they should come to see him, and unite their forces on the plains of Kian, near Tabreez, where he and his nobles would acknowledge Miran Meerza as their lord, according to right and justice.

After the death of Timour Beg,[1] who expired in the city of Samarcand, the Meerzas and confidential friends of the late lord concealed his death, until they could secure the treasure; but they could not keep it so close, but that some of the knights and followers knew it. There was present in the city of Samarcand, on the death of Timour Beg, one of his grandsons, a son of Miran Meerza, named Khuleel Sultan;[2] who, as soon as he heard of the death of his grand-

[1] In February 1405.

[2] Khuleel Sultan was crowned at Samarcand in March 1405. He was the slave of a passion for Shad Mulk, a depraved intriguing woman. In a short time he dissipated all the imperial treasury amongst the basest profligates, and the Ameers were disgusted with his government. Finally he was sent a prisoner to Kashgar, and his beloved Shad Mulk was led in chains through Samarcand. Shah Rokh, the son of Timour, and ruler of Khorassan, was then called to the head of affairs at Samarcand, in 1408. He generously liberated Khuleel Sultan, restored his love to his arms, and sent him into Khorassan. The lovers were

father, collected as many friends and followers as he could, and went to the three Meerzas who held the palace and treasure of the lord in their possession. He killed one of the three, named Botudo Meerza, a son of that Janza who had been beheaded by Omar Meerza, and the other two fled to the land of Khorassan, which was ruled by a son of Timour Beg, named Shah Rokh, who lived in a great city called Herat.

When Khuleel Sultan had killed his grandfather's intimate friend, he went to the castle, and got possession of the treasure and the city. He then caused the body of his grandfather to be buried, and sent a message to his father, Miran Meerza, asking him to come to Samarcand and take charge of the treasure, and he declared that he should be lord, as his father had been. All the Zagatays, he added, would join him, if he possessed that great treasure; but others said that Gansada, the wife of Miran Meerza, who had returned to Timour Beg, would prevent this, as she was the mother of Khuleel Sultan, and was with her son at Samarcand.

This Khuleel Sultan is a youth, of twenty-two years of age, and he is fair, and stout in his person, like his father. He was very hospitable to the ambassadors when they were in Samarcand.

It had been twice before reported that Timour Beg was dead, to see who would rebel; and he had presently fallen upon those who rebelled, and crushed them; so that men would not now believe that he was dead, and afterwards news came to Tabreez, where the ambassadors then were, that he was alive, and marching with his army against the Sultan of Babylon.

Miran Meerza, as soon as he knew for certain that Timour Beg was dead, and had seen the head of Janza Meerza, which his son had sent him, left the city of Baldan, with

buried in one grave, in 1409, Shad Mulk having stabbed herself over the body of her husband.

his son Abubeker Meerza. He knew that his son Omar Meerza had collected a large force, and had sent to the cities of Tabreez and Sultanieh, to prepare for his arrival. When the father heard this, he became jealous of his son, and would not join him. But when his other son Abubeker heard it, he said to his father that he would go to his brother, seize upon him, and bring him before Miran Meerza, but his father would not consent to this.

Abubeker Meerza and Omar Meerza were own brothers, and their mother went to Omar, and said, "My son! thy father ought to be lord, and every one wishes it, yet you hinder it." He answered, "God forbid! I am ready to obey his orders." The mother then returned to her husband, and told him what had happened, and Miran Meerza determined to send his other son, that both brothers might arrange how to secure the sovereignty to their father. As soon as Omar Meerza knew that his brother was approaching, he came out of the tent, took his hand, and led him in; but when he was inside, he ordered him to be secured; and about five hundred followers, who attended him, fled back to his father.

He sent his brother in chains to the castle of Sultanieh, and then marched against his father, to take him also, but he fled to the land of Rei, where Culemax Meerza, his brother-in-law, and other Zagatay knights, were assembled.

The mother of Omar Meerza and Abubeker Meerza, when she knew that the one had imprisoned the other, went to Omar Meerza, rending her clothes and weeping, and said, "I bore you, my son! and now you wish to kill your brother, knowing that he is your own brother, and that he is well beloved by all men." He answered that he had only imprisoned his brother, because he was mad and insolent, and that he only desired that his father should be lord.

After he had taken his brother prisoner, he found that he was beloved by the Zagatays; but he still endeavoured to secure his father, and marched after him, on the road to Samarcand. When he could not capture him, he proposed to his uncle, Shah Rokh, to divide the sovereignty between them. When Miran Meerza heard that this agreement had been made, he stayed in Khorassan. At this time Omar Meerza sent a letter to the ambassadors, who were in the city of Tabreez, saying that they should not be impatient, because they were not dismissed, for that they would very shortly be sent away.

On Tuesday, the 29th of April, being the day of St. Peter Martyr, the ambassadors being in their lodging, an officer of the city came to them, with a scribe and many other followers, and said that the lord had ordered that they should give up everything they possessed. The ambassadors answered that they were in the lord's power, but that the king their lord had sent them to visit Timour Beg as friends, and that as that great lord was dead, they could do as they pleased. The officer replied that the lord did not wish to do them any harm. He did not, however, intend to act as he spoke, but in quite an opposite way. He took away everything they had, as well money as horses, clothes, and saddles, leaving them only the clothes which they had on; and placed them in another house, under a guard. The same was done to the other ambassadors, who were robbed of all their property.

After twenty days, Omar Meerza sent to say that they must not be annoyed at what had been done, as he should be delighted to please them, and that they must come to a place near Tabreez, called Assarec, where he would be encamped, and that he would dismiss them. But this was not the truth, as he had not caught his father yet, and the Zagatays could not ascertain where his army was; for these people are deceitful, and never tell the truth. Thus the ambassadors had to wait until the lord Omar Meerza should arrive at Assarac.

At this time the king of Georgia rebelled, and entered the land of Aumian and of Asseron,[1] in Armenia, marching towards the city of Tabreez, and burning the villages, causing great terror amongst the people. The lord sent one of his knights, named Omar Toban, with six thousand cavalry, to this frontier, and ordered the people of Tabreez to join him, who made up a body of fifteen thousand cavalry. They marched out of Tabreez, and took up a position on the plains of Alatoa. The king, when he knew this, attacked them in the night, and defeated them with great slaughter, and those who escaped, fled to Tabreez. The noise and terror amongst the Moors of that city were great, and they were ashamed that the Kafirs should have conquered the Mussulmans, for they call the Christians by the name of Kafirs, meaning a people without laws; and Mussulman means those of the chosen and good law. Others said that this would not have happened if their lord had any luck, but that the fortunate Timour Beg was now dead.

When Omar Meerza was unable to capture his father, he returned to the city of Sultanieh, where he kept his brother in prison, and ordered him to be poisoned; and he then started for Assarec, to collect his army, and dismiss the ambassadors. While he was on the road, the news arrived that his brother Abubeker had escaped from prison, killed the guards, and robbed the treasury; so he returned towards Sultanieh, and sent a troop in chase of his brother, which could not overtake him.

Omar Meerza had left orders that his brother should be poisoned; but some of his men knew of it, and told Abubeker Meerza, and arranged to assist him in escaping. They settled that his horses and arms should be got ready, and that they should give him a sword, so that when his gaolor entered, he might kill him, when they would come quickly to aid in his escape from his prison; and this was done: for

[1] Erzeroum.

the next day in the morning, the knight who guarded him entered his prison, with three other men, and said: "Sire, your brother has sent me to say that he wishes us to take you from this place, and give you plenty of money, and other things which may please you; and, on account of this news, I beg you will drink wine with me." He brought this wine with him, and in it there was the poison which was to kill Abubeker, and their custom is to drink wine before they eat. The knight went down on his knees, and, offering the cup of wine, asked Abubeker to drink; but he excused himself, and then seized the sword, and gave the knight a cut on the head, which killed him. The three others who were with him ran out, and alarmed the people in the castle, but Abubeker's followers came in and cut his fetters, which were of silver; so he mounted his horse, and rode away with his followers to a place where the dues were collected, killing a treasurer whom they found there. At this noise a number of people came to him, and demanded good horses, which they took from the merchants and other people, and as many as five hundred horsemen were collected. So he returned to the castle, and divided the treasure amongst them, giving to each as much as he could carry. He loaded a hundred camels with what remained, and went in search of his father.

When he found his father, he told him that his brother, Shah Rokh, would not let him pass, on his way to Samarcand; but he marched on that night, with his own followers, and those of his father, and went to the place where his father's brother was, seizing him, and bringing him before his father; and many people joined him. Every day, also, the followers of Omar Meerza came over to him; so Omar made friends with his father, and Abubeker and his father took the road towards Samarcand.[1]

[1] In July, 1406, Sultan Ahmed, the Eelkhanee of Irak, and Kara Yusuf, a Turkish chief, retook Bagdad, and also occupied Tabreez, Omar

Omar Meerza marched with his host to the plains of Vian, six leagues from Tabreez. He then sent to the cities of Tabreez and Sultanieh, to say that he wished to make a feast in memory of his grandfather, for which purpose they must send sheep, bread, wine, and horses, and three thousand robes, which he wished to give to his followers. He also ordered that all the property of the ambassadors should be returned to them.

On Thursday, the 13th of August, Omar Meerza sent two Zagatays to the ambassadors, with a letter ordering them to come and see him. On Friday they started, and slept in the open air, and early next morning they came to the encampment of the lord at Vian, and pitched their tents near a little brook. On Saturday the lord came out of his tent, and went to a great pavilion, where he received the ambassadors well, and afterwards they were ordered to sit under an awning and eat. On Sunday, the ambassadors were conducted to the pavilion, and men preached before the lord, in praise of Timour Beg. The ambassadors gave him a present of cloth and silk, and a handsome sword, which he valued much. The custom is that he refuses to see those who bring him no present, and the first thing that the ambassadors were asked, was whether they brought any present for the lord. On Tuesday, the 17th of August, he gave the ambassadors some robes, and a guide to point out the road, but he ordered the ambassadors from the Sultan of Babylon, and from Turkey,

Meerza retreating before them. Abubeker Meerza marched rapidly from Sultanieh and retook Tabreez, Ahmed retreating to Bagdad; but in 1407 Abubeker was several times defeated on the Araxes, by the Toorkmans. He finally fled to Sultanieh, and collected a fresh army.

In 1408 he marched, with his father Miran Meerza, towards Tabreez, and attacked Kara Yusuf on the 22nd of April; but Miran was killed in the battle, Abubeker's wives were captured, and he himself fled. Kara Yusuf was completely victorious, his conquests including Azerbijan and Irak. Abubeker fled to Kerman, and thence into Seistan; but was killed in a petty skirmish with the governor of Kerman, in December, 1408.

to be thrown into prison. On Wednesday, they returned to Tabreez, and prepared for their journey.

On Friday evening, the ambassadors being ready to depart, the Darogah came, with officers and scribes, and many people armed with maces and staves; and said that they must bring out all the property they had, as he wished to see their things. This was said with much noise and insolence, and he took certain satin cloths of Cathay, and a scarlet robe, and other things, which he said the lord had ordered him to take, as he had none in that land of such good quality, but they were paid for, and when this was done, they departed. The ambassadors then consulted with those of Turkey, who had been released, and they agreed to set out next day, for they said that if they remained these robberies might be repeated.

On Saturday, the 22nd of August, before dawn, the ambassadors, in company with those of Turkey, departed from Tabreez, after having been in that city for five months and twenty-two days; and the Zagatay guide went with them. They soon overtook a caravan of two hundred horses, laden with merchandize, which was going to the city of Boursa, in Turkey, and they travelled together, for fear of robbers.

On Monday, at dawn, they arrived at the city of Khoi, and here the land of Persia ends, and Armenia commences. While they were at Khoi, they received news that a Toorkman knight, named Kara Toman, had rebelled, and was in the field with ten thousand cavalry, robbing and plundering the people. He was formerly a vassal of Timour Beg.[1] He had

[1] Kara Yusuf, a Turkish chief of the tribe of Kara Koyunlu (black sheep), afterwards defeated Miran Meerza, and his son Abubeker, establishing a dynasty in Azerbijan in 1408. In 1420 Shah Rokh marched from Khorassan to avenge the death of his brother Miran; and in November of the same year Kara Yusuf died at Tabreez. In 1421 Shah Rokh captured Tabreez and Erivan, and defeated the sons of Kara Yusuf near Lake Van. In 1429 he again invaded Azerbijan, and defeated Iskander, the son of Kara Yusuf, with great slaughter. The historian, Ali of Yezd, was present at this battle. In 1477 Jehan Shah, another

marched against the city of Arsinga, and for this reason the ambassadors left the direct road, and took one on the left hand side.

On Tuesday, at the hour of vespers, they left Khoi, and travelled all night, and all Wednesday. At noon they gave some barley to the horses, and went on, day and night. On Thursday, at the hour of vespers, they reached a village inhabited by Armenians, with a small castle, which was subject to Omar Meerza. Near this place there is a race of Moors, called Turks, who rule the land, and live amongst the Armenians. The country abounded in bread and wine. While they were here, news came that Kara Toman had left Arsinga, and was on their road, so they sent a man ahead to find out if he was really there. On Friday, in the afternoon, the man returned, and said that the road was safe; so they departed, and slept in a meadow, near a village; and they passed many well peopled villages, with handsome churches and cemeteries, with large stone crosses over the tombs. These crosses were as high as a man, and well made. They were again told that Kara Toman was in the road before them, so they left it at noon, and took another more to the left; but the more they went to the left hand, the more they went out of their way. They went on until Sunday, without coming to any habitation; and it is to be remembered that the Christians lost Armenia, on account of the quarrels of three brothers.

On Tuesday, the 1st of September, they reached a great city nearly uninhabited, and with the wall in ruins, which had once been very broad and high. At one corner there was a castle, breached in many places, with people living in it. This city was called Alesquinar, and there were many great edifices, and streets of houses built of stone. The am-

son of Kara Yusuf, invaded Khorassan, and actually besieged Herat; but in 1488 the dynasty of the black sheep was destroyed by Uzun Hassan, chief of the Ak Koyunlu (white sheep).

bassadors dined here, and they were informed of the reason why this city was in ruins.

In this land of Armenia, there was once a great and powerful Armenian king, and he died, leaving three sons, who divided the land in this manner:—the eldest took this city of Alesquiner, the second had the city of Aumian,[1] and the third had the city of Asseron,[2] and these are the three chief cities of Armenia. The eldest, seeing that he was master of the city of Alesquiner, which was very strong, wished to take the other cities from his brothers, and they rose against each other, and made war. After the war had continued some time, they brought in strangers to assist. The lord of Asseron brought a race of Moors called Toorkmans, and the lord of Aumian did the same, and they marched against their eldest brother. When he knew that his brothers were going to attack him with strange troops, he also sent for strangers to help him, and brought in a race of Moors, who were his neighbours, called Toorks. These made a parley with the Toorkmans, who were with the younger brothers, and who gave up the city, murdering the elder brother. They then killed the other brothers, and took the cities of Aumian and Asseron, and their territories. Thus these cities, and all Armenia, fell into the power of the Moors. When they destroyed this city they killed so many Armenian Christians, that they have never inhabited it since.

While they were here, the ambassadors had certain news that Kara Toman, with his army, was on the road before them, so they determined to take the road of Aumian. This counsel was fortunate, and they presently departed, and travelled for four days and nights through a desert country.

On Saturday, the 5th of September, they reached the city of Aumian;[3] and on Monday they went to a castle, to see the son of a great knight, who held that land for his father. He was a Zagatay, named Toladay Beg, and the lord Timour

[1] Erivan? [2] Erzeroum? [3] Erivan?

Beg had given him that land when he conquered it. They gave him a robe, for such is the custom, and he told them that Kara Toman was in the land of Arsinga, through which they would have to pass, and that he was robbing the people; but he added, that for the honour of the king their lord, and for the service of Timour Beg, whom they had come to visit, he would guide them into a safe road, and he sent the ambassadors from Turkey by another road. This castle of Aumian was very strong, built on a high rock, and inside it was supplied with water from a fountain, and it was well provisioned.

On Tuesday, the 8th of September, they departed in company with a Zagatay, who went with them by order of this lord of Aumian; and they left the road to Arsinga on the left hand side, and passed the night at a village belonging to the lord of Aumian. Next day they rose early, and travelled over a very high mountain, and when they were on the other side, they found a castle called Tarcon, on a high rock. It had been taken by Timour Beg, and paid him tribute, and it is in the land of Georgia. They slept in a village about a league further on, and travelled through these mountains for two more days.

On Friday, the 12th of September, they reached a castle called Vicer, which belonged to a Moorish Mollah, and *Mollah* means "doctor" or "learned man." This Mollah received them with much honour, and they dined with him. All this country was ravaged by Kara Toman. The ambassadors departed, and the guide said that they must visit a lord, who was in a city called Aspir, for that he had letters from his lord to him; and from Tarcon to this place, the road led over mountains. The lord of this land was named Piahacabea, and it is plentifully supplied with provisions, though mountainous.

On Saturday they went to see this lord, and gave him a robe, and dined with him, and he gave them a guide to take them to the territory of the emperor of Trebizond. On

Sunday they ascended a very high mountain, without trees, which was four leagues in the ascent, and the road was so rugged that men and beasts went up it with great difficulty. On this day they left the land of Georgia, and entered the land of Arraquiel. The Georgians are fine handsome men, and their religion is the same as that of the Greeks, but they have a different language.

On Monday they dined at a village in the land of Arraquiel, and slept at another village. The reason why this Moor is lord of Aspertenia and Arraquiel, is this:—the people of the country were discontented with their lord, whose name was Arraquiel; and they went to the lord of Aspir, and offered to give him the lordship, so they seized the lord of Arraquiel, and put a Moor in his place to rule over the Christians. This land is very rugged and mountainous, and in it there are difficult passes, in some places the road being continued by wooden bridges, stretching from one rock to another. In most parts of the land beasts of burden cannot pass, and men carry the burdens on their backs. There is little bread, and the ambassadors were in great danger in this land, as the Christian Armenians are an evil race, and would not let the ambassadors pass, until they had given up some of their property.

They travelled for four days through the mountains, and reached some houses near the sea, being six days journey from Trebizond.

It was a very bad road, until they came to a place called Lasurmena; and all this land of Trebizond, near the sea, consists of very high mountains covered with fine trees, and there was a vine creeping up every tree. They make wine from these creepers.

On Thursday, the 17th of September, they arrived at Trebizond, and found a ship about to sail for Pera, laden with nuts; but there was a foul wind, and she had put into a place called Platana, six miles from the city. The ambassadors obtained all they required, and took a boat, in which they went to the ship. The captain was a Genoese, named Nicolas Cojan. They sailed, and were twenty-five days in reaching Pera.

On Thursday, the 22nd of October, they arrived at Pera in the night, and found two Genoese carracks, which had come from Caffa, and were going to Genoa. The ambassadors sailed in one of them on the 4th of November, and reached Gallipoli, where they took in a cargo of cotton, and then sailed to the island of Chio. On Monday, the 17th of November, they sailed again, and passed the island of Sapienza, and the cape of St. Angelo. On Monday, the last day of November, they arrived at the island of Sicily, and anchored.

On Wednesday, the 2nd of December, they sailed, and, after encountering a great storm, came to the city of Gaeta, in the kingdom of Naples, and remained there five days; when they sailed, but, meeting another great storm, they again put into Gaeta.

On Tuesday, the 22nd of December, they again set out, and, meeting another storm, were obliged to put into Corsica, where they passed their Christmas; and on the following Sunday they were off the port of Veane. On Sunday, the 3rd of January, they reached the port of Genoa; and the coast, for six leagues before reaching the city, is lined with beautiful houses, and gardens, which is a very pleasant thing to see. The city is well peopled, and has beautiful houses, and on most of the houses there is a tower. The ambassadors went to Savona, where the Pope was.

On Monday, the 1st of February, they sailed from Genoa, in a ship commanded by Master Bienboso Barbero, and they met with such violent storms, and such bad weather, being worse than any they had encountered in all their voyages, that the voyage lasted from the 1st of February, when they left Genoa, to Sunday, the 1st of March, when they landed at San Lucar, and took the road to the city of Seville. On Monday, the 24th day of March, in the year of our Lord 1406, the ambassadors reached the court of their lord, the king of Castille, which they found in Alcala de Henares.

LAUS DEO.

End of the chronicle of the great Tamerlane, and of the itinerary of the voyage which the ambassadors made, who were sent by the most serene king Don Henry: with a relation of the notable and marvellous things which were met with in all the land of the East. Printed in Seville, in the house of Andrea Piscioni, in the year 1582.

THE END.